BOOTH'S BOOTS

Booth's Boots

The beginnings of Salvation Army Social Work

by

Jenty Fairbank

United Kingdom Territorial Headquarters of The Salvation Army
101 Newington Causeway, London SE1 6BN

Copyright © 1983 The General of The Salvation Army
First published 1983
Reprinted 2001
ISBN 0 85412 425 X

LIEUT-COLONEL JENTY FAIRBANK (R)

became a Salvation Army officer in 1964 and served as a corps officer in the British Territory until her appointment to the Public Relations Department, International Headquarters, in 1970. Three years later came service in the Army's teacher training college at Howard Institute, Zimbabwe, before she returned in 1978 to the international centre as Director, Information Services, and Press Officer. She was transferred to the Literary Department, IHQ, in 1980 subsequently becoming Director of The International Heritage Centre. In 1997 she became Editor-in-Chief and Publishing Secretary at UK Territorial Headquarters, from which appointment she retired in 2000. She is also the author of God's Soldiers.

Cover artwork by Jim Moss

Printed in Great Britain by
Halstan and Co Ltd

Contents

Chapter   Page

Prologue   vii

1   The destitute poor and the suffering saints (poor relief)   1

2   Saving a girl for seven pounds (rescue work)   10

3   The double difficulty (maternity work)   27

4   Strictly confidential! (investigation, anti-suicide and
    reconciliation work) 41

5   Emma's orphans (children's work)   49

6   Adequate boy-mending machinery (work with juvenile
    delinquents) 67

7   To make us bad 'uns good (prison work).   73

8   Strange bedfellows (shelter work)   83

9   The worshipful company of out-of-works (employment)   99

10 New coats for a drunkard's stomach (work with
    alcoholics) 121

11 The great machine (The Darkest England Scheme)   131

12 Where angels might be glad to find employment (farm
    colony, small holdings, oversea colony and emigration)   157

End piece. 184

Leaders and governors. 185

Sources 187

Index. 198

'BUT if this tendency of departments to overlap does make a mere chronicle difficult, it is just the difficulty one must meet in writing contemporary *history,* for history is a warm, vital, progressive setting forth of the doings of live people.'—Major Susie Swift, in *A Brief Review of the First Year's Work of The Darkest England Scheme* (1891).

Prologue

TOWARDS the end of his long life William Booth, Founder and first General of The Salvation Army, said: 'I have been trying all my life to stretch out my arms so as to reach with one hand the poor and at the same time keep the other in touch with the rich. But my arms are not long enough. I find that when I am in touch with the poor I lose my hold upon the rich, and when I reach up to the rich I let go of the poor. And I very much doubt whether God Almighty's arms are long enough!'

As a 13-year-old pawnbroker's apprentice hurrying to the Nottingham pawnshop to keep his daily encounter with the poverty of the 1840s, this religious Robin Hood became aware of the tremendous gulf between the new rich spawned by the Industrial Revolution, and the ever-present poor whom he was later to describe as the 'submerged tenth' of the population. No hope, no rights, no nothing for the poor of Victorian England; nothing, that is, but the poverty, hunger and misery which offered little chance of survival beyond the ploys of pickpocketing and prostitution. Quickly William Booth learned that the pawnbroker's pledge was the poor man's overdraft, and within his newly aroused heart burned a desire to lighten the darkness of the poor with the love of Christ.

Some 20 years later, as a methodist minister, Booth became for the first time aware that his arms were not long enough. If he were to lose touch with one or the other, it must be the rich, for the poor tugged all the more strongly at his heart. Resigning from a comfortable living in the North of England, with a wife and a handful of children increasing by the year, Booth now joined the vast number of Britain's unemployed. Here was the life of faith he had so often preached about, and in the course of it he came at last to Mile End Waste in the East End of London, where the poor had never been poorer and the need had never been greater.

He began by preaching in the open air where shows, shooting ranges, petty dealers and quack doctors rivalled each other in attracting the attention of East Enders. This tall dark preacher was to them an attraction equal at least to Punch and Judy or the giant baby.

In 1867, two years after Booth's Christian Mission had been born, its first annual report showed this latest of Christian denominations to be something more than just another church. Though his creed was that of the great Christian communions, Booth quickly realised that in the face of the East Enders' dire wretchedness his methods needed to be less conventional. So it is that this report gives evidence of evening classes, ragged schools, reading rooms, penny banks, soup kitchens, relief for the destitute and sick poor by distribution of bread, meat and small sums of money. All this and preaching too.

Whether God Almighty's arms were long enough or not, Booth now found that economy dictated he must reach out to the rich if his efforts on behalf of the poor were not to founder for want of finance. That this was accomplished was largely due to the oratory of his wife Catherine, at once poignant and persuasive, and in consequence many influential opposers of The Salvation Army's early methods offered eventual acceptance of and practical support for its work.

Whilst Mrs Booth was ministering in genteel fashion to the 'up-and-outs' of London's West End, her husband continued his more rugged efforts on behalf of the 'down-and-outs' in the East End. Early in the 1880s a woman salvationist had opened her tiny home (already overcrowded with her own six children) to young girls seeking an escape route from the miseries of prostitution. In the winter of 1887 the plight of homeless men sleeping on the Thames embankment led to the establishing of the Army's first 'shelter'—a warehouse, offering a modicum of food, warmth and bedding.

Becoming convinced that poverty was a grave impediment to salvation, Booth was to turn to yet more stringent methods of social reform. In 1890, hard on the heels of H. M. Stanley's *In Darkest Africa*, came William Booth's no less compelling *In Darkest England—And The Way Out,* being a comprehensive ground plan of the social scheme which was to lead to the eventual establishment of Britain as a welfare state.

Booth's Boots attempts to tell something of the gripping story behind these facts. There would have been no such telling, however, were it not for the lively penmanship of bygone salvationist writers, whose careful recording of contemporary history did much to point *this* writer in the appropriate direction. No chronicler of Salvation Army history these many years would have been adequate to the task without recourse to the unfailingly enthusiastic professionalism of Lieut-Colonel Cyril Barnes (R), originator of the Army's archives at IHQ. This writer is no exception, and gladly records her gratitude, as does she also to Miss Catherine Sturgess, whose exceptional powers of memory have proved invaluable, and to Major Elsie Wanstall of Social Services Headquarters, who revealed the hitherto unexplored source material which has formed the basis for chapter 3. Colleagues in the Literary Department at International Headquarters have simply done their daily task in helping yet another book towards publication. It is a daily task which does not go unappreciated.

J. J.

1
The destitute poor and the suffering saints

A RAW winter's day in the 1840s, and an orphan—hungry, shivering, penniless—stood on London Bridge eyeing the comfortably-dressed, smug-looking man coming towards him.

'Spare us a copper, mister?' whined Boy Flawn. 'I'm so 'ungry!'

'Get out, you little devil!' snarled the man of affairs impatiently.

The 10-year-old gazed after him, rage and hatred rising in his mind; above all swelled the sobbing vow, 'When *I'm* a man, I'll see if I can't feed all the boys like me!' [1]

Significantly, it was in the City of London's Pudding Lane (where began the Great Fire of 1666, and a stone's throw from that boyhood bridge) that James Flawn set up his vow in the form of a refreshment room. There, not only did he attempt to feed 'all the boys like me', but he also catered for more specialised tastes. During the summer of 1865 and 'until the Booth family moved to Hackney in November, William Booth lunched on Sundays with Flawn at the refreshment room', Booth taking his own food and Flawn making him a cup of cocoa. 'After lunch Booth would rest on a sofa in a back room until it was time for him to return to the Mission.' [2]

'Little indeed thought the cook-shop proprietor . . . that in the future it should fall to his lot to use his business capacity and experience in pushing on a great salvation scheme, originating from the brain of that very man whom he then curiously watched upon Mile End Waste.'

'The cholera year, 1866, will never be forgotten by those of us who lived in London at the time', wrote George Scott Railton 20 years on, '. . . and the extremity of that East End misery had a

1

great deal to do with many of the early arrangements in connection with the General's work.'[3]

In *The Revival* of 31 January 1867 William Booth writes that at the Union Temperance Hall, High Street, Poplar, 'We are now giving away soup and bread, and propose doing so while the distress continues and funds are sent us.'

The plight of the ship-building operatives was so dire that by mid-February Booth reported to *Christian World* the opening of an actual soup kitchen in Poplar, 'supplying nearly 200 quarts of soup and a proportionate amount of bread per day'.[4]

The East London Christian Mission's acquisition of the one-time Eastern Star beer-shop at 188 (now 220) Whitechapel Road as its first headquarters in July 1867, and the fitting up of part of the premises as a soup kitchen, meant that by early 1870[5] 'as many as two thousand poor fellows . . . most of them paying pennies of their own'[3] could be provided with soup in one day. Flawn's vow was already assuming impressive proportions.

And if there was an outcry then, as now, that nothing was given free, Railton had his answer: 'Free breakfasts were given now and then on Sunday morning to people to whom tickets had been carefully distributed by men, once of their own class, who carefully hunted them out one by one until the tables were crowded with the poor, and maimed, and halt, and blind. But after soup and after breakfast came prayer, the prayer of men who meant to prevail, together with appeal upon appeal, urging to immediate surrender to God as the only remedy for their miseries, temporal and spiritual. Those prayers and appeals did prevail to the salvation of many,'[3] maintained Railton. Indeed, just a year later, *The Christian Mission Magazine* of February 1871 records that after a free Sunday morning breakfast for 500 of the poor, 'men from the working classes address the listeners (one of them himself converted through a free breakfast two years ago at the theatre)'.

Before the end of the decade, however, Booth was to have second thoughts about gratuitous handouts. 'A free tea is certainly a method of gathering together many who could in no other way be induced to come and listen to the gospel of Christ. But we look with great doubt and little hope upon crowds who come to seek the bread that perisheth, and who even when the Master himself dispensed it, generally went away unchanged spiritually.'[6]

2

Surveying it all stands Flawn, manager of this not inconsequential undertaking, working out his boyhood vow. Beside him works Bramwell Booth, eldest son of William; at 15 years of age, little more than a boy himself. Manager of four or five Food-for-the-Million shops, his role is to provide the poor with 'Hot Soup Day or Night, Three-Course Dinners for 6d.'

Meanwhile, *The East London Evangelist* of 1 June 1869 assures us, 'The Sick Poor Visitation Society still pursues its quiet and unobtrusive way. In no more useful way can money be spent in relieving the poor than in visiting them when sick and dying. A little help is very welcome and ensures a quiet hearing for gospel truth', for from the earliest days of soup distribution all cases helped were visited and followed up. Prime mover in this vital ministry was Miss Jane Short who, having come under the influence of Catherine Booth's preaching at Margate in 1867, became not only a lodger in the Booth household and one of the Mission's district visitors, but 'in addition had charge of the collection and distribution of old clothing and boots'.[7] Those boots were to become a recurring motif in the ever-evolving story of Salvation Army social work.

Jane Short's priorities were uncompromising. She it is who gives us one of the first clear statements of intent as far as the relationship between evangelism and good works is concerned. Writing in *The Christian Mission Magazine* of April 1870 she explains: 'While the chief object and aim of The Christian Mission is to bring sinners to Jesus, we feel it a duty and a privilege to minister to the bodily wants of the necessitous. . . . Parcels of old clothing, and old boots and shoes will be most gratefully received.'

Clothes, boots, shoes—and now blankets. The Blanket Loan Society's[8] ingenuity was to be outdone only by the introduction of maternal bags (this at Stockton in 1876); although at Whitechapel as early as 1869 'Mrs Coates . . . went to the mission hall for a box of clothes for the baby as a loan for a month.' Meanwhile at Hammersmith teas were given for the oil-cake makers, the road-scrapers and the washerwomen.

Thrift clubs and mothers' meetings abounded, and of them Railton was later to write: 'I should not like to investigate too closely the question as to how many stitches were put into the garments then in course of completion at those meetings, in any given hour. There is no doubt that many a poor mother was

3

enabled, with the aid of a few pence carefully saved, to procure clothing, which would otherwise have cost many shillings. But in all the conversations I have had with those who made themselves generally useful in connection with these meetings, I have never once heard anything about sewing. All their memories of the mothers' meetings relate to mother this and sister that, who, after a great deal of persuasion, were induced to come to such-and-such a meeting, where they were got upon their knees and transformed into lovers of the Lord before they left the place.'[3]

'I can say religion is a good thing,' testified the husband of one such woman at Poplar, 'my body is stronger, my soul is saved, my wife is happier, my children are clothed, my house is better furnished, and, having signed the pledge and given over smoking, I can say, "Godliness is profitable for all things".'

More succinctly, at Hanley some years later a convert claimed: 'I had not any clothes when I got converted, but since I have joined the Army I have spent five pounds six in clothes in a few weeks. Glory to Jesus! And I'm saved into the bargain.'

Socially elevating though salvation might be proving in some cases, Booth's rapidly expanding Mission found its steps increasingly directed towards the 'destitute poor' who, through these ministrations, were fast being turned into 'the suffering saints'.[9]

In a London reported in *The Revival* of 1874 as containing '100,000 winter tramps, 40,000 costers, 30,000 paupers in the unions, with a criminal class numbering 110,000,'[10] Booth might well assert, 'Only the Government can give effectual assistance,' whilst regretting their lack of initiative in doing so. 'The whole subject of poor relief is beset with great difficulties; but whatever controversies there may be as to the mode of its administration, there cannot be two opinions as to the duty of those who have wealth—specially those who name the name of Christ—to stretch forth a helping hand. . . . Ought we to allow our brothers and sisters in Christ to stand shivering at the relieving officer's door, to end their days in the union, or to be buried in a pauper's coffin? Let those who have wealth answer.'[11]

Those who had wealth continued to answer in ones and twos, never in very great numbers; but it was left to the visionary William

Corbridge, Christian Mission evangelist at Hastings, to declare: 'We shall become God's relieving officers.'

Two years after the historic 1878 change of name from The Christian Mission to The Salvation Army, the first officer cadets were received for training. From all walks of life they came, but mostly from the labouring classes; small wonder that in a day when state grants were unheard of for any kind of education—let alone for such combat-style instruction as was the lot of salvation cadets—a standard advertisement for 'clothing for the cadets' began to appear in *The War Cry* over the name of J. Flawn, to be rapidly followed by an appeal for: 'Two lads, active, godly, willing to make themselves generally useful. Good character indispensable. Only those accustomed to kitchen work need apply, by letter only, to J. F., Congress Hall, Clapton.'

By this time he was known as 'Commissary Flawn', the caterer for both training homes, Booth's mid-1870s policy decision to relinquish soup kitchens and food shops[12] having freed Flawn for this equally essential work. If the war against sin was to be effective, then it must be thoroughly fuelled—on 'Ten Sacks of Potatoes, from A Friend, Thundersley, Essex; One Barrel of Apples, from Rector Rose; One Sack of Potatoes, from Mrs Webb, Barnet; Two Pecks of Flour, from A Friend; and Four Bushels of Peas, from Mr Lawpard', if one acknowledgement of donations to training home supplies stands as typical fare.

Even so, Flawn's boyhood vow had yet to reach the height of its fulfilment. Was it Flawn's boyhood bridge Booth was being driven across late one bitter winter's night towards the end of 1887 when he became conscious for the first time of the niche-dwellers—men huddled in the alcoves of the bridge, with only torn newspaper between their emaciated frames and the stone, the damp and the biting wind? Certainly it was Flawn's Food-for-the-Million manager, now in his early 30s, and The Salvation Army's Chief of the Staff, who was confronted the following morning by his hairbrush-waving father commanding: 'Go and do something! We *must* do something.' 'What can we do?' 'Get them a shelter!' 'That will cost money.' 'Well, that is your affair! Something must be done. Get hold of a warehouse and warm it, and find something to cover them. But mind, Bramwell, no coddling!'[13]

Within weeks that 'something' was being described in *The War Cry* of 21 January 1888 as: 'A New Departure. For some time

6

now', the statement read, 'the starving condition of great numbers of the London poor has appealed imploringly to us for help. Not only are there thousands who walk the streets of this great city with its palatial mansions, abounding wealth and costly luxury, not knowing where to find a meal of bread, but there are numbers more who have nowhere to lay their heads save in the shadow of the railway arches, in the recesses of the bridges, or in the seats in the public parks and squares. . . . We have now decided to do something towards alleviating this dreadful misery, and have taken large premises in the West India Road, Limehouse, in which we propose to establish a very cheap food depot, and also to furnish a sleeping shelter for the night.'

Six hundred pounds was appealed for to launch the venture, with the pledge that even the smallest sums of money would be acknowledged in *The War Cry*—as indeed was: '6d from A Sympathizer' and '1s from Mrs Eliza Brown'. 'A Useless Sympathizer' even managed ten shillings. At the formal opening of the 'New Departure' in February, the offering, appropriately, was taken up in sugar basins.

The first 'regulations' concerning the Food and Shelter Depot appeared in *The War Cry* of 25 February, stating that: 'packets of tickets for single meals or for lodging, supper, and breakfast, can be had for distribution by Christians not members of the Army, or by other organizations, although no Salvation Army officer will be allowed to give away such tickets. This regulation will prevent the danger of 'charity' being the hindrance it too often is to ascertaining the genuineness of professed conversions. No one will come to our penitent forms for soup and coal any more than before!'

Writing of this 'New Departure' some years later, Bramwell Booth explained: 'Whole districts are occupied by sections of population who never can eat a decent meal—they try to live on bits and drops. Thousands of pounds a year are thrown away by the wretched system of buying tea in decimals of an ounce, and coals in brown paper bags, and light by the farthing dip. To meet in some degree this need, the food depots were established. . . . Nor is this all. Large numbers of the poorest people earn a scanty livelihood by work which is done in their homes, that is, in the one, or at most, the two rooms in which a whole family is brought up. Matchbox making, covering of tennis balls, artificial flower colouring, pulling the fur from rabbit skins, and various kinds of

7

needlework, are among the trades so followed. In order to gain the merest subsistence in these occupations every moment of every hour must be put to the best advantage. So that, apart altogether from economical reasons, which always make fires a costly luxury, the preparation of food is looked upon as a nuisance, for the simple reason that it takes *time,* which should be used to increase the joint earnings of the whole family. As a result a custom of buying cooked food has grown up and rapidly extended. To supply wholesome food at minimum prices to this class was one consideration which led to the creation of our food depots.'[14] Flawn's Food-for-the-Million shops had simply been resurrected as the 19th-century forerunners of fast-food and take-away stores.

'Planted just outside the entrance to the docks', the Limehouse Food Depot provided—during the dock strike in the late summer of 1889—the focal point of the kind of relief work for which The Salvation Army has since become well known. 'The huge strike of 120,000 of the most poorly paid, and fed, and clad, and housed, labourers in the world has . . . produced upon the great metropolis an impression deeper than it has received for years past. The mere question of a penny per hour, more or less, has been completely over-shadowed by the larger question as to what this tremendous upheaval of the poorest may, any day, foreshadow. What changes in social arrangements might not the people bring about within a few weeks should they suddenly combine together, in their millions, to act, with one consent, resolutely, yet calmly, and without any breach of law?'[15] *The Times* observed: 'The Salvation Army are [*sic*] continuing to do a vast amount of work at their depot in the West India Dock Road, and it is the opinion of the leaders of the strike that had it not been for this place of relief the distress would have been much greater.'[16] *The London Daily News* went as far as to say that: 'it has been impossible to move about in the neighbourhood of the Docks lately without feeling one's self under a debt of obligation to them'.[17]

Two more food depots had been opened at Clerkenwell[18] and Marylebone[19] earlier in the year, but in the face of the dock strike emergency measures needed to be taken. The Whitechapel barracks were briefly used for this purpose[20] (before being closed and altered into a regular food and shelter depot), as were Poplar barracks;[21] and here, as at Limehouse, Canning Town and Stepney barracks, special religious meetings were held three times a day during the strike.[22] 'We have avoided, as usual, anything like mere charity doling,' reported *The War Cry,* 'but have offered all meals at half the usual price. . . . In supplying meals at half-price we are naturally losing half the cost of each meal. It is gloriously remarkable to find our Australian forces quicker in coming to our help upon this occasion than the wealthy inhabitants of this country.'[23] Two hundred pounds had been sent by the Army in Melbourne for this purpose. 'Mr Flawn, the energetic and hard-working manager of the Limehouse Food and Shelter Depot, tells me that if the dock strike lasts much longer he will be finished. The place is simply besieged from morning till night.'[22]

Mr Flawn, of course, was *not* finished. He thrived on all this hard work. With the launching of Booth's Darkest England Social Scheme in the early 1890s came more and more food and shelter depots, and descriptions of their openings are sprinkled with comments by 'the universal provider, Mr Flawn'. At the end of 1893, when 3,886,896 meals had been provided that year, 'Manager Flawn declares the removal of the Social Headquarters to 272 Whitechapel Road has had the effect of bringing to the counters of his food department hordes of the most miserable and wretched, the chilliest and hungriest human beings whom it has ever been his lot to encounter.'[1]

To his father in 1906 Bramwell Booth writes: 'Flawn. Yes; he is living—very much so; he is in receipt of a pension, and shows no sign of dispensing with it! He will be most proud to see you.'[24] James Flawn 'remained a keen salvationist till his death at over 80 years of age in 1917'.[25] In that year alone 6,038,702 meals were supplied at Salvation Army cheap food depots in the United Kingdom.[26] Could a 10-year-old, sobbing on London Bridge 70 years earlier, have imagined such an outcome to his vow?

2
Saving a girl for seven pounds

SPEAKING of the beginnings of Salvation Army social work to officers gathered in council in 1911, the Founder said: 'My dear wife's heart had been particularly drawn out on behalf of the fallen outcasts of society, who, often more sinned against than sinning, appealed peculiarly to her large and tender sympathies. More than once she found opportunity for extending help to individual cases of misfortune. . . .'[1] Four months before her husband 'found his destiny' on Mile End Waste, *The Wesleyan Times* for 27 March 1865 carried a report of Mrs Booth addressing a Christian community tea meeting held in George Yard Ragged School, Spitalfields. In part it read: 'We again conclude that a considerable number of those who remained' to make decisions for Christ 'were young unfortunates' who 'would willingly enter a home if one were available. . . . Mrs Booth and the chairman were so moved that the latter left with her a sum of money and she submitted it to help provide some means of escape for these women.' This, before ever The Christian Mission—let alone The Salvation Army—had come to pass.

At about the same time as Miss Jane Short joined the Mission staff, Mrs James Reid, widow of a presbyterian minister, moved to East London in order to give all her time to Christian Mission relief work.[2] A letter to *The Revival* of 13 February 1868, signed by Flora Reid, appeals for donations towards the setting up of a refuge for women who have 'prayed to be saved from a life of infamy. . . . In these circumstances', continues Mrs Reid, 'we have taken a house and earnestly request assistance to furnish it in a humble way and offer them shelter until we can do better.' Two weeks later William Booth reports to the same paper: 'We have just taken and fitted out a coffee-house on the corner of Worship Street, Bishopsgate, Shoreditch. Here we shall have . . . on a small scale a temporary refuge for the poor, friendless, penniless girls who are so constantly crossing our paths.' By April, however, Mrs Reid was reporting failure to her readers: 'As little over £20 has come in and as my health is giving way under the amount of work I have already had in hand, I have been persuaded to abandon the attempt, and with the consent of the subscribers to pay over the amount received to the Rescue Society on condition of their accommodating girls sent on by us.'

No more is heard of any attempts at rescue work until William Corbridge reports from Hastings in 1871 that four 'poor fallen girls' had 'professed to find peace . . . in a fortnight'. Two years later, in January and February 1873, teas were given 'for the fallen' of Hastings, this being the first Christian Mission station to embark upon any form of organised rescue work.

Some time between 1874 and 1876 Catherine Booth was addressing a holiness meeting 'at Fells' Cook-shop, opposite the Blind Beggar where the Founder used to have his first open-air services'.[3] This turns out to have been that part of The Christian Mission's original headquarters fitted out as a soup kitchen in the late 1860s and purchased in 1874 by Mrs Booth's one-time maid, Honor Fells, and her husband William Burrell.[4] To that meeting in the former Eastern Star public house came baker's wife Mrs Elizabeth Cottrill. A resident of Christian Street, Whitechapel, she had until then been only 'a formal Christian', she explained in 1921 at the age of 81 years. 'At the penitent form I took the feather out of my hat and came home like a drowned rat, crying and weeping for joy, and from that day I went forward, not to *sing* "Rescue the Perishing", but to do it!'[3] Evidently there was more to Elizabeth Cottrill's profession of faith than the giving-up of feathers, for 'I said, "Lord, I'll do whatever you want," and I went visiting lodging-houses and thieves' kitchens.'

Was she present at a midnight meeting for the fallen of Whitechapel in February 1875 when 'some 10 or 12 came forward, willing to forsake their course of life, and to give themselves to the Saviour'? Certain it is that, whenever her conversion, she was early introduced to the concept of 'salvation *from*' being firmly linked with 'salvation *to*'; or, as salvationists of a later generation would put it, being 'saved to serve'. 'I was sent to deal with those at the penitent form, and one snowy February night a girl penitent asked, "How can I be Christian—the life I'm living?" I said, "You must give up that life." It was very late that night, 10 to 11, when she gave her heart to God. I took her down to a home where they'd taken such girls before, but the matron looked out of the window and said, "I can't take girls in at this hour. We don't keep open all night."' (Let it be hoped this wasn't the Rescue Society to which

Mrs Reid handed the conditional £20 in 1868!) 'Then I went to a coffee-house. The charge was 2s 6d, and I only had 1s, and they would not trust me till the morning. I tried another, and was told, "We don't take females." So I said, "*I'll* take her home." I lived at No. 1 Christian Street, Commercial Road, next door to a pawnbroker's. It was nearly 12, and my husband and six children were asleep. I gave her some supper—coffee and a little bit of cold meat, and bread and butter. I didn't want any myself. I wanted to get to bed. I was full of prayer and thankfulness, thinking about her broken-hearted mother and how glad she'd be. I made her up a bed in the kitchen on some chairs with old coats and dresses—the best I could get without waking the others. I couldn't undress her. She was a clean girl. She had run away from her home near Brighton with another girl, expecting to find London streets paved with gold. They went to the Tower Hill to see the soldiers, imagining they'd find a husband straight away, but only got into trouble. I took her home the next day. I said, "You must ask your mother's forgiveness, and if she won't take you in I'll bring you back." Of course, her mother *did* take her in, only too thankful to see her safe. After this, the soul-saving work amongst these girls went on, and I would get four and even eight in my little place. So I began to pray for a bigger house.'[3]

Mrs Cottrill's account gives no clue as to the year this important beginning was made, but before his death in the mid-1940s Colonel George Holmes (whose family lived on the top floor of the Cottrills' house) remembered it to be in 1881—his 14th year.[5] This would seem to be confirmed by a *War Cry* report of 1884 which stated: 'Some *years* ago a devoted soldier of the Whitechapel Corps became very interested in the poor, fallen girls who sometimes came to the penitent-form there.' We therefore make pause in Elizabeth Cottrill's story to note that before this 1881 milestone, occasional sorties into rescue work had been undertaken in response to 'our poor, fallen sisters' seeking salvation from their sins at the penitent forms of Limehouse, Soho, St Leonards, Chatham, Cardiff, Newcastle and Plymouth from whence Captain Dowdle reported: 'One poor prostitute got saved, and Mrs Dowdle took her away to a home.'

Whilst Mrs Cottrill in Whitechapel was still praying for a bigger house, a midnight rescue brigade was being organised in Glasgow—with such success 'that we have found ourselves literally compelled to face the establishing of a home to meet our requirements', wrote Major Henry T. Edmonds in Scotland's first annual report.[6] 'No sooner had we made up our minds to this than one gentleman offered the first year's rent of a house . . . and by the opening day, the 25th of May 1883, the whole amount necessary for the furnishing and other expenses connected with the work had been raised, and something left in hand to commence housekeeping with.'

If Mrs Cottrill's back kitchen constituted The Salvation Army's first residential social 'institution', Henry Edmonds' Victoria House Home of Rescue certainly ran a close second, having been specifically acquired for that purpose. Unfortunately, with his transference from Scotland at the end of May 1883, enthusiasm for financing the home seems to have ground to a halt, and nothing further is heard of the Glasgow scheme until Edmonds' re-appointment to Scotland in 1885,[7] when re-energised rescue efforts culminated in the opening of a newly established 'Home of Help and Love' by Mrs Bramwell Booth in April 1886.[8] But this is to overtake Mrs Cottrill in her praying!

In the spring of 1884 'The Lord answered my prayers', her memoirs continue. 'Mr Bramwell Booth had said, "Look for some rooms," but nobody would let rooms for that purpose. I hunted and hunted in vain. Then, walking along Hanbury Street one day, praying as I went, I said: "Lord, the earth is thine, and the fullness thereof. Oh, do let me have a house! You know these dear girls are thy children." Then, when I'd cast it on him, I thought: "I'll go home and have a cup of tea." But at that moment I lifted my eyes and saw an empty house, and a notice up, "This house to let." I forgot my tea, and went to inquire. The agent was in the same street, and a clerk showed me over, and I saw it would be suitable. But the rent was 25s. I said, "Will you let me have it for £1?"' (A good East-Ender was Mrs Cottrill!) 'Ever so many Jews were after it and ready to pay the 25s. The Rev William Tyler, congregational, was the landlord, and when he understood he said, "Let this woman have it for £1. I wish there were a few more who had such a heart towards the poor girls." But he said to me, "Don't let there be any tambourines, because I may be preaching!" His church was next door. He gave me 10s to get the girls something to eat. You see, God *does* answer prayer. I got the right sort of landlord! The Army Mother' (as Mrs William Booth had come to be known) 'went to a sale and got four single beds and some other things. There was a double bedstead in the lot, and I said, "Let me buy that for myself," but she insisted on giving it to me . . . I loved her so much. She was so thoughtful and so careful. . . . She taught me

13

so much, and did her utmost to build me up. Mr Bramwell let me have some old chairs from the Grecian Theatre (which had just been taken over), and I got the girls to scrub the house down and to scrub the chairs. We made bed-ticks and pillow-cases out of old cotton skirts, and stuffed them with wool and paper the girls had cut up. Sometimes I'd put four of those pillows together to make an extra bed. I begged clothes of all I knew. Often I had to rig a girl up before she could be put to bed. They were smart outside, but—underneath!'

'Some of the men who were after the girls I'd got would wait for me, and get hold of my bonnet and drag it off; or they'd throw me into a passage; or kick me in the shins, and when a man is wearing blucher boots they can give a bad kick. My husband used to say, "I shall have you killed one of these days."'[3] But in spite of such daily hazards Mrs Cottrill was to live to the age of 87.[9]

Back in 1884, however, the Hanbury Street cottage rental posed no small problem in the mind of Bramwell Booth, the Army's Chief of the Staff.[10] Should The Salvation Army take on rescue work officially?[11] Since the abandoning of soup kitchens and food shops in the mid-1870s, its work had been solely evangelical. But these girls were coming to its penitent forms as a direct result of its evangelism. Should not they then be helped? Yet how was this 'New Undertaking' to be financed? True, there had recently been received 'Five shillings from two working men in Earl's Court for rescue work' and 10 shillings from the Hanbury Street landlord 'to get the girls something to eat', but what kind of shoestring was that?

In some measure the problem presented its own answer. Writing less than four years later of the rescue work, a salvationist journalist pointed out: 'It is all very well to rejoice that Middlesbrough's makes our 12th Army rescue home. We thank God for every one of the hundreds snatched from a life of infamy, touched, softened, *saved* through our rescue workers. But to ensure a girl's being "saved to stay", you must also be able to ensure her an honest livelihood.'[12] Whether it was this kind of psychology, or the force of economic necessity, or a blend of both that led her to it, Elizabeth Cottrill 'toiled all her spare time to get them into situations, sometimes walking many miles a day'. 'Red jerseys were just being introduced as uniform' (for salvationists) 'and Mrs Cottrill secured the marking of these with "The Salvation Army" in yellow wool. The girls were taught to do this in cross-stitch, and

14

3s 6d per dozen was thus earned. A little washing was secured for others to do, and so the rent was paid and food procured.'[3]

With the hindsight of the years, this simple step was to be described in 1928 as 'Another of those foundation axioms' of Salvation Army social work—'that every woman and girl capable of doing so should help towards the cost of her own redemption.'[13]

Seeing the hand of the Lord in it all, Bramwell Booth took oversight of this work on 22 May 1884,[14] thus quite unconsciously marking what was to be celebrated 100 years later as the official launching of Salvation Army social work.

At a future stage his father, General William Booth, was to be asked in interview: ' "What about The Salvation Army proper? Has it suffered from the competition of the Social Work?" A smile flitted over the General's face at the mention of the word *proper,* but he replied: "I know what you mean; but in my estimation it is all The Salvation Army *proper.* We want to abolish these distinctions, and make it as religious to sell a guernsey or feed a hungry man as it is to take up a collection in the barracks. It is all part of our business, which is to save the world body and soul, for time and for eternity!" '[15]

Meanwhile, back in 1884 'The law of Salvation Army gravitation was at work as hard as ever.' On 26 May, when Elizabeth Sapsworth, 'a Clapton lady of middle age and independent means, was waiting on the steps of Clapton Congress Hall, she had a five-pound note thrust into her hands by the young Chief of the Staff, with instructions to go and finance the work and keep the books. . . . "She had a brain like a statesman's for strength and comprehensiveness," ' Bramwell Booth's wife was later to write of this 'cultured, methodical scholar in Greek, Hebrew and mathematics',[16] and now was added to her other qualifications that of being The Salvation Army's first rescue officer—before she had even been made a soldier![17]

'On June 30th, 1884, I went to Ireland,' recorded the young Mrs Bramwell Booth. 'On returning . . . I heard of the work which had begun in the East End of London among outcast girls. . . . The Founder said: "Flo had better go down and see what she can do in her spare time. Let her superintend." The next morning, July 18th, I left the trees and greenness of Clapton Common and journeyed by tram to Whitechapel, alighting in the High Road, to find the

15

cottage in Hanbury Street, a side turning. I felt depressed and unhappy. Whitechapel seemed so far away from Castlewood Road for a work which I realised would need daily attention. I felt, too, that I was entirely ignorant of the conditions into which I was to inquire.'[18] Later she was to confess: 'I had not then even realised that there were such people as prostitutes, nor defined to myself what this evil was.[19] Heavy with these thoughts I walked slowly, but was aroused by a blow from a missile hurled at me by a costermonger's boy who had taken a potato from his barrow. The effect was electric. This assault seemed to dispel my fears. I interpreted it to mean opposition and knew that the devil does not waste his ammunition!

'The first days were spent in interviewing those already in the cottage. God had shown me "my corner", but what a very dark and dismal corner it seemed. . . . When I heard from the lips of these young girls just in their 'teens the stories of their destruction; when I understood that women kept houses of ill-fame in which other women were practically prisoners; and that if they were 13 years of age, or if there were reason to believe they had reached that age, the men who destroyed them could not be punished; that for these outcast women there seemed left no place of repentance on earth, and the majority, even if they wished to return, were cast out of their homes and no one would give them employment; I felt this was a mystery of iniquity indeed.

'My faith was sorely tried, and but for the opportunity of pouring out my grief at home to one so strong in faith and so full of compassion for the sinful, I wonder what might have become of me. How acute were the contrasts in my life at this time; such bliss at home, the purest love of husband and my darling baby in her cot, and then suddenly these terrible revelations. This underworld seemed indeed a scene of diabolic confusion and darkness.'[18]

Eager to become as knowledgeable as possible upon every aspect of her new work, Florence Booth visited rescue homes run by other organisations. She was horrified by what she saw. 'Women were kept in these places for one, two, and even three years, and if they failed to run well, were never given a second chance. Bolts and bars, bare, dismal rooms, high walls, no occupation but that of laundry work, seemed to explain this discouragement. I could not imagine myself becoming any better for a long stay in similar circumstances.'[18]

16

In this last statement lay the strength of the Army's early rescue work. Both Florence Booth and her mother-in-law, Catherine, continually put themselves in the place of those they were helping, and in this way strong bonds grew between the helper and the helped. *The Wesleyan Times* report of 27 March 1865 instances this. Of Catherine Booth's address at George Yard Ragged School it says: 'She identified herself with them as a sinner, saying that if they supposed her better than they it was a mistake, as all sinners were sinners against God.'

Florence Booth 'determined therefore to make, at first, no rules for the refuge. I realised that there is no power in a mere removal from certain circumstances to reform the heart, and especially I felt that what these women most needed was a real home, for they were homeless, and that they needed support in their first efforts to earn their own living and return to respectable society.'[18]

By the end of 1884 she was writing: 'The large proportion of young girls who come is a hopeful fact, as our chance with these is much greater than with older women, because drink has not such a firm hold on them. I am firmly convinced of the wisdom of leaving them all free to quit the refuge at any moment. Those who do not *desire* to stay are better away. Of the five who have run away *four* have come back to us, literally seeking again a place for repentance, with tears'.[20]

Within months of the opening of the refuge, warnings were appearing in *The War Cry* to the following effect: 'IMPORTANT! Captains must not send any cases to The Salvation Army Refuge for Women, Whitechapel, without first ascertaining whether there be room to receive them, as they will have to be sent back, which causes great inconvenience and disappointment to all concerned.'[21]

Meanwhile, what Florence Booth called her 'experiments' continued. 'The occupation of a teacher in the scholastic realm is intensely interesting, though I suppose the large classes often make it impossible to follow up closely individual cases, *but the education of heart and conscience is more enthralling still.* . . . It was intensely interesting to see the light gradually dawning as the things of God were personally explained.'[18] Nor was she to be browbeaten into accepted practices simply because they *were* accepted. 'Miss Ellice Hopkins, a lady of perhaps the widest experience in England with this class of women, says that of all the employment open to them, laundry work is best. In her own words,

17

"As a rule, it stands to reason that the wild restlessness, the lawlessness, the animal passions and excitement of the old street life are best worked off by muscular exertion, and laundry work is on the whole the best and most profitable."'[22] 'We keep *off* the laundry work', insisted Florence Booth, 'because we wish opportunity for more personal influence over the girls.'[23]

And always, behind the personal influence, throbs the recurring motif of the social work:

> Assistance is greatly needed in two ways: IN MONEY . . . ALSO IN CLOTHES . . . and, above all, BOOTS. . . .
>
> The need of a clock is very badly felt. Good books would be especially welcome also, and the officers tell me that of various articles of clothing *boots* are what they stand in need of most.
>
> We thankfully acknowledge the following gifts: . . . three pairs of boots, no name or address. . . .

Before Mrs Bramwell Booth had gone on record as saying that, because of the firm hold drink had, their chances with older women were much less than with young girls, Captain Susan 'Hawker' Jones of Northampton read the warning to 'captains' in *The War Cry* and dutifully contacted the Whitechapel refuge regarding her latest house-guest. One of those salt-of-the-earth characters out of which the early-day Salvation Army was built, Captain Jones had seen a tall woman in 'a large blue hat with great blue feathers'[24] come into the meeting hall one evening and sit near the door. Her demeanour, as much as her hat, caused the captain to notice Rebecca Jarrett, for she was obviously ill. Before long the hot crowded meeting had its effect and she fainted. 'It was not the preaching that done the work in my poor soul, it was the care and trouble they all took of me,'[24] Rebecca remembered in her old age.

A brothel keeper in her late 30s, she had been introduced by her mother to a life of sexual promiscuity before she was 13 years old. Her father, a well-to-do rope merchant, used to give lectures against 'the drink' in a little hall in the Borough, squandering all his money on 'other women' the while. Finally he left her mother, who, with eight of her 13 children still needing support, soon 'took' to the very drink her husband had preached against. As the youngest child, Rebecca became not only the vehicle through which her mother was able to finance her constant drinking sprees, but also her mother's drinking companion. By the time she stumbled into Captain Jones's Northampton meeting in November 1884, 'I was too old to be reclaimed, besides, I was almost dying with the drink. Every doctor I went to said, "You must give up the drink!" How could I? It made me have a bit of life. . . . It was drinking to deaden your feeling, to meet the men. If you were not bright they would not come again. They paid your rent and supported you. No, you must drink, if it finished you up.'[24]

Nursing Rebecca in her own tiny room for several days, Captain Jones sent an SOS to Hanbury Street, and was given clearance to take her patient there. Wrote Mrs Bramwell Booth: 'Her very appearance was a challenge to my faith, for the marks of her dissolute life were very plain, the expression of her face almost repulsive, and showed plainly the ascendency that alcohol had gained over her.'[18] Nevertheless, when Rebecca's crisis point came, after prolonged treatment in the London Hospital,[24] Florence Booth had no qualms about handing baby Catherine into the arms of this 'challenge to her faith', whilst she herself went to make the inevitable soothing cup of tea.[25] Of that occasion she was later to write: 'When such slaves break away from sin and desire to lead a new life, they have no conception of the extent of their own weakness or the tenacity of the power of sin. To be finally saved they must go on to know "life more abundant", and open their hearts without reserve to the indwelling power of God.

'That Rebecca had sought for pardon and been wonderfully helped I do not doubt, but when she had been with us a short time I was greatly distressed one morning to receive a letter from her saying she "would not go on trying the new life any longer", and had made an appointment with a former companion in evil, and would "go back to the old life".

'I went at once to the refuge. My diary runs: "I spent the morning with Rebecca, and God helped me to put it all before her and show her how wonderfully the Lord had helped her." We kept her all day . . . pleading with her at intervals. Miss Sapsworth went to her before leaving in the evening, and going to take leave myself I overheard the words, "No, I cannot." I made an earnest appeal to her that if she left us she would go facing the truth that she turned her back on God and Heaven and deliberately chose sin and Hell.

'Rebecca suddenly fell on her knees sobbing, prayed earnestly, and as I listened I realised the Saviour had received her afresh. We called in the officers, and she told them of her deliverance, amidst her sobs, while I cried for very joy.

19

'In this way God prepared one of the instruments my husband and Mr Stead made use of to bring to light the evil in the underworld of London.'[18]

Rebecca's part in the *Maiden Tribute* drama has been well documented elsewhere[26] and need not be retold here. Suffice it to recall the 1871 Royal Commission recommendations: 'The traffic in children for infamous purposes is notoriously considerable in London and other large towns. We think that a child of 12 can hardly be deemed capable of giving consent and should not have the power of yielding up her person. We therefore recommend the absolute protection of female children to the age of 14 years.'[27]

The age of consent was eventually raised—to 13, not 14—but until 1875 any girl over the age of 12 years was regarded by English law as a consenting adult in sexual intercourse.[27]

Born too early to have benefited from even 1875's meagre protection, Rebecca Jarrett nevertheless played a strategic role in bringing about that 1885 Act of Parliament which raised the age of consent to 16, and to this day remains the protection of many a girl-child in similar circumstances. When Rebecca died 'full of years and piety' in 1928 at the age of 81, it was the baby Catherine Booth, firstborn of Bramwell and Florence and by then leader of the Women's Social Work in her own right, who assisted at the funeral service[28] of the woman for whom she had unwittingly performed her first piece of social service as a babe in arms more than 40 years earlier.

The Criminal Law Amendment Act of 1885 did not immediately render rescue homes redundant, however. In fact The Salvation Army's rescue work continued to mushroom in ever-increasing proportions. The staff of four in 1885 numbered 40 by March 1888, and 70 in a further three months. 'If that band of women cannot straighten up the transaction, it is no use anyone else trying,' remarked *The War Cry*.

'That band of women', as the Founder pointed out at the fourth anniversary of the rescue work in St James's Hall, Piccadilly, 'came from various classes—some, like the ordinary workers in The Salvation Army, from the very class we are endeavouring to save. This is a peculiarity of the movement . . . we turn the saved into the saviours of the class to which they formerly belonged. Others are motherly matrons, who lavish their affection upon these poor girls, and others come from higher ranks in life, having abandoned homes of luxury and refinement and devoted themselves entirely to the work.'[29]

Ten homes accommodating a total of 212 were by this time spread throughout the British Isles, 'and on average', claimed the General, 'we could save a girl for seven pounds.'[29]

Since September 1885 *The War Cry* had regularly carried 'An offer of help in seven languages', in which it invited 'parents, relations and friends in any part of the world interested in any woman or girl who is known or feared to be living in immorality, or is in danger of coming under the control of immoral persons, to write stating full particulars . . . and if possible a photograph of the person in whom the interest is taken. All letters, whether from these persons, or from *such women and girls themselves,* will be regarded as strictly confidential. They may be written in any language, and should be addressed to Mrs Bramwell Booth.'

By the time the first issue of *The Deliverer* (a monthly magazine featuring Salvation Army rescue work) appeared in July 1889, 2,099 women and girls had passed through the homes, of whom 1,676 had proved satisfactory. That year the Founder was reported to have remarked that 'as a rule, we took the very worst, and he was not sure but, as a rule, we succeeded best with the very worst'.[30]

Lest this should strike the Victorian reader as extremism, his daughter-in-law, Mrs Bramwell Booth, went on record as saying she considered that 'one of the first duties of a rescue officer is to take a stand firmly against the position that women guilty of immorality are *worse* than other transgressors. The Salvation Army has nothing but scorn for that code of morals which welcomes a repentant adulterer—if he happen to wear broadcloth—into the drawing room, and introduces him to the daughters of the house, while considering it the height of condescension to admit a repentant sinner of the other sex to be a kitchenmaid in the scullery.

'We believe absolutely in the salvability of every soul. The girl who enters the door of an Army home comes from a world where nobody, as far as she can see, believes in anybody else's goodness. She knows nobody to believe in, and she believes in herself least of all. The atmosphere which she breathes from the moment she crosses our threshold is full of that sort of faith in God which

21

involves high faith in the possibilities of every human creature he has made. Heretofore, from the time of her first fall, she has been expected to be bad. Now, she is expected to be good; and, as a rule, she *is* good. Considering the shattered nerves, the habits of drinking, the craving for excitement, the restlessness of mind and body with which a woman who has been for any length of time leading a sinful life comes to our homes, we could sometimes wonder ourselves as pronouncedly as do others at the large percentage who have been permanently reclaimed therein.'[31]

Grim though the subject be, these early rescue reports are not without their humour. 'Salvationists possess a compelling force which is exceedingly useful to rescue officers in some emergencies. For instance, a girl had been living in a brothel which was indicted, and had, with the rest of the occupants, to turn out into the streets. A companion told her that if she would go to The Salvation Army, they would help her to live a good life, and yet be able to earn a living. The girl took the address and started for Hackney, but a man who was determined to have her back persisted in following her all the way. After she had entered the home, he still remained on the pavement, collecting a small crowd in front of the gate.

'The officer who received the lassie was very anxious that he should be got away at once, and asked a captain near to send him off if possible. The officer settled matters sooner than could have been expected by kneeling promptly down at the gate and praying for the man. It will suffice to add that nothing has been seen of him since!'

'MRS Bramwell Booth would be very glad to get any information as to how she can assist those of the rescue girls who wish to emigrate, to do so.'[32] (And yet another chapter suggests itself.)

'WE want to have planted at every street-corner, like the houses of the fire-brigades or red lamps of the doctors' shops, women who would deal with the men as well as the women.'[29]

'WE propose to station officers at certain places in the street, Charing Cross and elsewhere, from eight pm, to one or two o'clock in the morning, that they may be at hand to offer help to those whom we are specially seeking.'[33] And the Army's midnight rescue work has spread from the East to the West End of London.

By August 1893 a refuge had been set up near Piccadilly Cir-

cus[34]—further proof that 'The Salvation Army is doing something
. . . to lessen this vast concourse of somebody's daughters',
estimated as far back as 1885 as numbering some 80,000 in London
alone.[35]

Towards the end of 1899 a similar midnight post was set up at
King's Cross, [36] forerunner of the famous Faith Cottage of half a
century later. Originally a builder's show house erected in the
forecourt of King's Cross Station before the Second World War, its
wartime use by The Salvation Army's Red Shield Services had come
to an end by the 1950s, and in April 1956 Captain Molly Scott
moved into it, naming it Faith Cottage,[37] set, as it was, "Mid all the
traffic of the ways', 'where three Underground lines converged,
two main lines had their termini, and half-a-dozen buses their fare
stages.'[38]

From there Molly Scott moved out into the small-hour life of
Soho, Piccadilly, Bayswater and Mayfair, her Salvation Army
bonnet a familiar sight to the prostitutes who regularly worked
those 'beats', and for the next seven years Faith Cottage provided
scores of them with the escape route for which in their better
moments they so desperately longed.

British Railways' re-possession of its forecourt property in 1963
meant that for some two years the midnight patrol was without a
permanent base; but whilst the international Salvation Army world
was pursuing its rejoicing way in the wake of the 1965 centenary
celebrations, Molly Scott was pursuing her own private rejoicing
way as she moved into the 'new' midnight post at 11 Argyle Street,
a block away from the old Faith Cottage.

Until the mid-1970s Faith House continued the tradition of
providing a gracious and homely atmosphere for women and girls
disillusioned with 'the game'. By then, however, altered legislation
regarding prostitution had driven them off the streets, rendering
midnight patrol work null and void, and Faith House was adapted
to other uses. By 1982, legislation not withstanding, prostitutes
were again very much in evidence on the streets of London's West
End, and in November of that year two more young but experienced officers were appointed to midnight patrol work.[39]

'Oh, God', prayed Molly Scott, embarking on this work in 1954,
'don't let the things I see and hear defile my own mind. It's only as
I am kept clean in my own soul that I can help others. Oh, Lord, I

am going into this work for thy sake—I trust thee to keep me holy in the midst of it!'[40]

'This work needs special prayer', was the brave quiet of an entry in the notebook of a 'Cellar, Gutter and Garret Brigade' girl engaged in similar work in 1885.

It was fast becoming obvious by that time that this work needed not only special prayer, but special training too. The training of officer cadets for evangelical work had commenced in 1880, but, as *The War Cry* of 28 July 1888 pointed out: 'Large and important factor as the rescue work is getting to be in the constantly complicating Army sum, it has grown so gradually and so quietly from a sort of side issue into a definite department, that it has only been organized after a kind of "from hand-to-mouth" fashion to meet the needs of every day.'

That month, therefore, saw the first commissioning of rescue officers by Mrs Bramwell Booth. Presumably by this time Miss Sapsworth (that Clapton lady of middle age and independent means) had been made a Salvation Army soldier, for on this occasion, 'as Mrs Bramwell's earliest ally and comrade in the work', she received her commission as staff-captain.[41]

The training of the first rescue officers had been very much *in situ*—getting on with the job, commissions being issued as an afterthought. By June 1889, however, the rescue training programme was in full swing under the roof of the erstwhile receiving house at 259 Mare Street, Hackney, with Mrs Major Rose Simmonds in charge (her husband holding his own appointment at International Headquarters).[42]

Addressing rescue officers in January 1888, William Booth had explained that 'because of the newness of the work and the general inexperience in it they had refrained from laying down very definite orders and regulations concerning it; but the time would come when the results of their experience would be gathered and their work more completely systematised.'[43] That time came at the beginning of October 1892, when the first *Orders and Regulations for Rescue Homes* were issued. Eminently practical they were—despite certain Victorian trappings which strike the modern reader as quaint. For example:

1. The quarter of an hour before dinner should, whenever the weather allows, be spent in the garden. . . . The girls should be encouraged to

24

take exercise, and should be allowed to run, or skip, or play innocent games; or they may do a little gardening, or chop wood, etc. . . . no noisy annoyance to neighbours, no rude horse-play, no screaming and shouting, can be permitted.

2. Public and Bank holidays will employ the ingenuity of officers to the utmost. The whole or part of the day the girls will attend, where possible, the Salvation Army public meetings . . . the one aim in view being to make these occasions—so associated in the past with hours of wildest revelry and sin—days on which they can look back as bright and sunny spots of pure and wholesome enjoyment. *Chapter* III: *Section* 4: *Paragraph* E.

Chapter IV: section 1: paragraph 10 maintained:

The old girls are sure to come and visit the old home, and many of them will make the captain the bank for their wages, and will consult with her how best to lay out their money. This should be encouraged as much as possible.

One such way of laying out their wages had been suggested to them by Mrs Bramwell Booth at the Army's 26th anniversary celebrations the previous year. 'At the Crystal Palace tea for women and girls who had been helped by the Women's Social Reform Battalion' (a title which, fortunately, very quickly went out of use!) 'Mrs Bramwell Booth made a proposition to her old rescue lasses, which was most cordially received and warmly applauded. She stated that, of the 5,000 girls who had been dealt with through the Rescue Headquarters, at least 2,000 could easily contribute one penny per week towards the support of a new rescue home, thus forming an annual income of about between £400 and £500 a year, which would support a home accommodating about 25 girls. . . . Really and truly,' the report goes on, 'the fund was started by the numerous coins put into Mrs Bramwell's hands before she left the tea-table. . . . Here is a beautiful chance for all saved rescue girls to repay, in some sense, the toil, the care, the love, and the expense which has been so freely and gladly expended upon them.'[44]

As was always her gift to do, Florence Booth managed to make the same facts sound so much warmer and more personal: 'For a long time I have been desiring to find some practical plan by which you could each one be enabled to take a definite part in the work of helping some who are still in the bondage from which you yourselves have been released. . . . It is proposed that we should open a home, for the support of which you as a family shall become responsible. . . . I do not intend to receive subscriptions for this home from anyone except through you. *It is to be yours.* Some of my friends think it is hardly safe to rely on you, but I think I know you best, and I believe you will respond to this call from me without hesitation and without delay.'[45]

By 1894 the 'Out-of-Love Fund' idea had grown to embrace the aim of '*repaying* what has been spent upon them, so as to wipe off their debt to the friends of the rescue work, by refunding all that has been spent upon them over and above what they had been able to earn while in the homes'. Wrote Florence Booth: 'I had the pleasure of giving a nicely-bound Bible to five whose contributions to the 'Out-of-Love Fund' had already accomplished this, and thus gave them the first places in the list of what we propose to call our roll of honour.'

Another roll of honour there is, unwritten, and for the most part unsung, upon which appear not only the names of Elizabeth Cottrill, Florence Booth, Elizabeth Sapsworth and Molly Scott, but those of Caroline Reynolds, Caroline Frost, Adelaide Cox, Mrs Goldsmith, Marianne Asdell and countless 'rescue' captains and lieutenants whose anonymity simply lends strength to the impact of their selfless service in the cause of 'somebody's daughters'.

Although the 51 'Rescue and other Homes' listed in *The Salvation Army Year Book* for 1916 had, by 1917, been designated 'Industrial and other Homes', rescue work in essence did not diminish. Indeed the 'other homes' were early an outcome of that work: maternity homes, mother and baby homes, children's homes, industrial homes—not to mention police court work, the poor man's lawyer, an adoption department, an emigration department and a servants' registry. ('If you can't adopt a baby, can't you have your next servant from Dalston?')

'*Reclaim London*' had become Mrs Bramwell Booth's registered address for the rescue work by 1886. 'Reclaim the World' might well be the modern-day slogan of her globe-spanning salvationist social service successors.

3
The double difficulty

AMONG the original six girls received into the Hanbury Street refuge in May 1884 was one so fondly attached to her baby that she dreaded being separated from it. During the first little meeting held in the kitchen she found the Saviour and began to give steady proof of a real change of heart. Work was procured for her at a laundry, and a few things provided to furnish a room, the baby being kept at a neighbouring crèche during the day. But since the young mother seemed incapable of graduating to ironing, she was only able to earn eight shillings a week, and to do that stood at the wash-tub 12 hours a day.[1] Inevitably her health broke down and the rescue officers had to find lighter work for her, as well as assisting with rent and the support of her baby.[2] This proved to be their earliest involvement with that Victorian euphemism known as 'the double difficulty'.

By the time the Army's organisational powers caught up with its rapidly expanding rescue work four years later, and produced commissions for the first already-on-the-job rescue officers, the 'double difficulty' off-shoot had become an integral part of the work. Among the captains commissioned on that historic occasion were Mr and Mrs Frost,[3] a Channel Isles couple, he with a lifetime of professional soldiering behind him, she a certificated midwife before she was 17. Having become salvationists, they had turned their Guernsey home into a miniature receiving house, from whence girls were sent to the Southern Division rescue home on the mainland. Preparing for a visit to the island, Mrs Bramwell Booth sent word that she especially wished to see Mrs Frost. This intimation Carrie Frost received with a flood of tears.

'"What's the matter?" asked the astounded captain. "Don't you want to see Mrs Bramwell?"

'No, she didn't.

'"Why not? Are you condemned about anything?"

'"No—oh, no!"

'"Are your books all right?"

'"Quite right."

'The captain pondered. "I believe you're under conviction for the work," he said at last, "and ought to go right in." Mrs Frost did not know "if that were it". She only knew it was midnight in her soul. She felt sure Mrs Bramwell would never want such a stupid, blundering worker as she felt herself to be, but if Mrs Bramwell did, she knew she never would go.

'She had to meet her first at dinner.

'"I feel as if you belonged to me," said the sweet voice of the rescue chief. Mrs Frost wished she wouldn't feel so!

28

'She had never known quite how it was, but when, at night, Mrs Bramwell said, "If I wished you to come and help me in London, would you be willing?" She answered, hardly knowing what she said:

' "If I can be of more use to you in London than here, I'm quite willing to come."

'The darkness fled in a moment. Light and peace were round her. She saw she had been resisting God's will. She went home to her husband' (already a staid elderly soldier when he had married his 16-year-old child-bride). 'Together they knelt and said:

' "Now, Lord, here we are. If you want us in the work, open the way."

'She had a dozen engagements ahead, but somehow the way was cleared, and in six weeks she and her husband were launched in London rescue work at Chelsea, where she acted as our first regular midnight officer, as well as having charge of a home.' Significantly the 1889 *War Cry* article which tells their story is headed 'Captains William and Caroline Frost of the Rescue Work'; no question here of 'Captain and Mrs'—it was Carrie who was needed to spearhead this important work, and because he was married to her, William came too.[4]

During 1982 an important find came to light in the subterranean regions of the Army's Social Services Headquarters at 280 Mare Street, Hackney. Some four-score hand-written record books, dating back to 1886, carry detailed accounts of every girl passing through its rescue homes over the next 40 years. This material shows the official account of the beginnings of mother and baby work to be inaccurate when it states: 'Homes had been provided . . . where mothers and infants could stay until able to go out to situations or otherwise face the world again. The first was established in 1889 in Pimlico. It is also said that it had been situated previously in Chelsea, having been taken over from a friend, Mrs Walker, who began this work in 1888.' (*The History of The Salvation Army,* Volume 3, page 53: Nelson, 1955.) In fact the hand-written record bears evidence to a girl being sent to the Chelsea home as early as 16 March 1886,[5] the first mother and baby appearing there in August of that year.[6] The book also witnesses to the fact that Mrs Frost herself sent a girl from Guernsey to London on 12 July,[7] another following on 8

29

October—on Mrs Bramwell's advice—by which time Mrs Frost is not only the sender, but also the 'friend to whom reference can be made', her address being given as 52 Blenheim Street, Chelsea.[8] A week earlier *The War Cry* had carried first word of the proposal 'to station officers at . . . Charing Cross and elsewhere, from eight p.m. to one or two o'clock in the morning . . .',[9] and a 3 November record book entry tells of Florence Spalding, aged 18, having been 'rescued at Charing Cross the first night Mrs Frost went out'.[10] The first pregnant girl was sent to Chelsea from the receiving house at the end of November, her confinement taking place on 24 February 1887, the place of birth being recorded as '52 Blenheim Street, Chelsea (Home)', and the final statement being signed by Marianne Asdell (of whom more in chapter 5).[11] The last clear reference to the Chelsea home is on 27 March 1889,[12] although a somewhat ambiguous entry appears a month later, which could suggest it was still functioning in April.[13] Clearly then, the mother and baby work at Chelsea commenced a good two years earlier than has hitherto been recognised, and much the same can be said for Pimlico.

More than a year before references to Chelsea ceased, Pimlico began to make its appearance in the record books. On 3 January 1888 (not 1889 as the official *History* states) a girl was sent 'to Pimlico, Mrs Frost's'.[14] Had Blenheim Street been situated at the Pimlico end of Chelsea, the entry under discussion might well have referred to the Chelsea home; but although Blenheim Street is no longer in existence, a glance at a 19th-century street map shows it to have been at the opposite end of Chelsea from Pimlico,[15] and therefore the two names would not have been interchangeable. In April the first pregnancy was sent to the home at Pimlico[16] (for which, unfortunately, no address has yet been discovered), and the first confinement took place in July,[17] although after the end of that year no further confinements are recorded as having taken place there, it being used rather as a home to which mothers came with their babies after the births had taken place elsewhere. In October 1888 the term 'No. IV Home'[18] began to be used as an alternative designation for Pimlico, until by the summer of 1889 it had taken over completely, so that there is nothing in the record books after June of that year to indicate that the Pimlico home had ceased to function, every pertinent entry thereafter being labelled 'No. IV Home'. Fortunately the first issue of *The Deliverer* magazine came to birth in time to inform its readers of the late June move of the mother and baby home from Pimlico to Notting Hill— where it was still to be known as 'No. IV Home'.[19] 'The move is an

30

improvement,' wrote Mrs Bramwell Booth. 'At Pimlico we did not possess a blade of grass, back or front, and the dear babies did not thrive. At Notting Hill they will have a tiny garden, and the secretary is, I know, praying and believing for a tent umbrella that they may be out in the air as much as possible this summer. I hope friends will remember her "cradle fund", when the baby has grown out of long clothes and short clothes. We have to supply most of ours with all the necessaries they do not bring with them!'[20] When, after a few months, the mother was placed in a situation (usually domestic work), her mistress would be encouraged to make regular contributions to this cradle fund, and a sum of 6d per week was granted out of it for the support of the child where no maintenance money was forthcoming from its father. The child would either be cared for by the girl's family or a 'nursing mother', or would be adopted. The same issue of *The Deliverer* identifies the new home as being at Ladbroke Grove,[21] whilst six months later we learn that its house number was 90.[22]

To return to Mrs Frost. That confinements no longer took place at Pimlico after the end of 1888 can be explained by the fact that on 21 January 1889 the hand-written records give first mention of 'No. V Home' at '27 Devonshire Road, Hackney', to which Mary Ann Elliott, aged 14, was admitted, having been seduced by her own brother. Her confinement took place on 7 May at that address, and her final statement (together with all succeeding statements involving confinements at No. V home) was signed by Caroline Frost.[23] Again, the fact that the writer of the official *History* had not the good fortune to have come upon the early record books means that he does not acknowledge the existence of the Devonshire Road home. Instead, he assumes that the first Hackney maternity home was Ivy House, which he records as being opened towards the end of 1889.[24] 'Our salvation accoucheuse, Captain Mrs Frost', was, however, very much in business at the No. V (Devonshire Road) home as early as January 1889.

On 26 April 1890 Herbert Kidd is recorded as having been born to his mother, Eliza, at 271 Mare Street, Hackney,[25] which on 19 June the record books describe for the first time as Ivy House.[26] There seems to have been a period of a few weeks when *two* No. V homes were operating at the same time, for not only was Herbert Kidd born at Ivy House on 26 April, but Minnie Brooks gave birth to the stillborn child of Thomas McPherson on 11 May at 27 Devonshire Road.[27] Herbert Kidd's claim to fame as the first baby

31

to be born at Ivy House did not, however, stand him in good stead. He died five months later.

The Deliverer reveals the official opening of Ivy House to have been on Monday 2 June 1890, the premises being large enough to cater for 21 girls and their babies under Mrs Frost's guidance. A *War Cry* report several months earlier had stated that 'the house previously used for this work' (Devonshire Road) would be utilised to increase the accommodation of the receiving house[28]—Brent House, at 29 Devonshire Road[22]—whose secretary was yet another Caroline, and yet another married woman with an appointment in her own right—Mrs Carrie Reynolds.[29] (Contrary to popular belief, Mrs Reynolds was not a widow. Like William Frost, Mr Reynolds 'came too', although never holding rank.)[30] By 1896 Mrs Colonel Barker (see chapter 7) is reported as having charge of the *maternity* receiving house[31]—as distinct from the rescue receiving house. In 1909 Brent House was described as 'A home for hitherto well-conducted young women who have been led astray, and are about to become mothers.'[32] Such a one was Phoebe Atkins, although whether she was 'hitherto well-conducted' is a matter for speculation. 'Some comments have lately been made in the daily journals with regard to the statements of a girl named Phoebe Atkins, whose child recently died of malnutrition,' reported *The Darkest England Gazette* for 14 October 1893. 'With regard to the statements made, we should have thought it was thoroughly well known by this time that Salvation Army rescue homes are *not* managed according to prison system, the inmates being at perfect liberty to leave whenever they please. There was no difference whatever made in this case, Phoebe Atkins could leave when she pleased. Any statement, therefore, to the effect that the girl was "obliged to stay" in the home for three months is incorrect. Moreover, she never asked for cow's milk, nor was it necessary for the child to have it.

'It may be pointed out that Phoebe Atkins entered the rescue home from Poplar workhouse in February of this year. She obtained a situation to which she went on July 8th, so that at the time of the child's death she had been out of the rescue home for over two months. The child died at the house of a person who was nursing it, and who received it from the mother herself on the 7th of July last.

'Since, therefore, both mother and child left the home in the early part of July, we entirely disclaim any responsibility for the condition of the child, which, it seems, although originally very puny, thrived during its stay in the home, and never had any illness there whatsoever.

'Further, some time after the child had been thus placed out to nurse by the mother, the officers of the home, acting entirely from the purest motive of philanthropy, called on the nurse in question, and being dissatisfied with the child's condition, arranged with the mother that it should be removed. Subsequently, however, the mother altered her mind and wrote saying she "wished the child to remain where it was". Consequently, our rescue officers were unable to take it away, and, so far as they were concerned, the matter entirely dropped. . . . We may add that a properly qualified medical man gives most careful oversight to the babies' home, sees all the babies frequently, and is always sent for in any case of illness.'

Whether it was this same 'properly qualified medical man' who informed Mrs Bramwell Booth as early as 1887 that a small hospital of 15 beds could be 'obtained complete, with all necessaries, for £400',[33] will never be known; certain it is that such a project, though dear to Florence Booth's heart, was to be long in its fulfilling, despite the gift of 'some valuable diamonds to aid in its erection', the donor suggesting that the little hospital be built entirely by such gifts. As he was yet again to do in March 1890 regarding the future use of 27 Devonshire Road, the writer of the 'Headquarters' column in *The War Cry* 'jumped the gun' regarding 'a lady, who is an MD' offering to undertake the medical work in connection with the proposed hospital. This 'leak' appeared in the 11 May 1889 issue, but was not announced publicly by Mrs Bramwell Booth until the fifth anniversary celebrations of the rescue work in London's Exeter Hall early in June. 'In this hospital', it was reported, 'they would be able to train salvationist nurses, for, of course, salvation would be first in this branch of the work as well as in every other.' The November issue of *The Deliverer* reveals the 'lady who is an MD' to be Dr Edith Huntley. It also reveals the need not for boots, but for 'any old linen and blankets, things so much needed both in the hospital and in our maternity home'. By the following March, however, Florence Booth is disclosing: 'I am very disappointed that we have been unable to carry out our hospital scheme. In spite of all our endeavours, we are still forced to look upon it as a plan for the future. Multitudinous difficulties have prevented our finding a suitable house; and, in addition to this, our funds have been, and are, so low, that we do not feel justified in incurring such heavy additional financial responsibility as would be involved in this scheme, for the present.

'Dr Edith Huntley has waited patiently with us as long as there was any hope of our being able to carry out our plans, and, in the meantime, has been acting as medical officer to our rescue staff and training home, and as many of the rescue homes as are within reach. She fully understands and sympathises with the difficulties that have so unexpectedly stopped us at the threshold of our hospital enterprise, and shares our disappointment in relinquishing it. To her regret, as well as ours, she is, therefore, shortly leaving us, to enter on another field of medical missionary labour, that will afford her the scope which we cannot offer at present.'

Meanwhile the men in the city colony were faring better than their sisters in the rescue homes. 'Captain (Dr) Hart to be Medical Officer for the City Colony, under Commissioner Cadman', announced an April 1891 edition of *The War Cry*. They evidently had less need of hospitalisation than Mrs Booth's clientele.

Sixteen months later: 'Mrs Bramwell is happy in having been able to secure the services of an efficient lady doctor for the rescue homes. This, as our readers know, has long been Mrs Bramwell's earnest wish. Our dear friend, Doctor Wilson, who has hitherto acted in this capacity, and for whose kind services we have been most grateful, has consented still to act as consulting surgeon.

'Mrs Bramwell feels that many ladies in the neighbourhood may, like herself, be glad of the services of a medical Christian lady. She is glad of this opportunity of furnishing them with her address, as below—

Mrs FRAZER NASH
(LRCP and S Ed, LFP and S Glasgow),
246, Richmond Road, Hackney.' [34]

Still no sign of a hospital. Things were, however, developing upon another front. An August 1891 issue of *The War Cry* had carried the following 'advance word' by its gun-jumping 'Headquarters' columnist: 'Mrs Bramwell Booth has decided to immediately extend the nursing work which she has for some time been organising, and will be glad to have applications for appointment as Salvation Army nurses from any young women who feel able to undertake that.' But not all her goods had been displayed in *The War Cry*'s shop window on this occasion it transpires. In the following month's edition of *The Deliverer* (had *The War Cry* man seen the proofs?) Mrs Booth elaborates: 'One small department of our work, in which we have met with much success, has, I think, been scarcely mentioned in these pages, and I am anxious that friends should understand that we have now a competent band of trained nurses in connection with our maternity home, whom we would gladly send to any part of the country. . . . Hitherto . . . we have had most numerous testimonies from their employers, speaking both of the efficiency with which their duty has been performed, and of the comfort and happiness they have brought into the household.

'One lady the other day told us that whereas she had on previous occasions found the advent of a stranger to be a trying ordeal to herself and other members of the household, the moment the salvationist nurse entered the room she felt as though the sunshine of Heaven came in with her, and the four weeks they spent together had been of the happiest description. It is needless for me to say our charges are always moderate, and though varied according to the circumstances of the employers, I would like to remind salvation officers that for them we make very special terms. Any young woman who would like to be trained to fill this capacity should apply to me at once, as we are making arrangements for a large increase of this branch of the work.' This appeal, we are informed in the following issue, was well responded to by young women anxious to be trained as nurses, and by the Christmas number there are tidings that 'Mrs Bramwell has recently added a small nurses' home, and training operations are now being set on foot, not only for the nurses we need for our own cases, but for many hundreds of friends and soldiers outside. . . . Though this scheme is only a few weeks old, 170 converted women have applied to be trained as nurses; . . . The little nurses' home will be in full working order in a week or two. It is needless, I should think, to add that we shall arrange for the most thorough training.' The nurses' home was at 225 Richmond Road, and adjoined [35] the corner property of Ivy House at 271 Mare Street, [36] thus coming under Captain Mrs Frost's ever-expanding jurisdiction. 'Six probationers and five nurses are at present in residence. . . . They are trained for six months in the most thorough and severe manner in the maternity home, where each probationer will have an opportunity of watching from 60 to 100 cases. After this they will live in the nurses' home, close by, and give their services to whomsoever the head of the home sees fit—receiving only board and lodging, uniform, washing, and from three to four shillings per week pocket money. They may be sent out to paying patients, in which case the fee will go towards the home, or they may be sent to care for a woman among the poorest of the poor.' Interestingly enough we gain from the same report the information that unmarried mothers were not received at Ivy House indiscriminately. 'The maternity home . . . usually . . . receives only cases of first confinement, under peculiar circumstances.'[37] The 1892 *Report of the Committee of Inquiry upon the Darkest England Scheme* gives a slightly different emphasis, finding that 'To the maternity home any woman is admitted upon payment of a subscription of 1s per week for 10 weeks, the object being rather to train nurses in midwifery than to afford charitable relief.'

By May 1894 Florence Booth is writing in *The Deliverer* of the proposed 'transformation, after careful consideration, of our maternity home into a hospital. . . . By transferring elsewhere the work of the rescue home proper, the finding of situations and the mothering of the family of both old and new girls [ante-natal and post-natal cases], we shall be able to almost double our accommodation for maternity cases at Ivy House. . . . My friend, Major Sapsworth, is taking up this cause for me, and will act as superintendent to the hospital when it is opened.'

'Not to be at an entire disadvantage herself as the future superintendent, the remarkably fresh-minded Elizabeth Sapsworth, now in later middle life, had begun taking a course of lectures in midwifery—through her ear trumpet! (She eventually passed all the theory examinations.) It only impressed on her more deeply the indispensable need for a matron with the necessary training and experience, also native nursing gifts—plus The Salvation Army essentials, self-sacrifice and "love for souls". How and when would such a woman be found?' Let Madge Unsworth continue the story, as it is found in the December 1944/January 1945 issue of *The Deliverer:* 'There came to Ivy House one morning a skilled nurse seeking a specially trustworthy assistant. Having been called to a difficult maternity case at the residence of a duke, the nurse needed another reliable pair of hands. Elizabeth Sapsworth received the visitor. She discovered in the course of conversation that Nurse Mrs Sowden had previously been in charge of a large maternity hospital. Promising to send her an assistant, after Army fashion she then prayed with her—unwittingly meeting another, though secret, need of the capable but spiritually untaught stranger.

'The "assistant" who went next day from the humble little East London home to the peer's mansion "lived salvation" under her superior's interested and astonished eyes. When the difficult case was successfully over, Mrs Sowden called again at Ivy House, this time to see Elizabeth Sapsworth on her own account. She now told the salvationist something of her story—how, left alone years before to support and educate four boys, she had studied and taken up maternity nursing as a career, succeeding beyond every hope. The boys were now off her hands and all things prosperous; yet Mrs Sowden was conscious of lacking the true fulfilment of her vocation.

'Greatly interested, and with a dawning intuition of things to come, Elizabeth Sapsworth invited the visitor to tea at her own home next day, saying that there they would have more time and freedom in speaking of "things spiritual". Now the austere surroundings of "259", and the colonel's plain uniform dress, had deepened some vague ideas previously formed by Mrs Sowden as to the poverty of all salvationists. Fearful, therefore, of encroaching on a possibly scanty food supply, she took with her in a basket bread and butter, eggs, jam and tea to the address given! With growing surprise she found herself walking up the drive of a large house and being ushered by a smart parlour-maid into a beautiful home. Hastily she revised her ideas, and left the basket with the umbrellas in the hall! She was thinking furiously. Here were two sisters who had the means to spend their days in all the comfort of this the mother's family mansion if they had so chosen; instead, they were devoting their time entirely to the poor. Could she do less, when the plight of the matronless hospital-to-be was put before her?

' "Afternoon tea" turned into a dedication service. Mrs Sowden consecrated herself to God and humanity. Abandoning her hard-won position among a wealthy and influential clientele, she accepted the meagre allowance of a Salvation Army captain and the oversight of a small hospital for patients of the poorest and most pitiable type.

'For 16 years the hospital superintendent and the matron, soon fast friends, were to work unitedly through trying days, financial crises, and that not less difficult period of transition when the requirements of the London Obstetrical Society were being adjusted to those of the new Central Midwives' Board.'

By the time The Mothers' Hospital, Lower Clapton Road, was opened in 1913, both Elizabeth Sapsworth and Annie Sowden had retired, but as they had been able to build so securely on the foundation laid by Caroline Frost, so Miriam Castle (first matron of 'The Mothers'') and her successors to the present day have continued to build well, extending the ministry of the hospital to include not only the needs of the unmarried mother, but those of poorer married women, as well as a limited number of wealthier fee-paying patients. High-standard training in midwifery continues to be a feature of the hospital—not least for Salvation Army officer nurses contemplating overseas service in that chain of maternity hospitals and clinics which encircles the Army world.

This 1894 development of the maternal home into a fully-fledged maternity hospital meant that Caroline Frost was free to pursue fresh paths in the cause of the East End's ever-expanding population. 'Eighteen months ago', ran an 1896 *War Cry* report, 'Mrs Bramwell Booth appointed Ensign Mrs Frost to inaugurate a scheme, which was first called "The Slum Maternity Work". During the short time since then the work has so prospered and branched out that "District Nursing" is now a more appropriate name than the original one.

'At first the nurses undertook only maternity cases, but now they go to all who need them. The London Hospital is kind about allowing them to attend their lectures, and Mrs Frost says that the respectable poor make an excellent training-ground.'[38]

A year earlier the address given as the base for slum maternity work is 46 Tudor Road, South Hackney,[39] and an 1897 *All the World* article outlines in some detail the need for such a ministry. 'Some unskilled and often intemperate neighbour—a lineal descendant of famous Mrs Gamp—is the usual attendant at a poor woman's confinement. The mother suffers all her life from the effects of neglect and wrong treatment, and the beginning of life to the baby is the beginning of dirt, hunger, unsuitable food, and sips of gin and brandy. The Salvation Army district or slum nurses attend confinements with or without a doctor, many being thoroughly qualified midwives.

'Of the lives they save there is no record—it is an ordinary matter to them to be called to women sinking under their trial for lack of medical aid, and the necessities of everyday life. The case-books compress stories of human woe and sisterly help into something

38

like the following: "Called at Poverty Row at 2:30 a.m. Woman very exhausted. Baby born. No food but dry bread. Attended to mother and child. Sent milk and eggs. Cleaned room." . . .'

' "We always make a charge if the people can pay anything at all," said 'The Mother' (as Mrs Frost is called by her nurses and her patients), "and what they give goes to buy food for those who have neither money or food. What do we want? . . . Clothes. We have people barefoot and half-naked. . . . And we don't *give* them always. We make them up in penny and two-penny bundles. People like to buy, and we like them to feel they are not paupers receiving charity. . . . Then we want old linen. And baby-clothes of all sorts. . . . And money. . . . And boots. And flannel. And meat for soup, and eggs, and so on. And work for women and men."

' "Anything else?"

' "Yes! *Everything.* Nothing comes amiss to poor people who have only wants." ' [40]

Small wonder that within 18 months this valuable asset was transferred to New York City[41] with the rank of adjutant (her husband being given his promotion at the same time and accompanying her). [42]

'The Thirty-fourth anniversary of the Women's Social Work, celebrated at the Central Hall, Westminster, . . . was associated with an incident which will be marked down as historic in the annals of that important department,' declared a 1918 *War Cry* report. Since no such 'marking down' appears to have been indulged in until now, we pause at this point in our narrative so to do. 'It was none other than the announcement by the President of the Local Government Board, who chairmaned [sic] the meeting, of a Treasury grant of £2,000 towards the cost of a section of Women's Social Work which has a direct bearing on national welfare.

'Maternity and child welfare, of course, has long been one of the prime concerns of The Salvation Army, and Commissioner Adelaide Cox [now leader of the Women's Social Work] is to be cordially congratulated upon the sure and efficient manner in which that branch of Women's Social endeavour has been developed.

39

'It now forms part of a bold and enlightened government programme for rebuilding the nation, and this new departure in the direction of state endowment is a matter of immense encouragement to all concerned.'[43]

This first gesture by the British Government in the form of state aid for Salvation Army social work was, as *The War Cry* noted, long in coming. Having come at last, however, it was to set a precedent in that kind of support funding which has, through the years, proved so vital to the maintenance and expansion of the practical ministrations of those who follow in Booth's boots.

Since this book was first published, the location of the Pimlico maternity home (see page 30) has been established through the birth certificate of a child born there on 10 October 1888, as being at 33 Cumberland Street.

4
Strictly confidential!

POOR Harry Stott! 'Sixteen next April, rather tall for his age, brown hair, full grey eyes, cut at corner of left eye, pigeon breasted, right knee bent inwards a little . . . black Scotch cap, black coat and waistcoat, light grey cloth trousers, lace-up boots . . . about three months ago . . . went to the Salvation Army barracks at New Wortley, Leeds III, where Captain Dobson was then in command, whose faithful words broke his heart, and brought him to the feet of Jesus,' reported the 2 February 1882 *War Cry,* under the caption 'Missing!' 'His new born faith could not be restrained; so he went home and made it known that he was saved, and that in the Army. His father, upon hearing this news, which should have cheered his heart, at once commenced to curse and swear, threatening to break his neck if he went there again. But he continued to go, which caused his father to be more enraged and to pour upon him more oaths, curses, and threats, upon which the lad, who could get no peace at home, ran away and has not been heard of since, 12 weeks today. . . . Any captain or soldier, or anyone who reads this would oblige by keeping a look-out for him, who, if found, may be informed that his father has since not only been brought to repentance for his cruelty to his son, but has also been brought to the feet of Jesus, and got a Saviour's pardon. A few hours before he got salvation he was on the verge of sending into eternity his wife and seven children. Getting into words with his wife, he got soon into blows, and then dragged her about by the hair. Then he thought he would murder her. He felt for his knife, but here God took hold of him, and that night he was found at the same barracks where his son got saved, weeping on account of his sins. His heart was broke whilst Captain Milner was singing— "Heaven's beautiful city, I long to be there." He is now going there with joy, but is sorrowing on account of his son, who he so cruelly drove away from home.—Captain Harrison. (The General wishes the above notice to be given out in every station.)'

Harry's was the first missing person's appeal to be carried by *The War Cry,* and resulted in a letter from Ninfield the following month, headed 'The Missing Salvation Lad', and saying that he was making his way home.[1] By 1884 such appeals were being made fairly frequently, the most pathetic of which concerned 'a *minister's wife,* aged 60, grey hair, height about five feet, very stout through disease, who left her home on the 7th November. If she should be heard of at any station, please report'.

During 1884-5 *The War Cry* featured a weekly letter from the General 'To the Soldiers of The Salvation Army Scattered Throughout the World'. Letter No. XXXI, dated 11 July 1885, was on the highly topical subject of 'Fallen Women', this being the very week in which W. T. Stead was publishing 'The Maiden Tribute of Modern Babylon' exposé in the *Pall Mall Gazette.* Giving the subject most thorough and explicit treatment, the General finally comes to the point that 'here is a host of mothers and fathers and guardians who want information about lost children. If there is an army of fallen girls what an army of broken-hearted mothers there must be who lie awake through the long night hours on their beds weeping over their lost girls! And what a multitude of fathers there must be who never mention them and in whose presence no one dares to repeat their names! How they must long for information and help! What can they do?

'Something *must* be done. Something *shall* be done, and *at once.* . . .

'In London a house of help and enquiry must be at once provided, to be *open day and night* . . . to which parents who have lost girls can apply for information.'

A week later there appeared under the heading 'Help and Enquiry' the invitation to parents, relations and friends in any part of the world, which was to be featured regularly from September onwards as 'An Offer of Help in Seven Languages'. (See page 21.) It concluded with assurance that the 'Letters will be regarded as strictly confidential.'[2]

Having been successful, in conjunction with W. T. Stead, in bringing about the passing of the Criminal Law Amendment Act in August of that year, the Army immediately launched a 'New National Scheme for the Deliverance of Unprotected Girls and the Rescue of the Fallen', which proposed, among other things, 'The immediate formation of a central office of help and enquiry in London', one of the functions of which was that it should be a place to which 'parents, guardians and friends can apply for information respecting their children and others whom they may have reason to believe have gone astray or are in danger of doing so'.

'Where would such an office of enquiry be situated?

1. The chief central office must, of course, be in London.

2. Auxiliary offices of enquiry would be opened as soon as possible in Paris, New York, Chicago, Toronto, Melbourne, Sydney, and ultimately in all the principal cities of the world where the Army is at work.

3. At least one officer of The Salvation Army, or an auxiliary acting as one, can at once be appointed in most of the towns where the English language is spoken, who can be relied upon to co-operate with the central office of enquiry.'[3]

In May 1886 comes the first definite reference to the fact that these plans had been implemented and an enquiry department had been set in motion. An anonymous letter sent to Mrs Bramwell Booth gave evidence that a girl 'leading a bad life' was anxious to leave both the address mentioned and the type of life she led there. Carrie Reynolds was dispatched from the receiving house to seek out the address, 'and was flatly told that no such person was known there. Mrs Reynolds walked home praying for guidance in the matter', the upshot of which was that 'it was decided . . . an officer connected with the enquiry department (an ex-policeman) should go dressed as a gentleman and enquire for the girl. He did so, asking for her by the same name . . . and was readily admitted and shown into the parlour, while the girl was called down to meet him. . . .

'"I do not remember to have seen you before, sir," she said, as she took a seat at his side. "Probably not, but you see me now and I see you," was his answer, and the officer having assured himself that this was the girl he was seeking, threw off disguise and told her his errand, viz.: that of rescuing her from her life of shame. She listened attentively to all he said, and he went away. The girl's mother was communicated with and taken to the house. The keeper dare not shut the door against her as she could have done previous to the passing of the new Act [see page 20] and in a few minutes the mother and daughter were clasped in each other's embrace . . . while the woman of the house hurried out of the room with an unlawful visitor, whose pipe and grog were left standing on the table.'[4]

'We do not know of any unpaid agency other than our own which undertakes to trace and hunt up and bring back missing ones,' declared *All the World* in June 1886. Sometimes the tracing and the hunting up called for all the skilled ingenuity the ex-policeman and his comrades could muster. At other times, as in the case of 15-year-old Annie Knowles, that all-prevenient grace about which salvationists know a great deal rendered such sleuthing unnecessary. On 23 March 1886, Book I of the unpublished receiving house statements tells us, 'whilst Mrs Bramwell was speaking to Annie a telegram was put into her hand—from Brighton—saying Mrs Knowles' little daughter was missing. On finding it to be the very girl she was then speaking with, Mrs B. Booth wired to her mother to meet her at Brighton station'.[5]

'You don't need novels if you come to The Salvation Army,' declared William Booth at the fifth anniversary of the rescue work in 1889. 'There is nothing in any of them so romantic as the things that are happening every day among us. . . . Our ability to find lost people is on the increase. During the first four months of 1888, there were 250 sought for, of whom 60 were found. During the first four months of 1889, 318 persons were sought and 116 found.'[6] By Christmas 1891 the annual number of people found had risen to 600,[7] the increase without doubt being attributable to publicity surrounding the publication of *In Darkest England and the Way Out.*

The terms of reference of the enquiry department had, by 1892, widened considerably: 'This department will *search* in any part of the world for missing or runaway relatives and friends; will seek to *bring to justice* men who have ruined or wronged girls or women; will *enquire* into the respectability of people, houses, or situations, and generally advise and help, as far as possible, those in difficulty. Beyond the above, it is prepared to undertake detective cases and investigation of certain descriptions, for those in a position to pay, at moderate rates.'[8]

A multiplicity of emigration programmes in the early decades of the 20th century and the social disruption caused by two world wars led to an even greater demand upon the skilled services of the Army's missing persons departments around the world, until by the 1980s an average of 5,000 enquiries was annually received by the London office alone, with a 70 per cent contact (rather than success) rate—for not everyone contacted *wants* to be 'found', and the 'strictly confidential' clause of 1885 is still rigidly adhered to.*

*For a fuller treatment of this subject see *Missing* by Richard Williams, published 1969 by Hodder and Stoughton.

THROUGH the years other departments have been set up closely relating to the problems of missing persons. In 1907, for instance, General Booth was asked to undertake an effort to check the increasing spate of suicides, and an anti-suicide bureau came into being, headed by Colonel Isaac Unsworth and Colonel Mrs Barker, widow of the Army's prison work pioneer. Such a 'success' did it become that branches were opened in the principal cities of the United Kingdom, and similar agencies were established overseas.[9]

LAUNCHING his 1890 *Darkest England* social scheme, William Booth described one of his most novel ideas in the chapter entitled 'Assistance in General' for the submerged tenth of the population whom he reckoned to be below the poverty line: 'While I have been busily occupied in working out my scheme for the registration of labour, it has occurred to me more than once, why could not something like the same plan be adopted in relation to men who want wives and women who want husbands? . . . Of course, the registration of the unmarried who wish to marry would be a matter of much greater delicacy than the registration of the joiners and stonemasons who wish to obtain work. But the thing is not impossible. I have repeatedly found in my experience that many a man and many a woman would only be too glad to have a friendly hint as to where they might prosecute their attentions or from which they might receive proposals. . . . In the natural life of a country village all the lads and lasses grow up together, they meet together in religious associations, in daily employments, and in their amusements on the village green. They have learned their ABC and pot-hooks together, and when the time comes for pairing off they have had excellent opportunities of knowing the qualities and the defects of those whom they select as their partners in life. Everything in such a community lends itself naturally to the indispensable preliminaries of love-making and courtships, which, however much they may be laughed at, contribute more than most things to the happiness of life. But in a great city all this is destroyed. In London at the present moment how many hundreds, nay thousands, of young men and young women, who are living in lodgings, are practically without any opportunity of making the acquaintance of each other, or of any one of the other sex! The street is no doubt the city substitute for the village green, and what a substitute it is! . . . I am not engaging to undertake this task—I am only throwing out a possible suggestion as to the development in the direction of meeting a much needed want.'[10]

'A day or two since,' reported *The Social News* of 5 December 1891, 'Colonel Barker showed us a letter just received. . . . A young working man, a Christian, and earning good wages, solicited the aid of the Social Wing in procuring him a young woman of similar age, who would be willing to make a comfortable home for him and herself. He cared not how poor she might be, whether a rescued or "submerged" lassie, and even would not object if she had one child; but having been a salvationist, he would like "none other" than one like-minded.

'"What are you going to do?" we asked Colonel Barker.

'"Oh," he said, "I think I can manage it!"'

Two months later, in the same paper, comes the question: 'Are you really going to establish a matrimonial bureau? Yes, we are! There have been some anxious enquiries, and some reassuring replies, after this style. The aid of the bureau is invoked by a wife-wanter in one of our colonies, who has considerable means; while from nearer home comes a request for help in a similar matter, though in the other direction. The young woman is a reader of *Social News*, and concludes that she is perfectly safe if she can get a partner through The Salvation Army, for "I knew the Army would know what the man really was!" The favoured one must be a Christian—an out-and-out salvationist preferred!'[11]

A month later, Colonel Barker was well into stride: 'Safety matches are now made by the Social Wing without sulphur or phosphorus, which will flame without striking. What do we mean? Just this. That if you are unmarried, and do not know where to choose a partner, you can communicate with—

COLONEL BARKER,
Matrimonial Bureau,
101 Queen Victoria Street,
London E.C.,

and he will most probably supply you with just what you want—somebody loveable and good.'[12]

However, Colonel Barker's stride seems eventually to have outreached itself, for apart from the following Trade Headquarters advertisement of 1895, little more is heard on the subject.

If the link between a marriage bureau and the hunt for missing
persons seems but tenuous, we mention it solely as an introduction
to that more pertinent subject, the reconciliation bureau. God might
indeed bless the unions of those married couples who purchased
their doormats through The Salvation Army trade department, but
there were a good many couples left who, through ignorance of
that emporium, enjoyed no such blessing upon their relationships.
With them in mind, therefore, General Bramwell Booth announced
in March 1926: 'I am anxious to establish a reconciliation
department in addition to the anti-suicide bureau. There is a special
need for reconciliation, such as between a man and wife who have
been separated. Someone is needed who will step in wisely and

47

kindly, bringing about a reconciliation instead of leaving the parties concerned to the miserable procedure of divorce.'[14]

In the first year the bureau dealt with almost 10,000 applications. Analysis of the first 300 cases shows that about two-thirds represented difficulties between husbands and wives, and the remainder were disputes between relations, or employers and employed. The outcome was as follows:

Reconciled	69
Advised and helped—by employment, clothing, and financial aid	171
Passed to other departments qualified to aid them	38
Assisted by legal, medical or other aid	22
	300[14]

'We cannot always effect a reconciliation. It would not be well if we could,'[14] observed the first annual account of the work of the reconciliation bureau. Indeed, Lieut-Colonel Reginald Chapman, bringing to the newly-formed department all the accumulated experience of his previous appointment as head of the investigation and anti-suicide bureau, declared: 'Recently we have been asked to bring about reconciliations which could only mean worse trouble later. Kindly, but firmly, we were able to show that separation or divorce was really best in the interests of the innocent sufferer, or the welfare of the children,'[15] for as a *Salvation Army Year Book* article pointed out 25 years on: 'Reconciliation work has to do its best with the imperfect human material with which it has to deal. This means that less than an ideal arrangement has, at times, to be accepted and, among people outside Christian influence, the work of reconciliation is extremely difficult.'[15] Difficult it may be, yet it is a work which, under the auspices of the missing persons department, continues with increasing frequency in an age when divorce has never been easier and the marriage relationship never so fragile; for, in the words of its 11th General, Arnold Brown, the Army believes that 'the family is essential to the stability and continuity of society. . . . Legislation cannot abolish selfishness, intolerance or waywardness, which in our view contribute more to the breakdown of marriages than poverty or poor housing. The Salvation Army's experience suggests that a great many of the marriages that now break down could be saved and the parties find fulfilment for themselves and security for their children, given a willingness to persevere and a measure of social support at times of crisis.'[16]

5
Emma's orphans

MARRIED in 1855, William and Catherine Booth brought eight children into the world between the years 1856 and 1868. All of them were to follow in their parents' evangelical footsteps.

At The Christian Mission's 1877 conference Booth reported: 'My eldest daughter who is here with us . . . purposes to give herself up to labour in the Mission, and I trust that by next conference we shall have another son ready for the work. I think you must all see that the entering of our children into this enterprise is no small token of our confidence in the future and of our willingness to lay aside earthly ambitions and positions in order to promote its extension and success. I believe I can say for my dear wife as for myself that we have no greater joy than to see our children devote themselves to the redemption and salvation of the masses. May God accept all the *nine* for this service! I believe he will.'[1] (Author's italics.)

A quick head count of the Booth offspring must have left the more astute of the Christian Mission membership wondering. Was Mrs Booth, at 48, *enceinte* again? If not, who was the *ninth* of the eight? A Mexboro' newspaper reporter of 1878 confused matters even further by stating: 'Mrs Booth . . . gave a short address . . . she also stated that they had *nine sons* all 'coming on' ready to fight in the great conflicts against sin, the flesh, and the devil'[2] (author's italics). The 'sons' mistake could be forgiven, reporters being what they are; but 'nine' was the constant factor; never has it been known for *both* parents (even of a large Victorian family) to overcount the number of mouths to be fed.

A year later, at The Salvation Army's London Council of War, 'A navvy from Canning Town . . . told how . . . he thought them funny people, and they are so, for they will actually pray for you to your face. However, he was just coming away when the General's little son got hold of his hand, and would not let go. So he was forced to give in and get converted, and now he could sing beautiful.'[3]

49

The youngest Booth boy, Herbert, was by this time 17—hardly the 'little son' of the navvy's conversion story. Who, then, was this young evangelist? Four years elapse before we find more specific reference to his person. 'Miss Emma Booth (the Principal of the Women's Training Home) had been announced to be present [at a meeting at The Grecian, Hoxton] but was prevented from coming by indisposition. Mr Herbert Booth, in mentioning this circumstance to the audience, said that she had sent to represent her her younger sister and brother, Lucy and Georgie Booth, who would now sing in public for the first time. . . . Little George did his part manfully, and when his sister sat down he told us that though he had been very nervous too, he was glad to know that he was also one of the Lord's little soldiers.'[4]

The fact that it was Emma, the Booths' second daughter, who sent along Georgie to represent her at the Hoxton meeting of 1883, is both light upon our path and confusion to our darkness, for he was obviously at this stage one of 'Emma's orphans'. Whether Georgie was also that ninth child referred to by both William and Catherine, and whether he was 'the General's little son' of the Canning Town incident, is thrown into question by the following recollection from Bramwell Booth's earliest East End days: 'Near my father's house on the border of Victoria Park there was a little street of workmen's houses. . . . In the course of my early work in the Mission I frequently visited in this street, especially the sick, which as a lad I was rather fond of doing. In one of these houses I came across the wife of one of our own people, belonging to our society at Bethnal Green. The man was a foreman in a cardboard-box factory in the City. They had a numerous family, and the wife, who had lately given birth to another child, was very ill. It was soon evident that she was sick unto death. . . . Her last request to me was that I would take charge of the baby—the latest of her family. Perhaps not altogether realising what I was undertaking, I promised that I would. Naturally I turned to my mother for assistance, and after a certain amount of negotiation the little boy—Harry, we called him—was brought into our own home and placed under the care of my sister Emma . . . who was at that time in delicate health, and who found in the training of this baby delightful occupation. The child grew and prospered, and gave early evidence of being a child of God. While still in his teens he developed a singular gift for caring for the sick. When in 1888 my sister was married to Commissioner Booth-Tucker and went to India, this lad begged us to send him also.'[5]

Harry Andrews, taken into the Booth home in 1875/6[6] to be cared for by 13-year-old Emma, could equally have been the Booths' 'ninth child' of the late 1870s, and 'the General's little son' of Canning Town. Certain it is that both Harry and Georgie were numbered among 'Emma's orphans'; that Harry became The Salvation Army's first 'medical man' in India, serving almost 30 years there before dying heroically, while a medical officer attached to the Indian Army on the North-West Frontier in 1919, and being posthumously awarded the Victoria Cross; and that Georgie, by the summer of 1887, found himself among the pupils of William Kitching's school at Southport, where Theodore, the principal's son (later to become the father of the Army's seventh General, Wilfred Kitching), took a special interest in this alleged son of a nobleman.[7] An unpublished letter from the principal's wife, Louisa, reporting Georgie's safe arrival in Southport to 'My dear friend' (presumably Catherine Booth), discloses among other things that 'I find he has not brought any drawers—would you object to his having two pairs that he can change fortnightly?'[8] And on that hygienic note young Georgie Booth fades quietly into Salvation Army oblivion, save for a brief mention, in an unpublished letter of 1890, that he had arrived safely in New York.[9]

'Will anyone adopt the daughter of a saint in Heaven, and train her for the Army? An extraordinarily bright attractive child of six years. Reply to the General, 3 Gore Road, without delay,' ran a paragraph in *The Christian Mission Magazine* of September 1878. With both Georgie and Harry added to their own family, the Booths were hard put to it to accommodate any more. The only solution for the future care of this 'daughter of a saint in Heaven' was to offer her for adoption.

With the rapid opening of a succession of rescue homes after 1884, the need for adoptive parents weekly paraded itself across the 'Rescue Notes' page of *The War Cry*. 'I should like to say here that in every possible case I feel it right to let the mothers provide for their own children, but these are exceptional cases,'[10] explained Mrs Bramwell Booth, under whose jurisdiction this booming extension of the rescue work naturally fell. 'Very few other rescue homes, of course, allow a mother who wishes to enter, to bring her child with her. Mrs Bramwell has been so anxious to help those for whom no other help was provided, that while exercising all possible care in the selection of such cases, she has never let the fact of the possession of a little one stand in the way of its mother's admission

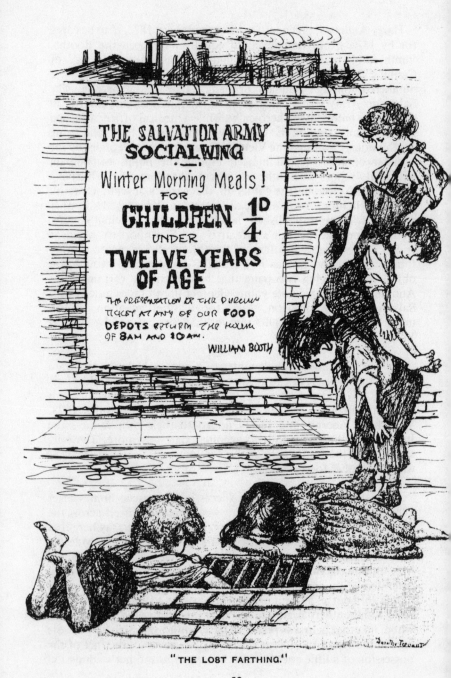

"THE LOST FARTHING."

to *her* homes. But what to do with the babies when their mothers are ready for service? It is seldom that one of her servants can earn more than £8 to £10 a year. No proper home can be procured for a baby at less than £12 a year, except when a salvationist is willing to take one for love—not money!'[11]

By 1891 an adoption department was in full swing at the Rescue Headquarters, 259 Mare Street, Hackney,[12] which later developed into the Children's Aid Department, giving special attention to affiliation cases by establishing the paternity and maintenance responsibility for illegitimate children. During the year 1898/99, for instance, 336 cases were dealt with. Through legal action or other means 100 men were made to support their children, and 10 children were adopted.[13]

But there were always the Nannies of this world whom no one ever seemed to want to adopt. 'Nannie's earliest recollection of life is being "put to the Union" when she was five and father died. . . . When she was eight, a woman came and took her out. "She said she was my mother, but I'd never seen her afore. I remember a stout lady, as I called Aunt Sally, when father was alive. But she said she was my mother, an' she took me away to a house which she kept for an old man, as she said was my grandfather. Then I used to wonder how many grandfathers I had, for I knew this wasn't one of the two I used to have."

'The grandfather arrangement was, however, only temporary, and Nannie's so-called mother plunged into a life of the most indiscriminate vice. The scenes that the child witnessed, night after night, and her familiarity with the phraseology of business-like iniquity, are beyond belief. . . . Then "the Army got her". It is impossible to tell you how or where. But Nannie is a happy, cared-for little woman today, and growing childlike, week by week.' A mere child, she was none the less being cared for in a rescue home, where the older girls could 'teach her nothing'.[14] One day, however, when her mind had become childlike again, Nanny would need the security of a more suitable home, with the companionship of other children. She, too, might become one of 'Emma's orphans'.

In 1884 Catherine Booth wrote in *The Salvation War*: 'Some three years ago, two or three little children were cast upon our sympathy and care by the death of their parents, soldiers of the Army. . . . We felt this to be a call from God to undertake the

53

charge of these little ones, to train them for him, and so originated our Army nursery which has since increased to the number of 16 children, ranging from 10 months to 12 years old. Four rooms on the women's wing of the training home have been appropriated to their use, and three devoted young women have given themselves, without fee or reward, to nurse and train them for Jesus, under the superintendence of Miss Emma Booth. . . . We believe in the possibility of little children being *saved* and trained and inspired with the single purpose and ambition to live and labour for the salvation of the world. . . . Consequently our nursery, as all other of our agencies, is conducted on salvation lines, and the children are fed, managed, taught and disciplined, and educated alone for the glory and service of our King. So far, the efforts of those engaged in this work have been crowned with greater success than we even dared to hope for, and our little nursery contains some as precious specimens of infant piety as ever we have read of in books or heard from mothers whose saintly children have been transplanted to Glory.' Such, then, was the quality of at least some of 'Emma's orphans'.

But while his womenfolk were busy consolidating the nursery work with *War Cry* advertisements for a sewing machine, a piano, a blackboard or large swing slate, 'The General had hesitated to sanction the opening of permanent homes for children, because he held in horror the Victorian institutions of the type described by Dickens, with their regimented "indigent orphans", clad in dreary garb of one pattern and their utter lack of home life, or anything but the most formal religious teaching.'[15]

Signs that Emma's daughterly persuasion was taking effect were to be discerned in the *Daily Chronicle* of Tuesday 13 January 1885, which reported: 'In regard to the orphanage, the General said a gentleman had called upon him at headquarters and promised to give a freehold building, large enough to accommodate 200 children, but he (the General) was unable, at the moment, to accept the offer. He, however, promised to pray over it, and there was every prospect that the donor's proposition would be carried out.' It was not. Instead, the General's praying led him to 'publicly dedicate to the Lord and The Salvation Army the Training Home Nursery' at a little soldiers' demonstration in London's Exeter Hall on the second day of March, during which Emma delivered an address on 'Saving the Children', and 'The White-sashed Nursery Brigade, led by Captain Rees, sang, "I'm pressing towards the golden gates".'[16] Then back to their Clapton home toddled

'Emma's orphans', totally oblivious of the fact (it is to be hoped) that before its purchase as a Salvation Army training home, it had been known far and wide as the London Orphan Asylum.

Meanwhile, William Booth's book on *The Training of Children* (published in August 1884) had turned him into somewhat of an authority on the subject. Reviewing it, the *Pall Mall Gazette* said: 'This is a remarkable little book, well worth being read and studied by parents who have no desire to see their children become either saints or soldiers of General Booth's pattern. Above all things, stereotyped uniformity of the Chinese type is to be avoided in the education of the young, and there are few who will not be able to pick up useful hints from the very direct and business-like directions of General Booth. Like the age of which he is one of the most remarkable products, General Booth is nothing if not practical. . . . Whatever may be the eccentricities or pecularities of the author of this volume, he is one of the shrewdest men alive. He has swallowed all formulas, and entirely untrammelled by custom or tradition, goes for his goal in the directest and most unceremonious fashion. A great deal might profitably be written on the ideal of life set forth within these pages, but that is not our present purpose. We only wish to call attention to a noteworthy volume which contains a great deal of common sense when all that is distinctive of The Salvation Army is eliminated. Of course we need hardly say that we have little or no sympathy with a spirit which "distinctly forbids 'Jack the Giant Killer', 'Goody Two Shoes', 'Jack and the Bean Stalk', and all the fairytale nonsense put together;" but after all these extravagances of extremes are weeded out, there remains sufficient to give many a useful hint to all who have to do with the training or the education of children.'[17]

A review of the book published in *The Schoolmaster* is here quoted, not only because of its assessment of Booth's views, but also because of the robust picture it paints of the Army of the 1880s. 'The Salvation Army has become a power in the country. Its drums beat, its colours fly, and its soldiers (Amazonian light infantry included) sing their songs of defiance and victory in nearly every town in the land. Men differ widely as the poles with regard to the value of its operations, but all acknowledge the vigour and success so far as sensation and notoriety go. The General of the Army is undoubtedly a great man, and a work on education by him must command attention.

55

'A careful examination of this book, with a mind unprejudiced either for or against the Army, has led us to the conclusion that it contains a good deal of sound common sense, which might well be attended to by parents and teachers of every denomination, and that its author is animated by an earnest desire to impart a Christian education based on the teaching of our Lord himself, and free from the technicalities of theology, though in accordance with the practices of The Salvation Army. General Booth's child would become an earnest Christian, a good citizen, an enthusiastic salvationist, and an enemy of the world with its ordinary tastes and pursuits. The book is written in the form of questions and answers, and treats of almost every topic which could be thought of in connection with home and school training. He is, of course, a bitter enemy of strong drink.

'We are pleased to notice that the General does not belong to the number of sham philanthropists who think themselves wiser than Solomon, and are utterly opposed to corporal punishment. Nothing could be better than the higher "motives to obedience" which he lays down; but he does not hesitate to say that with young children he "should be inclined to the old-fashioned method of 'a little whipping'." We have no hesitation in saying that the whole chapter on "Chastisement" is admirable, as regards both principles and precepts, and deserves to be read again and again by all concerned in the training of the young.'[18] It still deserves to be! The book was to go into its third edition by April 1904.

Back at the nursery, Emma was finding it necessary to insert a cautionary note into her *War Cry* appeals for pictures to bedeck its bare walls. 'We would like . . . to give a hint to those who are intending to send other pictures that we should like them to relate to scriptural subjects, so that the children may early be helped to learn the stories and great facts of Bible history.'

Four years later that salvationist journalist *par excellence,* American Major Susie Swift, brought to her reading public's notice a hitherto undescribed aspect of the Army's work with children. The Cellar, Gutter and Garrett Brigade of women cadets had begun visiting, scrubbing, washing and nursing in the Seven Dials district of London in 1884. By 1886 this practical expression of salvationism had developed into an established work, with officers living and ministering in several of the poorest areas of London. Known as the Slum Work, it quickly opened, alongside other doors of mercy, a 'London Crèche' at the Borough. There Major Swift met Freddy.

56

'Eighteen months ago, Freddy began to wink his eyes at the light and to learn that screaming sometimes brought him his dinner and sometimes only earned him a shake from whatever old woman might be tending him. He was a workhouse baby. . . . Today he is "getting ready for the war" at our crèche in the Borough . . . among the pale, thin little babies who are gathered in there every morning, and some of whom go to their chilly, dark homes very unwillingly, after being tended and cared for all day. . . . But one happy baby does not go home at night! . . . For Freddy is the crèche baby. Freddy is there "to stay". Freddy is given to Major Cooke for God and the Army, and is to grow up altogether "Army property".'[19]

Within weeks of this emotive article appearing, Booth's caution expressed itself in a 'General Order', printed in *The War Cry* under the heading 'No Orphanages: Whereas in several countries an inclination to accept the permanent care of children has been shown by various officers, and whereas upon trial such adoptions, where they have been ventured upon, have repeatedly turned out injurious to the general interests of the war, demanding for the care of a few children the entire attention of officers who might be much more effectively employed elsewhere, so that in some cases we have been compelled to get such children adopted by others: Now let it be clearly understood that in future no child may be adopted by, or received into, the permanent care of any headquarters or any officer without my previous consent. At some future time, when we have more fully met the urgent spiritual needs of the nations, we may be able to spare strength for efforts of this kind, which we should gladly undertake. Meanwhile, we must content ourselves with helping only those cases which appear to me of sufficient urgency to warrant our taking this responsibility.'[20]

How, one wonders, did 'Miss Eva' feel about such a pronouncement? As the Field Commissioner, the Founders' fourth daughter was already an evangelical force to be reckoned with. She was also the guardian of 'Chris, Dot and Jhai . . . who sing solos, speak occasionally in the meetings, and are taught to pray at home. They have travelled extensively, and small as is the number of their years—a total of 16 between them—they have already won battles in the arena of life. All have histories, and for each destinies have been ordained by the kind care of The Salvation Army.'[21]

The plight of homeless children threatened to move Eva's passionate nature beyond words and into action. Not content with taking on Chris, Dot and Jhai (there were to be others in later years), she saw in the opening of the Army's first men's shelter a pattern to be followed in the care of destitute children.

Captioned '*The Threepenny Doss*' a *War Cry* report for 3 March 1888 stated: 'Staff-Captain Eva Booth is already anxious to have another building started for the children, and offers to take charge of it herself.' Eva's talents, the General felt, could better be utilised elsewhere. The children's doss house—a project not dear to his heart—must wait.[22] Well might the *War Cry* report of a week later conclude with the disturbing question: 'Where are all those children sleeping?'[23]

Precluded from the night shelter they may have been, but their welcome to 'Manager Flawn's' wing of the Limehouse establishment was far from being in question. 'The children are beyond all possibility either of counting or describing! . . . "Tea" to these little ones stands for the only warm and palatable thing they know of, and we must be content to educate them slowly up to soup and rice and proper children's food.'[23]

During the prolonged distress of the 1889 dock strike, 18 months later, Mrs Bramwell Booth gave free teas to 1,200 half-starved women and children.[24] In some cases the poor mothers had carried the pawning of their clothes so far that they could not come out, and had to arrange to send their children in charge of the eldest one.'[25]

Yet even with the resolving of the dock strike, the need appeared as massive as ever. Writing in his now historic social manifesto of 1890, William Booth declared: 'As I rode through Canada and the United States some three years ago, I was greatly impressed with the superabundance of food which I saw at every turn. Oh, how I longed that the poor starving people, and the hungry children of the East of London and of other centres of our destitute populations, should come into the midst of this abundance; but as it appeared impossible for me to take them to it, I secretly resolved that I would endeavour to bring some of it to them.'[26]

By the winter of 1891 *The Social News Supplement to The War Cry* was carrying details of the first organised plan for 'farthing meals' for children. 'In one large East End school alone it is computed that 700 children attend in a breakfastless condition.[27] . . . We're giving 20,000 farthing breakfasts a week to school children at 16 centres,' reported Commissioner Elijah Cadman, one-time sweep's boy, now heading the Army's Social Wing. 'Big ones come carrying little ones. They mostly run their tongues all round the bread first, and get the jam out of the hollows when it's bread and jam. Then they settle down to eat it up.'[28]

If all this seems a long way from 'Emma's orphans', we remind ourselves that in 1888 she was married to Commissioner Booth-Tucker, going with him to India. Presumably the training home nursery continued to function without her, though references are difficult to find after 1886. Her father's attitude to the subject remained ambivalent, theory consistently outweighing practice for several years to come. Recognising a good quote when he saw one, he wrote: 'When an English judge tells us, as Mr Justice Wills did the other day, that there were any number of parents who would kill their children for a few pounds' insurance money, we can form some idea of the horrors of the existence into which many of the children of this highly favoured land are ushered at their birth.'[29] Yet less than 150 pages on in his social scheme we find him announcing: 'For the waifs and strays of the streets of London . . . we have no direct purpose of entering on a crusade on their behalf, apart from our attempt at changing the hearts and lives and improving the circumstances of their parents.' The atmosphere is hardly warmed by the grudging concession: 'Still, a number of them will unavoidably be forced upon us; and we shall be quite prepared to accept the responsibility of dealing with them, calculating that our organisation will enable us to do so, not only with facility and efficiency, but with trifling cost to the public. To begin with, children's crèches or children's day homes would be established in the centres of every poor population, where for a small charge babies and young children can be taken care of in the day.'[22] Something, after all, had resulted from the story of 'Crèche Freddy'.

To be fair, every other aspect of the Army's rapidly expanding social work was in a position to make a laudable gesture towards self-support. A children's home could not. Crèches or day homes, nominally financed by parents, provided part of the answer, and the first of these to be organised by Mrs Bramwell Booth (as distinct from the two already forming part of the Slum Work) was opened at the beginning of November 1890, next door to the Hanbury Street Women's Shelter, Whitechapel. Thus ended, for a handful of families at least, 'The government of children by children . . . a system to be found in the rookeries and slums of Whitechapel and the like.'[30]

A crèche, however, was hardly the setting in which to place 'a clear-eyed, intelligent, honest-looking boy, 14 years of age . . . entirely alone in London. Father and mother both dead, he had left his native town and come to London to find bread.' On the night an officer visiting a men's shelter noticed him and found he had been converted the previous Sunday, 'he had been in London about a month, and found it a hard battle, often getting no more than enough to pay for a penny doss—at 14 years of age!—compelled to mix with the indescribable characters (some of them) who frequent our shelters. He had decided upon enlisting for a military soldier on the Monday morning—he is tall and well-formed for his age—when I took him by the hand, telling him to come up to headquarters in the morning. I am happy to be able to report that we have secured him a situation with a certain well-known sergeant-major of Wood Green, who has a business house in the city, with whom, we hope and believe, the lad will do well. We shall keep a watchful eye upon him, and believe we have saved a good citizen for service.'[31]

Unfortunately there were not enough Wood Green sergeant-majors to go round when it came to boys adrift in London. In his annual social work report, *Work in Darkest England, 1894,* Bramwell Booth outlined a proposed 'effort to aid boys and youths in our great cities who earn their livelihood on the streets, and are only too often without any real home, or would be better off if they were. Such are the newspaper, bag-carrying and match boys; "Touts" who call cabs; "Tellers" who carry messages between those who do not, for various reasons, desire to show themselves in public houses or lighted thoroughfares; crossing-sweepers, boot-blacks, errand-boys, who gain a precarious living in connection with the great markets; and boys, who like men when out of employment, find life goes very hard with them indeed. *Keeping in mind the central fact that they must pay in money or labour for what they get,* I should like at once to open at least one comfortable shelter exclusively for them. I believe it would prove an immediate success.'

From page 2 of *The Social Gazette,* 9 February 1895, light suddenly blazes forth. Describing 'that child-heathen world which has its centres in our big cities and which is at once the disgrace and crime of the nation', it goes on to announce that the new 'apostle of waif and stray children' appointed to direct this work, is that same

Major Susie Swift who, as editor of *All the World,* 'wrote up' Crèche Freddy six years earlier. 'Behind her literary ability', we are assured, 'she possesses immense and as yet unused capacity for that class of work.' Indeed, as Bramwell Booth was quick to point out: 'She has some very remarkable qualifications, and among them she really thinks she can do anything that she sets her hand to'— including, perhaps, persuading the General that 'The Salvation Army ought to do something definite for the lost children of the streets'?

The object of this new junior shelter was threefold: (1) To enable enterprising lads to rise to better situations. (2) To provide a home for lads working in the City. (3) To prevent lads from drifting into paupers and criminals.'

Sentimentality, if not exactly abounding, was certainly present. 'Now if we can only get father or mother into the men's or women's shelter, and the brave little fellow into the junior shelter, and thus get the family saved, we can, by means of our labour bureau, accelerate their newly-implanted desire to ascend the social ladder, for the tendency of all saved people is to gravitate upwards and not downwards.'[32]

The reality was slightly more down to earth. Situated in Fetter Lane, next door to the chapel where the Wesleys came under Moravian influence,[33] and in the immediate neighbourhood of Dickens' *Bleak House,*[34] 'The new waifs' home will be in the centre of the boy gamblers' happy hunting-ground—the purlieus of the newspaper district at the rear of "The Daily Telegraph" offices— and within a few minutes' walk of the open-air betting clubs of Whitefriars.'[35]

One wonders how Major Swift's notions about games went down with these young gamblers. ' "Animal Snap is rather a nice game, I think. Do you understand Animal Snap? No?" (Volumes of personal pity experienced in the query.)'

Reported Bramwell Booth: 'An officer who spoke to me of a visit on a cold and rainy night assured me that amongst the 60 boys present there was not one sound pair of *boots.*' (Author's italics.)

Footwear—always a problem to the poor, because boots and shoes could not be made at home—took a turn for the better in the '90s, when boot-making machinery had become sufficiently widespread to bring down the price.[36] In the second-hand chain of clothing events, one has reason to believe, Major Swift's boys would before long feel the benefit where now they felt only the damp.

A beginning had been made in the way of residential care for boys, but what was to be done for small girls?

'Early one morning in 1884, Miss Marianne Asdell, a pretty young woman of 25, had gone to Waterloo station to meet—in accordance with a promise made to one of her new salvationist friends, wife of a retired military colonel—a young girl whom that lady was sending up from Salisbury, and to escort her to the refuge in Hanbury Street, Whitechapel.

'The traveller, on stepping from the train, proved to be the merest child in looks and speech. Sitting beside her in the bus as they travelled eastward, Marianne Asdell wondered greatly why this very young girl had needed to be sent so far away from her country home and her own people. On reaching Whitechapel she put this question to the officers; she received a kind, but frank, answer—they had been afraid of what might happen to Nellie in her own apparently respectable home!

'"It was the first time I had even heard anything about such horrors," she relates, "or indeed realised that these things could be done to a child." She adds characteristically, "I was troubled because I had *not* known—it was a shake to me." . . . Small wonder that . . . Miss Asdell was overwhelmed to weeping by the pit of misery of which she, a very new soldier, was having her very first glimpse that day! . . . But the ruined children, and those in danger of such a fate, won her devotion and became her passionate charge, both then and when, in 1902, the Army opened The Nest, the first home for little girls.'[37]

This mid-1940s retrospect differs somewhat from contemporary accounts of the early 1900s which give The Nest as coming into being as a home for mothers with young children,[38] already occupied by July 1901.[39] On the other hand, Lanark House (from whence Major Asdell and her family had removed to The Nest)[40] was known, by March 1902, as the Children's Home,[41] catering for both girls *and* boys, within a stone's throw of Emma's original nursery, and under the direction of Ensign Quarterman.

Keen vegetarians as both Florence and Bramwell Booth were,[42] it is of significance that the children of Lanark House 'have neither meat nor tea, but an abundance of nourishing food, including brown bread, milk and fruit'.[41] They attended the local Board School on weekdays, the Clapton Congress Hall Salvation Army meeting on Sundays,[41] and if their existence seems spartan compared with today's standards, it needs to be set within the context of the findings of a 1902 Home Office committee which estimated 'that the total army of little toilers, who spend the dawn of their lives between the school-room and the earning of wages, reaches the striking total of no fewer than 3,000,000. Of these, 1,000,000 are technically half-timers . . . (the age of partial exemption from school was, in 1901, raised from eleven to twelve). The remainder, a round 2,000,000, attend school by day for full time, and earn their little amount of wages, before and after school, and in the playtime of others.'[43] Lanark House, by contrast, offered 24 children the daily routine of 'an ordinary Christian family'.

Much the same approach was maintained at The Nest, where Major Asdell could accommodate about 30 mothers and the same number of children. A feature here was the service girls' room, furnished by contributions from erstwhile rescue girls, now in employment, whose children were being cared for at The Nest, and who used it as their club room.[38]

The Nest had not been functioning six months before the inevitable appeal appeared in *The Deliverer*: 'In common with all our other homes, The Nest is always in need of left-off clothes, *boots,* etc.' (author's italics). As if to emphasise the point, *The Social Gazette* from time to time carried such incentive-laden advertisements from the Army's Trade Headquarters as: 'To every purchaser of our *new regulation overcoat* at 40/- (net), we will give a 7/6 *pair of boots* absolutely free of charge.' It is to be hoped that the Nestlings benefited from such liberal largess.

Over the years changing fashions in child care (and footwear!) have been reflected in the administration of Salvation Army children's homes, but beneath and beyond all such adaptations have remained the bedrock principles upon which Emma Booth founded her training home nursery. Her sister-in-law, Mrs Bramwell Booth, in presenting a masterly paper to the 1921 International Social Council, articulated many of these principles:

'We must, as far as possible, avoid the herding together of children. If, for the present, in order to economise both with officers and money, we are obliged to bring numbers of children under one roof, then we cannot be too particular that the number of officers is sufficient. . . . The individual touch is absolutely necessary for young children. . . . Every child must feel that personal love and personal interest are bestowed upon him or her. . . . I think that the system to aim at is that of groups of cottages, each cottage with a home mother. . . . In the days when we shall have plenty of officers, shall we say that there shall be no officers over 40 years in charge of a children's home? God's plan for the children is that the mother should be young with them. . . . Again, his plan is that no mother should have the care of more than one infant—or at most a couple—under a year old. That ought to be the standard in the home. . . .

'Though human beings are so much alike, it is the differences that are vital. This is especially so with children; and this is why we cannot deal with children except individually. . . . One of the dangers of institutional life to be avoided for the physical, moral and spiritual well-being of children, is the danger of conventionalism—rigidly doing a thing the same way over and over again. . . . One of the chief charms to children is variety, the unexpected happening; and institutional life is so rigid! . . . Beware, lest the finest powers in the children are crushed and handicapped by institutionalism! . . . Keep as far as you can from hard-and-fast rules. . . . Rules should be made for the benefit of the cared for, and never for that of those responsible for their well-being. This applies to all institutions, but especially to those for children. . . . It is a child's nature to be happy, and our work is not so much to make the children happy in our homes, as to keep away and protect them from all that would destroy their happiness. To this end all regulations should be formed. . . .

'Let children be taught to understand and adopt the principle of obedience without violating their reason and intelligence. . . . Whenever you can, give a reason for your commands to children who are old enough to reason. . . . Beware of judging children by that which is outward. . . .

'There must be an absence of all favouritism. . . . Always remember that the cultivation of that which is good in character is of greater importance than the mere eradication of that which is evil. . . .

'The Unseen Presence must be made real to them. . . .

'Foundation principles of successful Salvation Army work among children are identical with the principles governing the care of children in Salvation Army families. ''The duty of parents (and therefore of officers) to children is so to govern, influence, and inspire them that they shall love, serve and enjoy God, and in consequence grow up to be good, holy and useful men and women.'' (The Founder: *The Training of Children*.)

'Great care must be taken not to create forms and ceremonies of religion for children. I always felt with my own girls and boys, especially whilst they were very young, that it was necessary to keep them away from large meetings, and from too frequent public meetings, so that nothing should become to them a mere form of ceremony. Children, being so quick to imitate, will pray as they hear grown-up people pray, using grown-up people's expressions. There is no reality to the child in such a prayer; it is mere imitation. Unless this is guarded against . . . children will readily accept a sort of parrot-like religion, which, being unreal, is like a great grave-stone put over the living development of their souls. . . . All services and prayers for children should be as varied and unconventional as possible. . . . Avoid the rut with adults, but avoid it as you would poison with children. . . .

'Nothing is better for children than to have moments in the day when they can be alone. . . .

'The development of the brain in young people is best accomplished in teaching them to use the hands and feet and the powers of hearing and vision—by movement, than by over-much application to books. . . .

'Ownership of property must be allowed to each child. He must have his own locker, where he can keep the little treasures he cherishes. . . . The property of the child must be respected. By this means the important lesson of respect for other people's property will be learnt. . . .

'If you want a clever child, an original child, he or she must have plenty to do, plenty to make. . . . Every child possesses a creative instinct in one direction or another: it is very important that this should be encouraged and developed. . . . A child must not only have something to do, something to make: there must be someone to admire the finished work. . . .

'Two errors into which little children and young people most easily fall are doing right for fear of punishment, and doing right because they want to be applauded, and to receive a reward. We must help them . . . to love right for its own sake. Search for the motive underlying the action and train the child to see the difference between doing right for love of right and doing right for any other reason. . . .

'Beware of any penalties or punishments which tend to destroy self-respect by making a child look ridiculous. . . . There must be some penalty for disobedience. The only safeguard is true love and interest in the children. . . . "Train up a child in the way he should go: and when he is old he will not depart from it" (Proverbs 22:6).'[44]—a useful point upon which to begin the next chapter!

6
Adequate boy-mending machinery

THE very first copy of The Christian Mission's *East London Evangelist* magazine, dated October 1868, carried presage of future events as far as 'boy-mending machinery' was concerned.

A report of open-air work in Shoreditch concluded: 'As we were leaving the Gardens, a young man, who had been standing at some distance, tapped me on the shoulder and asked if I would do him a favour. I said yes, if I could. He said, "There is a poor woman living down here who has got a boy. His father was a companion of mine; but he has got into trouble, and is in the country for a year or two. You know what I mean. Well, the mother must live somehow: so she is obliged to go out at nights; and her boy, who is about seven years old, runs the streets, turning somersaults alongside the omnibuses with a blackened face for coppers. If he is left to himself, the ha'pence he picks up at this game will not be enough for him soon; and though I am a thief myself, I should not like the boy to become one. If he once enters a prison he will not mind going there again. Now, sir, if you can get him into a reformatory you would save him from ruin, and perhaps prove a great blessing to his mother."

'I promised the man that I would do what I could, and appointed a time to meet him. Now, sir, if you can find a home for this boy I shall be very glad. (We hope to get the boy into the "Revival Refuge".)'

Not until 23 years later, however, were the wheels of The Salvation Army's own boy-mending machinery to be set in motion. With the opening of The Bridge prison gate home in January 1891 it was found necessary to set aside accommodation for 'lads given over to us under the provisions of the Probation of First Offenders Act'.[1]

A facsimile letter reproduced in the *Social News Supplement to The War Cry* of 7 May 1892 reads:

67

To Commr. Cadman.

Sir,

I had an interview with Col.
Barker this morning respecting my son
whom I took with me. He is nearly
fourteen years of age.

I am anxious to place him where
he would be under strict Christian discipline and should be glad if you will kindly
take him to learn a trade. He has had
two situations and robbed his employers
and also myself.

I am unable to keep him but wish
to save him being branded as a criminal.

Yours respectfully,

Column one of the previous page was headed '*To-day's Necessity—A Boys' Home*' and went on to insist: 'Just now the not-to-be-put-off n.cessity is a boys' home, and a home altogether different to the prison or the reformatory. Mothers come daily to the Social Headquarters, and plead with Commissioner Cadman on behalf of their dear, erring, boys. They see nothing between those they love and a ruined life but the agency of The Salvation Army.

'So a boys' home will speedily be established. A suitable property, some eight miles from London, with buildings and grounds and facilities the most promising, has been viewed and next-door to secured. . . . The ground will be capable of being utilised for a small farm, which, with various other trades which will be taught, will afford healthy and remunerative employment. The accommodation will suffice for 150-200 lads.

'Fourteen prospective inmates of this home are at present domiciled at Argyle Square'—the home for discharged prisoners. A month later: 'Premises for the boys' home are not yet secured; a large number of boys are.'[2]

There were now 15 boys among the discharged prisoners at The Bridge—which, in consequence, boasted a junior soldiers' corps.

'Magistrates would gladly fill our hands with mere children, who come under that merciful First Offenders Act, instead of sending them to prison, or the prison's vestibule and training ground—the reformatory or industrial school. . . . As it is, we can only receive the few boys who can be housed at The Bridge.'[3]

68

One was put into Salvation Army custody for stealing a bit of rope from the towpath. Another had been sentenced to seven years in a reformatory on his mother's charge of stealing a £10 note, which was afterwards found in her own pocket! 'After great difficulty his father got him out through the Home Secretary. But the lad's career was stamped. His mother entered an insane asylum, and the home was broken up. He got a succession of situations, but got into trouble of some sort repeatedly. At last he stole from his employer, and tried to get on an outward bound ship with his very moderate booty. Only fourpence was left him. In terror of the police, he did the very best possible thing—came to Headquarters, told his story, and asked to be taken care of. His employer said he would not prosecute him if he stayed for six months under our care. So he came to The Bridge. He worked well. He was fairly obedient. But he gave a great deal of trouble in many ways. . . . But the captain loved him, and prayed for him in secret, and strove, above all else, to throw about him the cheery, warm atmosphere of a Christian *home*, and to make him feel cared-for and wanted and cherished, big lad as he was. And one night a long-legged object tumbled itself down at the penitent-form in a home meeting, and cried its eyes out, and said it wanted to be good.'[3]

With her customary passion, Major Swift (editor of *All the World* at this stage) concluded: 'But oh! the boys we might give chances to if only the Social Wing were not so poverty-poor that the General is forced to be adamant to the appeals of our boy-lovers.'[3] Her own venture into boys' home work was still more than two years away.

In motion the wheels of the Army's boy-mending machinery may have been, but it was exceedingly slow motion. Fortunately there were other spokes in the wheels besides institutional care.

'Wanted! Young London Thieves!' advertised the editor-in-chief, Commissioner Nicol, and went on to appeal: 'Will the young thieves residing in the parishes of Clerkenwell, Islington and Holborn, who were kind enough to promise to attend my situation class, communicate with me? The winter is near, and I am desirous of starting you to learn reading, writing, arithmetic. I can get the use of a suitable room twice a week. Confidence respected. No peaching [ie informing]. The class is only for boys up to the age of 17. Any thief is eligible. Entrance-fee 1d; lessons free; monthly feed, and other social and spiritual advantages. Arrangements for quitting the profession. Write or call. . . .'[4]

69

Three years later: still no boy-mending accommodation, but a report in *The Social Gazette* to the effect that: 'The Committee of Inquiry into Scottish Prisons . . . has courteously requested The Salvation Army to give evidence at its sittings respecting the work of The Salvation Army amongst the criminal classes. . . . The Committee desired to know whether the General, if facilities were afforded, would undertake a reformation work amongst children, similar to the work which is being so successfully accomplished in Australia amongst girls and boys. The Committee was assured the General would, provided the means for doing it were forthcoming.'[5] Presumably they weren't, for it was not to be until 1952 that The Salvation Army undertook such work in Scotland.[6]

Another important spoke in the wheels of its boy-mending machinery was the Army's not insignificant contribution to the cultivation of public opinion, and the cultivation of that opinion into Acts of Parliament. The Children Act of 1908 is a notable example. Besides restricting juvenile smoking, excluding children from the bars of licensed premises and protecting young girls, it modified some 17 previous Acts and totally repealed 21 others.

The Probation of Offenders Act of 1907 embodied a principle for which the Army had long contended: that for a first offence, where character, antecedents, age, health, or mental condition of the person, or the trivial nature of the offence justified, the offender should be released on probation, and committed to the supervision of some responsible person for guidance and help, instead of suffering the disgrace of being sent to prison. Several officers had by this time been appointed as probation officers and attended court as necessity dictated.[7]

By 1909 the boy-mending capacity of the Army's men's hostels had been stretched to its limits. That year 555 boys were taken into care—making a total of 2,500 in eight years.[8] The situation was acute.

On Tuesday 28 June 1910 Mrs Bramwell Booth formally opened Sturge House, Bow, making available accommodation for 50 boys in the house from which that other champion of boys, Dr Barnardo, had been married.[8] 'The object is not to retain the boys indefinitely in the home, but only for so long a time as is necessary to equip them for situations in this country, or for emigration abroad.'[9]

A paper given at the Army's International Social Council the following year remarked: 'No doubt a great deal of the success is due to the character of the person in charge of the home. Not everyone is able to understand a boy, and manage him. Too often adults forget they were ever young and the escapades of their youth. Consequently they never get to the heart of the boy; never appreciate his point of view, and never succeed in winning his confidence.'[9]

Sturge House continued its valuable function until 1941 when a succession of air raids necessitated its residents being temporarily accommodated at the Poplar men's hostel.[10] There its work continued for a year or two until that hostel, in turn, was bombed.[11]

Boy-mending machinery was by this time recognised as a necessity, however, and in 1944 two approved probation hostels were opened in the provinces.[12]

Then, 53 years after the project had first been mooted by the Committee of Inquiry into Scottish Prisons, *The Salvation Army Year Book* carried information that the previous year 'In co-operation with the Scottish Home Department, work had begun among youths in Scotland in an endeavour to combat juvenile delinquency. At Kilbirnie, Ayrshire, a large residence has been adapted to house lads in need of good home surroundings and others on probation from the courts.'[13]

In 1959 the House o' the Trees, South Wales, was taken over by the Men's Social Work. Under the auspices of the Goodwill Department since 1932 (when it appealed for 'boots, shoes, a Welsh terrier, bicycles, tools, and wireless parts'), it had been designated an approved home for boys in 1942.[14]

Meanwhile the Army's girl-mending machinery, dating back through industrial and receiving homes to its earliest rescue homes, took on a more specialised aspect under 'The great new scheme for schools for young girl-probationers', brought in by the government in 1942.[15] And not only schools, but also approved homes and hostels. Longden House, Sheffield, was the first approved home to be opened under this scheme, with Newstead, next door, serving as an approved hostel. However, the Bristol girls' home immediately challenged this 'first' by claiming it had been the *very* first Salvation Army approved home,[16] having been officially recognised since 1929.[17]

71

By February 1943 the Army's first approved school (Woodlands, East Grinstead) was 'filling up fast. . . . The girls come to us straight from the courts and we are to have all the after-care when they have passed through',[18] explained Lieut-Commissioner Mrs Phillis Taylor, at this time leader of the Women's Social Work, and later to become wife of Albert Orsborn, the Army's sixth General. An astonishing 95 per cent success rate was claimed amongst these 14- to 17-year olds,[18] one of whom was heard to pronounce a few years after her Bristol stay: 'I myself think it is altogether a "changing-house"—where bad girls turn into good ones.' Adequate *girl*-mending machinery indeed!

7
To make us bad 'uns good

EVEN before Christian Mission evangelist William Corbridge had made his far-seeing prophecy about becoming 'God's relieving officers', he was 'on the job'—and not only with teas for the prostitutes of Hastings.

Declaring war on the nearby village of Battle towards the end of October 1871,[1] he 'issued a peculiar bill . . . which caused great excitement. This bill was taken before the Hastings magistrates, and condemned as a bill that would not attract respectable people. A gentleman present told them that was not our object; we wanted to rescue and save such men as Ponto, a man that had been before them that day for the 27th time. One of the town council told me of the remarks that had been made, and I said, 'Is it possible that in Hastings anyone has been into custody so many times?' He said, 'Yes.' I said, 'Then we will go in for his conversion, and plead with God till he is saved.' I told the circumstances to a few of our friends, who heartily united with me in prayer for this notorious character, and some of our friends invited him to our meetings. On the above date he appeared in our midst, heard the word, came to the penitent form and sought and found the Saviour. He has since then signed the pledge, and, by God's grace, intends to lead a new life. Will our friends pray that he may be kept steadfast against all the terrible temptations to which he will be exposed. This conversion will be a relief to the town and a blessing to the world.'[2]

Not until 11 years later does the next positive piece of prison work present itself—this time in a letter to *The War Cry* from the captain of Leeds New Wortley Corps, the scene of poor Harry Stott's saga three months earlier (see chapter 4). Dramatically captioned '*A young cadet aged 83 years. In Prison 200 Times. Now Saved. Glory to God! Shall she go to the Training Home?*' it continued:

'Dear Editor,
    Thank God we have captured the greatest sinner in Yorkshire—Jane Johnson, 83 years old, been in prison 200 times, and the parish hotel

scores of times, being taken, not in a carriage, but on a stretcher, borne by two of the Queen's officers.

This time, hearing she was coming out of Wakefield gaol, for the 200th time, I wrote to the governor of the gaol, and asked him to send her to me at 38, Hopewell Street, which he did.

Thank God, now she can give a bright testimony of all her sins being forgiven and of being ready to die. . . .

I am believing she will be the best cadet in the Army yet turned out. More to follow.

Capt. A. Hayward.'[3]

The 'more to follow' consisted in a correction being inserted the following week: 'In prison 200 times' should have read '240 times'!

It was to be another two years before steps were taken in any organised fashion to aid ex-convicts. Writing under the pen-name of 'Deborah', Mrs Commissioner Railton described the work of 'Our Prisoners' Rescue Brigade: Like each onward step of the Army our work for the salvation of ex-convicts has been begun with no cut-and-dried plan, but just as we have seen our way to reply to the cry of our hearts for the deliverance of these poor captives from the tyranny of the devil, without waiting to know how to do it.

'Stationing a saved thief outside the Wandsworth Jail gates, we have found no difficulty in catching one and another as they came out, some from only a short term of imprisonment, some after repeated convictions and a long life of guilt. But wishful to feel our way step by step, our decoy bird was only to bring one at a time to the house of the good sergeant whose wife was ready to provide breakfast and to pray with the newcomer. . . . We have no idea of giving any man "a new start in life" without a new heart. . . . We have no idea of providing for any man to live in idleness, nor of separating men from the busy world; but we have to arrange for a little temporary work at woodchopping so that each man can get at it without delay, whilst other labour is sought for. . . .

'As it seems one of the first necessities to save each one from undue publicity till he has got fairly started on the upward journey, we refrain at present from describing our first four captures or their present whereabouts.'[4]

Through relief work, rescue work, involvement first with homeless children, then with youngsters in need of special care, the 'Army' pattern of social service has been steadily emerging, until now, with ex-prisoners, it comes sharply into focus. Firstly, it is the unplanned response of an individual salvationist (often a soldier) to an immediate need. Secondly, it does not wait for 'official' premises to be made available when an East End back kitchen will serve the purpose just as well—if not better. Thirdly, a homely atmosphere and plenty of prayer are pre-requisites to that change of heart which is the essential need of every man. Fourthly, it works most effectively on the principle of like attracting like—'Set a (reformed) thief to catch a thief. . . .' Fifthly, 'God helps those who help themselves' is the firm basis of all Army self-help schemes. Sixthly, a further principle is now beginning to emerge—that of shielding the newly saved from the undue publicity surrounding Jane Johnson and her like, which, while ensuring that *The War Cry* makes compelling reading, has been known to curdle 'the sincere milk of the word' in the babe in Christ.

Reviewing the first six months of prison gate work in *The Salvation War* (December 1884), Commissioner Railton acknowledged the inspirational lead given to British salvationists by their Australian counterparts. Major and Mrs James Barker, fresh from the motherland, had commenced visiting Melbourne gaol early in 1883,[5] establishing the first prison gate home shortly after. By July of the following year Devonshire House, at 259 Mare Street, Hackney[6] (used between 1880 and 1882 as the training home for men cadets), was functioning as the first British prison gate home, Corps Sergeant-Major Ward[7] of Clapton Congress Hall Corps[8] being appointed as manager almost immediately.

'We are greatly in need of pecuniary help', pleaded Mrs Railton, 'to start the men in work—sometimes to provide railway fare, provision, till they get their wages, tools, clothes, *boots*, etc.—is no light consideration'[9] (author's italics). All the more heartening, then, to discover that 'One of our first cases has just paid back to us the last penny of the loan with which we set him up in work, and expressed a wish to be one of our subscribers.'[10]

At a January 1885 meeting in London's Exeter Hall, General Booth remarked that the prison work 'had of late somewhat flagged, Mrs Railton, who had the matter in hand, being at present on the ocean with her husband, dear Commissioner Railton, who had been advised by his medical advisers to make a sea voyage as

THE
CONVERTED BURGLAR,

Who has spent 40 years in Her Majesty's Convict Prisons.

WAS FLOGGED 8 TIMES,

50 lashes each time; he suffered in all 400 lashes with the Cat

Converted 19-5-89, at the Salvation Army Shelter, Clerkenwell, London

THIS IS OLD

DAD SLOSS

The Ex-Duke of Portland. Now a
Bridge, 30, Argyle-Square, King's

He stands at the Prison Ga
Morning, trying to help other
may have fallen.

the last chance of his recovery'. In consequence: 'A gentleman who had just thrown up his commission in the Royal Engineers, retiring with the rank of lieut-colonel, in order that he might devote his whole life to The Salvation Army, had been appointed to the charge of the prison work.'[11]

All sorts and conditions of men passed through the home—'from the educated gentleman who could speak four or five languages, and had once been an officer in the Queen's army, to the road tramp and the thief'. For that matter, 'Does anyone want a big, strong, coal-heaver? If so, apply to Devonshire House . . .' encouraged *The War Cry*. There was, it seemed, no end to the benefits in store for the saved ex-prisoner: 'One of the Prison Gate Brigade was extolling the beauties of salvation in his own style, and observed that he was happier now than ever in his life, and whereas he used at one time to have no money, now he has had six photos taken, sent three to his poor old mother, and kept three himself.'

Nothing if not practical, the Prison Gate Brigade good-humouredly rose to the challenge issued by 'a lady who had, a few months ago, the unpleasant experience of being in a house which was broken into by burglars. Having a natural desire not to undergo the same experience again, she writes to us, asking us to meet the man who was caught and sent to prison for his offence when he comes out, and run him in securely, where he will learn something better than house-breaking. We at once arranged to have someone at the prison gate.'

Arranging 'to have someone at the prison gate' was a skilled procedure: 'The officers who stand daily at the prison gates are two of very different types. One has been for 20 years a prison-warder. His experience is invaluable, not only as regards dealing with men, but also in respect of the confidence inspired by his long and unblemished record in the minds of prison officials. The other is old 'Dad' Sloss, mentioned on page 100 of 'In Darkest England' as having been more than 40 years in prison, undergoing eight floggings. He has an extended acquaintance among the men we want.'[12]

In contrast to the 'black maria' which delivered them to prison, a 'red maria' at the gates, serving 'coffee all steaming hot' as the men were discharged, was one proposal which met with an enthusiastic reception,[13] but which 'had to remain idle in the yard simply because we have no means of horsing it'. However, on 31 January

1891,[14] when the prison gate home was transferred from Devonshire House to 30 Argyle Square, King's Cross, there to be known as The Bridge, visitors to the opening ceremony 'were drawn to the front windows by exclamations of "Here it is! Here it is!" and upon looking out saw that the red maria—pair of horses, salvation coachman and all complete, and filled with a load of happy salvationists—had just driven up, where it remained, a source of unvarying interest for some little time.'[15]

Colonel and Mrs James Barker, pioneers of prison gate work in Melbourne eight years earlier, had by this time been appointed to the charge of such work in the British Isles,[16] the colonel's name appearing at the foot of the 'cards of hope' handed to the men as they left jail, inviting them to The Bridge. In the nine months to 25 September 160 men availed themselves of the offer.[14]

Comparing the prison gate home with the ordinary run of the mill men's shelters (see next chapter), Major Susie Swift pointed out: 'The dormitories, dining room, etc., are rather more comfortably appointed than those of the shelter. Whether this is correct or not, from a reformatory point of view, it is an absolute necessity. English criminals are accustomed to so much more comfort than English poor, that an ex-prisoner really cannot 'rough it' like a poor man who has always been forced to depend on what his two hands could earn, or on the alternative scant and chilly hospitality of his parish. But everything is, at the same time, of the plainest.'[17]

'The splendid services rendered to the state' by the prison gate home were given due recognition by Herbert Gladstone, son of the prime minister, when he re-opened the enlarged premises towards the end of 1893.[18] '"I cannot help realising what a different atmosphere I felt when I came in here to the atmosphere of the prison"', he said. '"No wonder that so large a proportion of those who once get into these Salvation Army institutions are delighted to stop there, and only wish to know how to make their stay satisfactory by learning better and better how to work, and to earn for themselves a further right to labour. Thus out of a total of 361 men received at the prison gate home in 1892, we find only 43 discharged as being unfit to go on further . . . upon the conditions . . . which the Army imposes."'[19].

Floating the Darkest England Scheme at the end of 1890,

William Booth had written of this aspect of the work: 'In order to save, as far as possible, first offenders from the contamination of prison life . . . we would offer, in the police and criminal courts, to take such offenders under our wing as were anxious to come and willing to accept our regulations.'[20] 'Now this is exactly what we have been able to do,' wrote his son, Bramwell, four years later. 'Of the 1,114 men received into our criminal homes since we began, no less than 135 have come to us under "orders" from Home Secretaries, judges, magistrates, governors and chaplains of prisons, clergymen and societies officially recognised for aiding prisoners. Naturally the business of creating confidence has been slow, but we believe it has been altogether satisfactory, and the number of such cases will increase now rapidly. At the Guildhall and the Mansion House Police Courts a notice is displayed, by permission of the authorities, and at a comparatively small outlay we hope to be able to help hundreds of prisoners who are now totally friendless, on their first appearance before the magistrate.'[19] Not such a new idea, then, were the Salvation Army bail units of the 1970s-80s.

First offenders or old lags, the good Salvation Army principle of self-support equally obtained. 'General Booth . . . takes a very concrete view of the world as he finds it,' reported the *Liverpool Daily Post,* 'and comes to the conclusion that if men are to be Christians they must have food, and if they are to eat they must work. . . . Two things only he insists upon—first, that those who accept his aid shall be willing to work; and next, that they shall obey orders. . . . His great rule all through is to be that, if a man will not work, neither shall he eat, and by rigidly adhering to this principle he hopes to ultimately make his scheme self-supporting.'[21]

Wood-chopping was the ex-prisoners' earliest means of self-support.[4] Then, by October 1885, having received £7 as a result of his appeal for £4 to purchase a costermonger's hand-barrow, Sergeant Ward of Devonshire House obtained one smartly painted in Army colours, putting the surplus money to buying materials with which to start the men in joinery work. Bootmaking, mat weaving, cabinet-making and tailoring quickly became part of their output, 'and perhaps no more satisfactory evidence of the change produced in these men can be adduced than the fact that during the year they have by their own labour produced no less than £354. 5s. 5½d. towards the cost of the work', reported the Christmas edition of *The War Cry* of 1886.

The costermonger's barrow was overtaken in 1891 by 'a most substantial salvage cart. It is painted red, and bears the Army crest on each side. If any of our readers should notice the same in their neighbourhood, will they kindly take the hint that broken victuals, clothes, old shoes, hats, etc., will be gladly taken in. Already it has been successful in securing us a fair supply of food, but we might here especially mention that we are in great need of clothes for our factory and shelter men. All clothes go through a kind of renovating process before being sold to the men at a nominal price; this makes them feel independent of charity.'[22] Salvage work was here to stay! (See chapter 9.)

The early 1890s were perhaps the heyday of the Army's work with ex-prisoners. Advertising ' "A Thieves Banquet" at Regent Hall, Oxford Street', The War Cry divulged that '600 ex-prisoners will be present. At the meeting, after supper, Commissioner Cadman will make some startling revelations of the work accomplished among the criminal classes.' 'The hundreds of well-dressed friends congregated in the galleries' to observe the spectacle were no doubt well used by now to Elijah Cadman's flamboyant approach. At his welcome as Social Wing leader 10 months earlier it was reported: 'Flinging off his cape as he walks, and thereby nearly extinguishing a gas jet, the new commissioner shouts "Hallelujah!" and coming to the front strips off his coat, as if for all the world he was preparing for one of his old boxing bouts, and takes hold of the meeting. And what a meeting it was! . . . He played upon his audience like a skilled musician upon his instrument, and laughter and tears, gladness and sadness, shouts and silence, followed each other in quick succession.'[23]

'Her Most Gracious Majesty Victoria, Queen of Great Britain and Ireland, Empress of India' was probably not amused to receive a communication from James Barker, Colonel, informing her that The Salvation Army intended gathering together some 600 of London's thieves for dinner. 'To do this successfully the sum of £25 will be required, and as there is no fund in connection with the social scheme for this, we are appealing to a few friends to help us raise the amount.' 'Her Most Gracious Majesty' evidently wished not to number herself among the friends of The Salvation Army. The Lord Mayor of London, on the other hand, felt differently, and sent a sum to help defray expenses.[24]

The 'guest' who was 'in such an unregenerate state that he picked a pocket outside the hall and was marched off to the police station instead of joining in the supper', missed the 'pile and a quart' served by caterer J. Flawn with his accustomed readiness, the singing of 'In evil long I took delight', another 'pathetic solo about wandering from God, home and mother, with refrains that went to the imperishable strains of "Home, Sweet Home!"' (accompanied by Puffing Billy's whistle), not to mention the little Testament presented to each man on departure.'[24] As the *Daily Telegraph* observed: 'Colonel James Barker and Commissioner Cadman . . . may certainly congratulate themselves upon the success which is attending their work.'

Writing in *The Deliverer* of April 1891 (now no longer confined exclusively to rescue work), Colonel Barker revealed: 'Circumstances have compelled us to confer with Mrs Bramwell Booth as to whether our present machinery could not be so enlarged as to do something for the criminal *women.* Temporary arrangements are made, and we hope soon to have a female prison gate brigade in full swing.'[22] Of that idea nothing more is heard, although three years later Mrs Bramwell Booth wrote that: 'The proposed establishment of a sisterhood . . . composed of those women of God who are at liberty to give their time and strength to work of this kind, would provide people who would be free to carry out various plans which we have hitherto been obliged to hold in abeyance. I hope, for instance, in the near future, to be able to appoint officers to attend the various police courts in this and other cities. In Cardiff we have been able to do this for some time . . . having the privilege of interviewing every woman both before and after she appeared before the magistrates. In a short time we hope to bring our plans for the formation of this sisterhood into shape, then we shall be in a position to communicate with any readers who may desire to become members of the order, which we propose to call "The Sisters of the Cross".'[25]

Returning from Plymouth in May 1895, Colonel Barker announced that 'the officer who would henceforth represent the Salvation Army in the police-court work of the great metropolis of the South-West was no other than Miss Soper, the sister of Mrs Bramwell Booth'. (Florence Booth herself was to be appointed a magistrate at a later stage.)[26] Recognising that 'it is useless to deal with cases unless we have somewhere to put them . . . deserving cases will be handed on to the local rescue home.'[27]

'The Sisters of the Cross' were not mentioned again, but the spirit of this still-born order bore much fruit. The first Salvation

Army service in a British prison took place in Plymouth in 1898,[28] and when, 50 years later, in co-operation with the Home Office the Army opened the first training centre in the country for mothers convicted of child neglect, Plymouth was the location chosen and 'Mayflower' was the eventual name of the home.[29] But the spirit of 'The Sisters of the Cross' spread even further than Plymouth. Towards the end of January 1898 the first home specifically for the accommodation of women charged with offences in police courts was opened in Glasgow by Colonel Adelaide Cox, chief secretary to Mrs Bramwell Booth (and later leader of the Women's Social Work).[30] Regular prison visitation (commenced in Paisley as early as 1889) was being undertaken in Glasgow, Ayr and Greenock.[28] By 1906 annual financial grants were being made to this work by the municipalities of Edinburgh, Glasgow, Aberdeen and Dundee.[31]

In 1902 the writer of the Army's annual social report felt it noteworthy that: 'A remarkable change has come over the feeling of the whole community towards the criminal. Some of the laws have been so altered in favour of a more rational and humane method of dealing with the prisoner that they are scarcely to be recognised. The Salvation Army has had something to do with this, and, among the changes for the better, is the new rule under which our officers are now admitted to interview any prisoners who express a desire to see them, while they are undergoing their sentences. We have reason to believe that this arrangement is working well.'[32] So well did it continue to work over the years that by 1983 *The Salvation Army Year Book* was listing almost 100 British prison establishments regularly visited by its chaplaincy service.

The 1902 summary of social operations throughout the world shows Britain as having one receiving house for ex-prisoners, one prison gate home and one prison gate works. No mention is made of the Glasgow home for women,[33] and by 1906 the three men's institutions cease to be listed, having been replaced by the following information: 'All our industrial homes and labour factories are available for the reception and employment of prisoners upon their discharge.'[34] Not until 1971, under the terms of the Xenia Field Foundation, was specialised accommodation once more engaged in.[35]

'"Oh, Lord, it was good of you to die to make us bad 'uns good!"' prayed a Clerkenwell shelter convert during Easter 1890. And that somehow more than sums up a century of prison work.

82

8
Strange bedfellows

'LONDON alone has more than 1,000 registered lodging houses, with accommodation for about 30,000 persons,' wrote Bramwell Booth in 1895. 'Some of them are, of course, well conducted and orderly houses, but of the low and lower classes it is difficult to speak too strongly. "Their keepers", says Mr Charles Booth's *Life and Labour of the People in London,* "can only be said to match the occupants. They, or rather their deputies, are too often men and women of the lowest grade, whose ideas of morality and conduct are exceedingly elastic—nor is this to be wondered at, for any householder can register his house as a common lodging-house provided he complies with the statutory regulations."'[1]

The Christian Missioners of Tottenham managed to gain evangelical access to such a lodging house as early as 1874,[2] and five years later the problem of homelessness began to creep off the streets and into the barracks with Elijah Cadman's report (when but a Coventry captain) that the Army had 'taken in' a gipsy who, having got saved, was turned out by those she lived with.

'The Salvation Army professes to go to the people,' challenged Staff-Captain Simpson in a forthright article in *The War Cry* (1884), 'but how many of our soldiers have gone into such places, and to such men, which even no band or singing ever draws from their hovels? . . .

'With permission from the deputies of these lodging houses, and with judgment, brigades could be organised to carry the war into such places as these. . . .

'Wait for nobody! Go straight at it! If you love these people you will find out where they are and how to get at them. But if you wait until it can all be arranged in a regular way by the corps there is no knowing how many will be dead before you get at them. They are your neighbours. Get them saved!'[3]

Two years on, and a full front page article, *'In and Out of the*

Lodging Houses', by S. F. Swift, concludes with the question: 'Doesn't somebody else's heart go out toward the scheme of a Salvation Army lodging house?'[4]

Adroit as she was at seed sowing, it was to be more than a year before Major Swift's General took that now historic winter's night journey which turned his heart in the direction of the niche-dwellers (see page 6). The sheer professionalism of the job description subsequently appearing in *The War Cry* must surely have justified the delay—even to her impetuous spirit. *'Night Refuge—Wanted Two Men* to take charge, must have good eyesight, good memory, and be willing to use both.'[5]

One of the two answering this classic description would have been Mr Hoe, making his début in the pages of *The War Cry* dated 17 March 1888, his good eyesight and good memory having noticed that 'two clocks, a vegetable cutter and one or two bread cutters, old clothes of any sort will be a great help' in the house of food and shelter opened at 21 West India Dock Road on 18 February.[6] No Christian name clue attaches itself to the enigmatic Mr Hoe in these early reports, but in 1962 his grand-daughter confirmed that this was Charles W. Hoe, father of the later Lieut-Commissioner Edgar Hoe, and a former Plymouth Brother, who 'was at that time working with the Founder and helping him with rescue work'[7]—a description which, taken in its broader sense, could certainly refer to running a night shelter for the destitute.

The house of food and shelter fast became known, in Limehouse parlance, as 'The Threepenny Doss', which *The Social Gazette,* 11 years on, helpfully translates as follows: 'The name "dosser", so commonly applied to the tramping, homeless outcasts of London, is probably a corruption of "dozer", that is, a man who hasn't the wherewithal to obtain a proper night's sleep, and must, therefore, doze in snatches when and where he can.'[8] Next door to the Home for Asiatics, the Threepenny Doss was a dormitory, with plenty of texts on the walls, situated above Caterer Flawn's food facilities. The 'dozing in snatches' was accomplished on 'bedsteads made by placing a number of forms on the ground on their sides, thus making a number of divisions, about six feet long by two-and-a-half wide. A little wooden locker with a sloping lid forms a pillow, and the mattress, placed upon this lid, is of leather stuffed with wool, while the top covering is made of soft skin, with a loop to slip on the neck, and has the great advantage that it can be kept clean by a daily baking.'[9]

'I have no faith in any pauperising of the people,' maintained Booth. 'People don't need to be paupers. They do not want to be saved, and never will be saved—English people won't—by doles of flannel petticoats or gruel. Give them salvation, and they will save themselves. . . .'[10] Consequently, 'it is proposed to conduct it in that strictly business-like way which will preserve or cultivate self-respect and manliness in its recipients. . . . Any applicant is received. If a man chooses—not unless—his name, occupation and references are taken, and the length of time he has been—if he is so—unemployed noted, with his own reasons therefor. His case is then investigated, with a view to finding him work.'[11]

'Our people can smell a man who is really destitute,' declared Commissioner Cadman, with his usual delightful *naïveté*. 'Once a young ex-barrister lieutenant was very near disobeying the orders of his wiser captain and letting in a man whose vows of poverty were of an extremely convincing nature; but, clinging to the sheet anchor of his instructions, his perseverance was rewarded by seeing the man sit him down on the pavement, pull off his boots, and then from the toe of his stocking extract the requisite fourpence!'

'Further, these shelters are a great help to those men and women who wish to serve God, and to do what is right. The moment that a man or woman of this class professes salvation they are subjected to tests of the most searching description. They have a fiery trial to go through, which nothing but the grace and wonderful power of God could carry them over. One of the chief points looked at is, whether these new followers of Jesus are saved as to their *tempers*. . . . Moreover, the morality of the shelters has its effect upon many who do not profess the name of Christ at all,' maintained an observer towards the end of 1889, when Mr Hoe's shelter had set the pattern for a chain of others. 'We can with confidence say that we are sure that we are on the right lines for the reaching of this class of people, in substituting for the notorious common lodging-houses in London these shelters, which are cheaper, cleaner and better in every respect, and where the influence is for good and not for evil.' Yet all was not self-complacency. 'What modifications and alterations may be made in our methods time will show.'[12]

No sooner was 'The Threepenny Doss' under way than Susie Swift set about sowing more seed: 'One out of many other women who beg piteously that we should shelter them as well as the men, came to us about half-past six, timidly proffering her coppers.

THE GRAPHIC

AN ILLUSTRATED WEEKLY NEWSPAPER

SATURDAY, FEBRUARY 27, 1892

A SALVATION ARMY SHELTER FOR WOMEN IN WHITECHAPEL

"They told me you'd take me," she said with a sort of dull despair, when we told her gently we had no place for women. There was nothing to be done but serve her with bread and tea for the coppers she had treasured for her lodging, and give her an address where they might be able to do something for her.' Then, after a detailed description of the Limehouse premises, comes one of those final Swift thrusts we have long learned to anticipate: 'The meeting closes about nine, the forms are put in order, the men stow themselves away, the night watchman takes his post, our "Day at Limehouse" is ended, and we go out into the gusty winter night, thankful that even so many of our brothers are safely housed for the coming Sunday, away from cards and liquor, shut in for a few hours at least, face to face with reminders of the promises they made their mothers in the past, and the promises their Father longs to make them for their future; albeit not daring to ask ourselves, "Where are the women we turned away?"' [13]

It was seed well sown. At the 1888 May meeting in London's Exeter Hall General Booth announced: 'We have already a generous offer of £400 towards the formation of a scheme for the women and children.' [10]

Captain Tassie, pioneer rescue officer in Glasgow, let it be known in November of that year that: 'She is anxious to set up a salvation lodging house, with a truly saved man and wife as "father" and "mother", where the girls who have passed through the home can live, while earning their livelihood at a factory', [14] and a few weeks later Mrs Bramwell Booth advertised in *The War Cry* for 'a motherly woman (or man and wife) to take charge of a boarding house for young women in business. Must be salvationists, and have highest references.'

By the beginning of March 1889 it was revealed that '*The Female Shelter* wanted immediately two or three tall, strong, godly women of good character. . . . None residing far from London need make application. They must be salvationists, hard-working and single.'

'"Is that the place where the murder was?"' asked a bystander, seeing a crowd gathering about the doors of 194 Hanbury Street on the day of its opening. A recent spate of crimes, known as the 'Whitechapel murders' had brought unsought fame to the row where a derelict swimming bath next door to the first rescue home had been fitted up as a shelter for 250 women and 50 children. A

87

crèche adjoining it would accommodate up to 150 children.[15] Corps Sergeant-Major and Mrs Ward, late of Devonshire House prison gate home, now make their appearance as Captain and Mrs Ward, managers of the first women's shelter.[16] They would find their hands full, for into their care would be passed those residents from 'next door' featured in the following graphic description by that Clapton lady of middle age and independent means, Miss Sapsworth: 'The "prisoner" and the "homeless servant" and the babies have nearly extinguished me. My deep conviction is that the prisoner is a double-dyed liar; the homeless servant is worse than prisoner, babies, and all the rest put together! Most certainly the mixing of such as she and the prisoner with our refuge girls will mar our work. . . . It seems to me that the older homeless women should have a separate place and those to work there should have the faith of Abraham. Other refuges will not take them, but I see no reason why, all things considered, we should not. What is to be our course?'[17] What indeed! Captain and Mrs Ward's experience at the prison gate home—when linked with the faith of Abraham—no doubt stood them in good stead.

'It was one of those old stagers who got up in her bunk in the middle of the first night and called out, "Lasses, I know who've we to thank for this place! We'd never have had it but for old Jack. God bless Jack the Ripper, I say!" . . . Still, we seem to be finding a way at these dark, sin-steeped *old* women. Several of them were weeping in this morning's meeting.'[18] 'Old Telegraph', however, would not have been among the weepers; neither would she have been among the 25 who professed conversion in the first six weeks. This elderly paper-picker, nicknamed Old Telegraph by her shelter comrades because of her frightful tendency to broadcast all the news she picked up,[18] came to the shelter the first night it was opened, and was never missing except when housed at Her Majesty's expense.[19] 'Every night for weeks, Captain Ward had to stand at the door, and, as he puts it, "jolly" Old Telegraph into washing at least the tip of her nose. "Come along, now! Go in and give your face a swim! . . . You'll not know yourself when you've had an 'all 'ot' in there. Get along in, old girl!"'

'One day, came a bundle of cast-off clothes containing a full outfit for a woman just Old Telegraph's size. . . . She was beguiled into the laundry and given what was probably the first thorough bath of her life. She made a terrible fuss about parting with the vermin-filled rags which had covered her so long, but she could only have the yellow frock on condition that she gave them up for ever, and at last they were borne away in triumph.

'"The old soul seems to be a different woman since she began to come here," says the captain. "But as to understanding salvation, it seems impossible for her!"'[20]

Nevertheless, the faith of Abraham prevailed, and when, 10 years later, Mrs Bramwell Booth reported in the columns of *The Deliverer*, 'Old Telegraph of the shelter is no more; she passed away suddenly during the dinner hour at the food depot in Whitechapel Road', she was able to add: 'Latterly there was considerable improvement in her behaviour. On the Sunday night previous to her death, the captain, in giving out the chorus:

> I do believe, I will believe,
> That Jesus died for me,

asked the question of the women, "Do you really believe it?" and instantly Old Telegraph answered "I do." Her death made a great impression upon the other women.'[19]

'Joy . . . over one sinner that repenteth' notwithstanding, there was a stark no-nonsense facing of reality by the Army's early-day social workers. 'Every inmate knows that her welcome, and such advantages as she can earn and pay for, are in no shape or form depending upon any profession she may make of a religious kind,' declared Forence Booth. 'She knows further that a strong tide of searching criticism will flow round her once she comes out on the Lord's side. Eyes and ears as sharp as her own, and moral standards of full measure will be brought to bear on her. The very worst of her fellow-lodgers have a high ideal of what a 'saved life' should be, and they are painfully frank in expressing their views on the subject in the face of any inconsistency. In view of all this I rejoice in humble gratitude to God that over 500 souls have been led to Jesus at the shelter, many of whom have, after suitable trial, been sent to their friends, to situations, or to some employment in connection with our own industries.'[21] This in 1893.

'All our friends are cordially invited to visit the night shelters for men and food depots. Ladies are always welcome to inspect the women's shelter,' ran an early advertisement with fine distinction. One such 'lady' provides us with a good deal of insight into the rationale behind shelter meetings. 'The evening service . . . to them is what the finest ritual—the most delightful oratorio—is to the

89

more cultivated. Grant all its noise and blare and want of refined taste—grant its questionable familiarities, its hysterical excitements—surely this rousing, rollicking service, with banjos, tambourines, loud shoutings and untrained gestures, is better than the flash songs of a penny gaff, or the obscene jokes and carols of a gin palace! When refined noses turn themselves up and sniff at intellectual dregs, they ought to remember the loathsome carrion for which this more harmless sustenance is substituted. . . . Sometimes, too, more permanent good is done. The right chord is struck and the conscience vibrates in unison with the appeal, outcast sinners rise redeemed as penitent Magdalenes. For such as these The Salvation Army has ever a glad welcome . . . and, we venture to add, a more rational way of dealing with them than is to be found in the strict seclusion and dull monotony of many penitential homes. For the methods of The Salvation Army are essentially movement, life, activity—light and colour and noise—the exchange of destructive excitements for these which are, at all events, harmless, when even not life-giving. And for women who have lived in the lurid glare and wild uproar of vice, this is better than the gloomy retribution of penance and penitence.'[22]

A small Salvation Army corps was formed in connection with the women's shelter. 'About 23 members signed articles of war, and were duly enrolled at the first meeting. These soldiers will consist of those who profess conversion at the shelter and who have afterwards given proof of their sincerity.'[23]

By the autumn of 1891 Captain Tassie's three-year-old dream of a 'salvation lodging house' had come true—not in Glasgow, but in Cardiff, where rescue work had subsequently taken her. Now she was to be its first manager.[24] Plans were afoot for a similar opening in Liverpool,[25] whilst the building adjoining the Hanbury Street shelter was being converted into a lodging house, or metropole, 'for women who have now risen, and are able to pay fourpence or sixpence for a proper bed'.[26] This elevating influence was making itself felt amongst their husbands and brothers also, in that a 'poor man's metropole', known as The Ark, had been opened earlier that year in the premises formerly used as the Army's first Trade Headquarters at 96 Southwark Street. 'This is for the men who have got a footing through the shelters, and are earning enough money to pay for something better than the wooden bunk and seaweed mattress for which the amateur casual is so profoundly ungrateful, and for which the genuine article usually gets a real affection! We saw a specimen of their neat little beds and punched its mattress with house-keeperly care. It was excellent.'[27] Two years earlier, with a year's experience of shelter work behind him, Mr Hoe made an assessment of the situation which may well have engendered the metropole idea. 'We have taken hold of a large number of men, both young and old, who have come to the shelter when, *for the first time,* they were destitute, before they had lost their clothing, and with all the signs of respectability still about them. We have been able to help many such men, and in some cases to get them immediate employment.'[28] Yet within two months of The Ark's opening, it was to be promoted from the *second* step of the elevating ladder, to the *third.* This was occasioned by the opening, in April 1891, of The Lighthouse, Quaker Street. This erstwhile walking-stick factory 'was a sort of second step in one of our ladders. There was first the ordinary food and shelter, to which any poor, hungry, shelterless person could come. . . . Having been cleansed bodily, they wanted to keep clean, and so did not want to have to associate at night with the ordinary occupants. The Lighthouse was the place for this class. . . . Above and beyond this came The Ark—for the third class,'[29] although by 1894 even this was found not to be an adequate enough spread for the complicated English class system. Reported Bramwell Booth: 'One of the difficulties which confront us continually is the dealing with men of the educated and upper classes who have through drink, vice or misfortune, lost all. We find it alike impolitic and impossible to mix them with the coarser types of submerged. One of the misfortunes of misfortune is that it makes such strange bedfellows. Commissioner Cadman is very anxious for the establishment of a small working retreat, into which such men could be passed straight from the streets. We do not find any serious difficulty in finding for them such employment as will provide their immediate wants, and we believe that with the extra oversight and personal care which this institution will secure, a very much larger portion could be reclaimed than is even now the case. At present so strongly do we feel the desirability of not mixing all together, that we pay, and pay heavily, for special accommodation in ordinary lodgings.'[30]

At the end of 1888 General Booth had presented a 'memorial' to the Home Secretary, outlining the Army's rescue and food and shelter efforts (both proposed and actual), and suggesting that 'the wretched condition of vast numbers of the men and women existing in the East of London, and in other large centres of population, seems to us to demand some special and extraordinary effort on behalf of the state'. This, The Salvation Army's first approach to a

British Government for financial aid (£15,000 was requested), found a precedent yet again in Australia, where the Government of Victoria made regular grants for similar work, without imposing conditions.[31] It was to be some years before the British Government saw fit to follow this example. Undeterred, Booth went ahead with his proposals.[32]

Providing the framework for that part of the still-to-be-launched Darkest England Scheme known as the City Colony, a swift succession of shelters opened in 1889 at Clerkenwell, Whitechapel and Westminster,[33] joined in 1891 (with the launching of the scheme) by additional London shelters at Clare Market,[34] Bethnal Green, Royal Mint Street,[35] Lisson Grove and Blackfriars Road,[36] together with one at Bristol.[35]

Lighthouses, Arks, Harbours—all of them playing a vital part in rescuing the victims of vice and poverty from the sea of misery and despair beneath which Booth's estimated submerged tenth[37] of the population was drowning. But Lighthouses, Arks and Harbours were nothing more romantic than common lodging-houses in the eyes of the police. Summoned at the Thames police court for not registering the women's shelter as a lodging house, the Army was cleared of the offence, the magistrate giving a decision in its favour. 'Mark the glorious uncertainty of law!' exclaimed *The War Cry* when, sometime later, at the same court, another magistrate fined the General 20 shillings and costs for not registering a men's shelter similarly.[38] The Lord Chief Justice overruled, however, and the Army claimed 'another legal victory'.[39]

Criticism being the easiest of trades, and the publication of Booth's *In Darkest England and the Way Out* having turned the public gaze firmly upon the nearest 'way out'—the shelter work—it should occasion no surprise that the two things met. This meeting came to pass at the Clerkenwell shelter towards the end of 1891, apparently, and the evening papers in consequence threw the kind of mud which is intended to stick.[40] *The Lancet,* the leading medical journal, reproduced these calumnious statements 'in perfect good faith'[41] (they hastened to assure the Army at a later date), whereupon 'seven gentlemen of position—and administrators of the Sanitary Acts to wit—visited the shelter in question.'[40] Humble pie was now the order of the day. Declared *The Lancet*: 'A fortnight ago, acting upon apparently reliable information, we directed attention to the alleged unwholesomeness of a Salvation Army shelter, and to its apparent influence in promoting a local increase in the pauper population. We have now the satisfaction of learning from a presumably well-informed correspondent that a recent official inspection of the shelter has, at all events, effectually disposed of any question as to its present sanitary condition. Within, it was found to be remarkably clean, well heated, and well ventilated. Several baths, with a sufficient supply of water, towels, and soap, were at the service of the occupants, and the sanitary conditions generally were the reverse of what they were at first supposed to be. "Adversity", says Bacon, "doth best discover virtue"; and certainly the salvationists of Clerkenwell have little reason to regret the light hardship of public suspicion, which finally appears to have discovered among them the healthy virtue of cleanliness.'[41]

If adversity *does* best discover virtue, then the shelters of the 1890s must have been hallowed places indeed. Two years after this 'unsanitary' outburst, *The Darkest England Gazette* carried an interview with Commissioner Cadman entitled 'Salvation Sanitation'.

'The old slander respecting the cleanliness of the shelters having been dished up once more by a religious print, our representative called upon Commissioner Cadman with a view to ascertaining what steps are actually taken to ensure cleanliness in the City Colony buildings. . . . The commissioner . . . exclaimed: "I say this, there are the shelters; you can see for yourself they are spotlessly clean. . . . Of course, if an individual is commissioned by a newspaper to write something spicey, he is bound to find fault, like an inspector who has not done his duty unless he says something is wrong. . . ."

'"Then the public are at liberty to inspect, commissioner?"

'"Most decidedly, and I will defy them to find any place dirty."

'"What about surprise visits?"

'"Anybody can come at any time to inspect. Mind you, I speak of the shelters. If a *man* comes with a dirty face, I won't be responsible for that. We exist more especially for men with dirty faces; are we to turn them away? Certainly not! We must bring them in and teach them cleanliness."

'"What cleansing work is daily gone through in the shelters?"

'"We have a big staff of scrubbers at every shelter. . . . When I say that we use one part of Jeyes' fluid to eight of water, that should be enough to convince the most unreasonable. . . ."'[42] It certainly should—particularly in view of the fact that the same paper printed a correction two weeks later stating that the proportion of Jeyes' fluid to water used in cleansing the shelters was not one to eight, but one to 80!

Echoes of Old Telegraph are to be heard in Bramwell Booth's annual report for 1895, where, in dealing with the subject of the homeless, he says: 'The intense hatred which the most degraded of them feel towards clean water has no parallel, except it be in their affection for strong drink. Their poverty alone makes them conservative in the matter of washing their clothes—if they have any to wash—for they imagine that to wash your shirt is an infallible method of wearing it out before its time. They wander aimlessly about from one place to another, the certain distributors of innumerable germs of disease more or less active, and no doubt largely responsible for introducing and extending the various epidemics from which our great cities are periodically the sufferers.'[1]

One such epidemic had caused the *Westminster Gazette* to report in August of that year: 'Charity may cover a multitude of sins, but it must not cover a centre of infection. Such was yesterday the conclusion of the Whitechapel Guardians on the report that 17 cases of smallpox had occurred in the Salvation Army shelters within their district during the last fortnight. The Guardians unanimously resolved to call upon the Local Government Board to put the shelters under the same regulations as common lodgings.'[43] '"So you think that if we were classified as common lodging-houses the plague would never appear, do you?"' rejoined Bramwell Booth. '"Why the very case which started the epidemic has been traced to a lodging house. And what happened? The patient was taken to the smallpox ship, the house was closed, and each of the patient's fellow-lodgers was turned out into the street— with what consequences we are all aware. . . . Does not all the misery and wretchedness of London gravitate to the Army— homeless, ragged, vermin-eaten outcasts? . . . If you shut up our shelters there would be more fevers and more smallpox—in my opinion. There is no germ-breeder like an outcast."'[43]

Lacking in cleanliness, source of epidemics, and now—guilty of overcrowding. The Blackfriars Road shelter, catering nightly for

800 men, was judged by a magistrate to be capable of holding only 550. Reported *The Social Gazette* for 7 December 1895: 'The Officer of Public Health for the Vestry of Southwark, having succeeded, to some extent, in casting adrift 250 of London's waifs, has gone to Eastbourne to recuperate his health.' The Army, on the other hand, determined to open another shelter in the vicinity of Blackfriars; 250 men were not to be so easily lost. Writing to *The Times* Bramwell Booth appealed for £1,000 to furnish and fit up a building of the necessary size to shelter them under proper conditions. Aware of his readership, Bramwell concluded: 'I venture to think they are worth it. Among them are men of good character, men who have seen brighter and happier days, men of education and of gentle breeding. And they are Englishmen!'[44]

Such an Englishman was Bill—albeit 'a blackguard, well-known to the police and the magistrate. His life was a reckless and drunken brawl. He was about 40 times before the magistrates and in prison nearly as often, and when at large was a nuisance in the neighbourhood in which he lived, for he was a desperado of a very violent type.

'He entered one of our shelters in a woe begone and bitter state of soul. The second night his heart was touched by the meeting, and he publicly confessed his sin and resolved to abandon it. His faith was soon put to a severe test. The police came to take him on a warrant granted some two years previously. Instead of resisting them as he had been accustomed to, he walked quietly to the police station, and in due course appeared before the magistrate. The inspector spoke to Bill's present good behaviour and the influence The Salvation Army had had upon him. Bill himself said he thought it was rather hard that he should be taken by the police, seeing he was doing so well now, and did not intend to drink any more. The magistrate said that he had intended sending him to prison, but gave him the option of a fine and 14 days to pay it in, and added that if Bill kept sober for three months more he, the magistrate, would give him a pair of new boots.

'During the 14 days of grace Bill earned enough to pay the fine, and the boots will soon be an accomplished fact.'[45]

The common lodging-house spectre continued to haunt the shelters at recurring intervals—often with amusing results. '"Just to humour a London vestry's passing whim,"' related Elijah Cadman, '"we once acceded to a request to register the name of every man who came into our shelters during a specified week. As each man came in he was asked for his name. Why, bless you, it was all a farce! We got the names of Members of Parliament, the nobility and royalty, Jack the Ripper, and other notorious personages! The men would give any kind of name but their own. We find that our shelter-men prefer our shelters to the registered lodging-houses, because their liberties are not interfered with in any way." We hope the vestry in question was satisfied. But we have our doubts.'[46]

At the turn of the century a paragraph entitled *'For Queen and Country'* made its appearance in *The Social Gazette*. It was to have far-reaching effects on the future pattern of shelter work. It revealed that 'Her Majesty the Queen has decreed by Royal warrant that all ex-soldiers under the age of 45 shall go back to the army again if they wish to do so. More than this, Her Majesty has appealed to them to re-enlist. This appeal is meeting with an enthusiastic response. Our shelter officers state that since the Royal decree was published scores of our shelter-men have come forward to ask for pen, ink, and paper, to write to their depot, offering to rejoin the army. A great many have already gone, and were right glad of the chance to be of some use to somebody or something.'[47]

After a resultant initial drop of some 3,000 in the annual statistics of the Army's 'cheap lodgings for the homeless', the figure gradually builds up again, until in 1908 it passes the two million mark for the first time. Even during the 1914-18 war years the shelter population fell by only a few thousand. But the pattern of its intake changed remarkably. Reported *The Social Gazette* for 12 September 1914: 'Up to last week no fewer than 400 men—including 100 Reservists—had left the Spa Road and Whitecross (London) social centres to join the colours, and since then there have been more volunteers. Many of the men are orderlies and prominent workers. According to Brigadier Aspinall, this patriotic exodus has heavily depleted the social working staff at Burne Street, Great Peter Street, Blackfriars, Middlesex Street and other social institutions. Many of the lodgers also are involved in the rush to the front.' Two weeks later the same paper carries first mention of Belgian refugees being received into Salvation Army social institutions in Cardiff.[48] Six thousand of them arrived in London in one day: 40,000 during one week. The men's home in Quaker Street immediately opened its doors to 175, and other institutions quickly followed suit.[49]

96

At the end of 1915 it was, significantly, the Australian High Commissioner who approached General Bramwell Booth regarding the problem of additional accommodation for convalescing Commonwealth soldiers. In consequence the Great Peter Street hostel was placed at the immediate disposal of the Commonwealth military authorities for this purpose,[50] and within weeks of this arrangement coming to pass several of the Army's Birmingham institutions were set aside to house munitions factory war-workers—in fact two additional buildings were taken over and specifically adapted to this end.[51] Then there were the families rendered homeless by air-raids; for instance, 42 such families from the same neighbourhood were taken into Army premises on one day.[52]

Following the long-looked-for Armistice announcement of November 1918, the General's 'Peace' letter published in *The War Cry* concluded: 'And now, my dear comrades of The Salvation Army . . . the days of peace will bring to us needs as great as the days of war.' That these needs were already engaging the thinking powers of the General and the Governor of the Men's Social Work, Colonel John B. Laurie, had been evidenced in the previous week's paper: 'In the solving of problems following the war The Salvation Army is destined to play a leading part. The General, who has devoted close personal attention to this matter, has formulated a far-reaching programme which includes the opening, in various parts of the country, of a number of superior hostels for men. This, it is felt, will provide for the needs of a class of workers who having no home of their own in the proper sense of the term, will require and be able to pay for accommodation and comfort in advance of what The Salvation Army is able to give at its poor men's shelters. And surely it was a happy inspiration which led the General to decide upon the opening of the first, and, at the moment, the largest of these new institutions at the earliest signs of a coming peace.' This was that suite of buildings known as the Victoria Homes in Whitechapel, taken over as a going concern, with a nucleus of 460 lodgers.[53] Similar projects were soon to follow in the provinces.[54]

IN the summer of 1921, more than 30 years after William Booth's original confrontation with the niche-dwellers of London, The Salvation Army held its second International Social Council in that city. To salvationist social workers representing 26 countries Commissioner David Lamb spoke on the subject of the homeless poor: 'When the "Darkest England Scheme" was launched the homeless poor in the streets of London were a disgrace to our civilization. The facts arrayed by the Founder were almost unbelievable; but they were beyond dispute. Even after men and women had been swept up out of the cold and wet by the thousand and sheltered by The Salvation Army in clean, warm buildings, there was still an open sore which continued to trouble the community. I suppose amongst the problems of a great city there will always be a fresh daily crop of unfortunates, who for one reason or another find themselves homeless, destitute and friendless. But there was more than that; and it required years of agitation in public and private to bring into existence the machinery necessary to reduce this blot to a reasonable minimum with a hope of its complete elimination. We increased the number of our shelters; we had our midnight soup kitchens on the Thames Embankment right under the nose of Parliament; we stirred up the responsible public authorities, we co-operated with them. . . . The eight years following 1904, when the first official census was taken, showed an average of over 2,000 destitute persons seeking the shelter of arches, staircases and the streets. The highest number recorded was 2,777 in 1910. Co-operation with the authorities brought the number to 532 in 1913 and to 491 in 1914. The war came, and conditions prevailing during that time demonstrated beyond all doubt that this disgraceful evil could be successfully grappled with, and that—as we have always said—when the community willed they could organize it out of existence. The numbers for the last seven years (1915-21) are: 192, 51, 32, 11, 10, 61, 76. I venture to predict that London will never see a return of its homeless poor to be huddled in doorways, stairways, and arches, in the cold, bleak, miserable weather, with the biting, cutting winds which mark our English winters. The next generation will never know what London knew 50 years ago.'[55] Fifty years on, in 1971, the official census revealed a figure of 745 such niche-dwellers in Greater London.[56]

9
The worshipful company of out-of-works

'HE who statedly employs the poor in useful labour is their only friend; he who only feeds them is their greatest enemy.'[1] Writing on the subject of the Poor Law in 1786, Townsend could scarcely have foreseen the fulfilment his words would find 100 or so years later in the work of The Salvation Army.

Within a year of The Christian Mission's original feeding programme being commenced at Poplar in 1867, a sewing class had been set up in the East End 'for the starving poor. Widows and wives of men incapacitated for labour by illness or accident attend three times per week, and receive sixpence per day and their tea'.[2] By February 1869, 120 women were regularly receiving two shillings each for two days' work. 'The true Christian is a real self-helper,' wrote William Booth the same year. 'In bringing the truths of religion before the suffering masses we are also assisting in the great work of social reform.'[3]

The following year a report appeared in *The Christian Mission Magazine* from Brighton: 'Two very poor young men who had been tramping about the country for 18 months, so ragged and dirty that their whole outfit was not worth more than sixpence, came forward seeking mercy. . . . Something had now to be done for their bodies. A dear brother, himself only recently converted, took charge of them, and got them a lodging for the night. Next day he got them a bath, and went out amongst his friends and begged them some clothes, so they were able to come to the prayer meeting at the Mission hall on the Monday evening very nicely dressed. The following day, having business in the town, we met a lady who was enquiring of a shopkeeper if he knew where she could get a strong young man as "boots". He not being able to inform her, the lady, who was a stranger to me, asked if I knew of one she might succeed in getting. I at once told her 'That the Lord had saved one for her on Sunday night at the town hall.' He was sought and brought to this Christian lady, who at once engaged him; surely,

> 'God moves in a mysterious way
> His wonders to perform.'

We are praying for a way to open for the other young man. What a blessing it would be if Christians saw what a work might be done by employing these poor reformed outcasts. Many are saved, and would become useful members of society if someone took them by the hand; but numbers, after being reclaimed, drift back through sheer starvation.'[4]

The September 1878 issue of the same magazine carried an unusual appeal: '*A good plain cook* wanted in a Christian Mission family. Privilege of attending Mission services. Liberal wages to a competent person.' It was to be the first of many such advertisements—all of which emboldened 'Emily' to place the following paragraph some years later: '*A little soldier,* nearly 15, wants a *situation* as nurse, where they love Jesus, and love family prayer. Apply to Emily, 101, Queen Victoria Street.'[5] Two-way traffic in a specialised kind of employment having thus been established, every promise was given of its fast becoming a 'going concern' with the November 1887 intimation that 'Any friends wanting respectable young women, salvationists, as *servants,* can be put in communication with suitable applicants by writing to Mrs Colonel Pepper, Milford Hill, Salisbury.'[6] Mrs Pepper, wife of a retired military officer, had come across Catherine Booth's *Papers on Practical Religion,* and whilst dearly desiring to meet her, was somewhat taken aback when asked by Charles Fry, bandmaster of Salisbury's much persecuted salvationists, whether she would entertain Mrs Booth at Milford Hill on her coming visit to the city. Growing involvement with the Army led Ellen Pepper to a conviction that she should become a salvationist. Pocketing her initial resistance, she informed Mrs Booth, who relayed the news to the General. He, however, 'rather threw cold water upon it. When Mrs Booth said, "Mrs Pepper feels God is leading her to work with our people," he answered, "I do not know if it will do," but said very little on the subject.'[7] Booth was constantly suspicious of what he termed 'the dangerous classes' entering his ranks.[8]

Nevertheless Mrs Pepper donned uniform and commenced Salvation Army warfare. 'With my comrades in the fight I shared the ill-treatment they then received in the streets, being often pelted with stones, mud, rotten eggs, and refuse of all kinds. . . . Another branch of work which engages me, is supplying Salvation Army servants with places in godly families where they can have the privilege of attending the Army meetings. This has proved beneficial in its results to both ladies and servants, as is confirmed by many letters received from both parties.'⁷

Occasional letters between salvationist servants and Mrs Pepper began to appear in *The War Cry,* her replies being full of common sense regarding household affairs. 'Dear Madam,' wrote a salvationist servant, 'I have been puzzled about working on Sundays. Does God mean that we are able to do no cleaning or washing-up on Sundays? We do some of our Sunday work on Saturday nights, but in a farmhouse there are a lot of milk things and pots to be attended to. If the washing-up were to be saved till Monday there would be such a lot, and it would upset the comfort of the family, and a place where there is a lot of people requires sweeping up. Could you tell me if it is wrong to sweep up and tidy a little on Sundays, and wash up?'

'If you read carefully Matthew 12:1-14', replied Mrs Pepper, 'you will see that Christ justifies his disciples in plucking the corn when hungry on the Sabbath-day. . . . Our Saviour's judgment pronounced it lawful to do well on the Sabbath.

'We see, therefore, that necessary duties may be performed on Sunday as shown by the Scripture; and cleanliness and tidiness are surely necessary duties. Putting off till Monday what should be done on Sunday would cause hurry, worry, and careless performance of work, and that would be wrong in God's sight.'⁹

Within months of Mrs Pepper's first 'intimation' appearing in *The War Cry,* the same paper informed its readers that '*Mrs Bramwell Booth* has *several girls* who have passed through her homes, whom she can confidently recommend, and for whom she wishes to find *situations* as *housemaids, cooks,* and *general servants.* Apply 259, Mare Street, Hackney, E.'¹⁰

The first issue of *The Deliverer* (1 July 1889) advertised the availability of domestic servants through the lately organised Situation Department, which by May 1890 was under the direction of Mrs Bird.¹¹ In no way in competition with Mrs Pepper's establishment, Mrs Bird's sought initially to place girls who had passed through the rescue homes, although later advertisements appealed for Christian servants generally to apply to the Situation

Department[12]—probably because demand was exceeding supply, such a good reputation had 'Mrs Booth's' servants.[11] In 1891, for instance, 1,956 mistresses applied for servants, as compared with 1,560 servants seeking situations, and £85. 4s. 9d. was passed to the rescue work from the one shilling fee charged 'when suited'.[13]

By the spring of 1892 additional registry offices for servants had been opened in Notting Hill and Cardiff[14]—this last being attached to the metropole for 'respectable women who go out charing or to daily work', and where spring mattresses were the order of the night.

An ever alert trade department saw in the problems of servant-mistress relationships a way to bring itself to the public consciousness. *'Problem for Mistresses'*, ran a *War Cry* column in 1896. 'Mary Jane is an excellent servant. Saved, wears full uniform, is truthful, good-tempered, hard-working and anxious to please. She cooks well, cleans well, is very fond of the children, can be trusted without fear with money or valuables (provided they are not breakable!). But Mary Jane has three besetting weaknesses which no efforts on the part of her mistress seem successful in altering—

(1) She sleeps very heavily, and cannot wake herself in the morning. When called she takes a long time to rouse, and is hardly ever downstairs in time.

(2) She has a terrible propensity for smashing. Hardly a day passes without some crockery being victimised, and her mistress, who used frequently to throw up her hands and exclaim, "What *is* that girl breaking now?" has grown so accustomed to the crashes that she only sighs wearily and waits till Mary Jane comes in tears to confess. But the expense for new cups and saucers, etc., is most serious.

(3) She seems to find it impossible to come back promptly when sent on an errand, and is generally home late when she goes to a meeting.

'Now, while Mary Jane has the aforementioned valuable qualities, and yet has such counter-balancing vices, what is a poor distracted mistress to do in the interests of both herself, her household and Mary Jane? The mistress who sends in the most satisfactory solution to this problem by Thursday, 30th January, will receive an award to the value of 3s. 6d. in goods from the Trade Department.'[15]

The Mary Janes of this world had other, and sometimes more pressing, needs. Not surprisingly, knowing how one thing led to another in the early development of the Army's work, the 'Social Wing' (as it came to be known in the 1890s) sought to meet those needs as well. Reported *The Social News*: 'Numerous as are the irons the Social Wing have in the fire, some more will be put in ere long. Can't help it! Last week a young servant came all the way from Lancashire to take a situation in the big City. She found that the girl whom she was to succeed was not leaving till a day later than expected, and the Lancashire lass could not take possession that night. What was she to do? Her little stock of money had been barely sufficient to cover the costs of the journey. She acted wisely, and found her way to The Bridge. Naturally, she was closely questioned, and it turned out that the girl was a salvationist. In reply to the query, "Is there anything wrong?" came the answer, "It was to prevent that that I came here." This, and daily occurring cases like it, demand a launch-out in the direction of a servants' home.'[16]

The 'launching-out' took place in February 1892, with a servants' home being opened in the same premises as the Notting Hill servants' registry at 90 Ladbroke Grove Road.[17] There, *All the World* readers were assured, Mary Jane would be 'boarded and lodged for the modest sum of 8s. per week, and mothered and loved for nothing at all! . . . "But who serves these lasses, tired with serving?" someone is sure to have asked before this. The answer to this question brings us to the nicest part of all. Over and over the writer [whose by now familiar style has already given away her identity] has sighed . . . for a home where little, useless, muddling children could be taught housework, in a way which would fit them for some kind of service better than dreary slaveyhood!

'"Her stepmother never had patience to show her, and she's been put in situations where she's been let go on in dirty, untidy ways, till now she's not fit for a decent place. What's to be done with her?" asked a sergeant of us, dismally, only last month, as she landed a round-eyed, 14-year-old girl in our kitchen, where she speedily assayed to show her goodwill by scrubbing up the floor with a pocket-handkerchief.

'The nucleus of something to be done with her like, may be seen in kitchen and laundry at Notting Hill, where six little lasses, from 11 to 14, are learning how to climb up to the ideal set before them

103

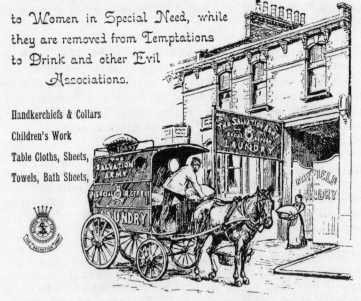
104

in the shape of the tidy, respectful, efficient nurse and parlour-maids and cooks and "generals" upstairs.'[18] So the one thing that led to another, led to another, and all as a means of stately employing the poor.

However, in spite of Mrs Bramwell Booth's confident and repeated recommendations of her rescue girls for domestic service, as early as February 1888 'S.F.S.' was asserting in *All the World* that: 'While there is a steady demand for first-class servants, there is *not* a constant supply of good average situations for good average servants, and the hurried training of the homes can hardly turn out girls who are more than that, if as much. Thoroughly good servants are seldom among their candidates for admission. . . . Some are too delicate. Some have little ones whose care hampers them. One, we recall, actually so ugly that no one would employ her! Every fresh trade which looks at all feasible is hailed by the rescue officers as likely to employ fingers and brains which have failed to be useful elsewhere. Bookbinding is proving one of the best. It is sheltered. It is fairly paid. It is quickly learned. It requires a concentration of thought and attention which is an invaluable shield and discipline. . . . Just now, six or eight girls are always "learning their trade" at a long table in Devonshire House's general work-room, under the superintendence of a lieutenant who has been five years in the business.' (Devonshire House was still in use as the first prison gate home at this stage.)

'Penny song-books—our little red ones—were on hand that morning. Each book, we were told, would pass through six hands; those of the "folder", the "gatherer", the "stitcher", the "wrapperer", and the "cutter". . . . "The beauty of it is . . . they feel they're earning something from the very beginning. . . ."'

In addition to the Devonshire House workshop there was another at Whitechapel. '"The bookbinding's coming on beautifully!" said Mrs Bramwell to us one day. "You know we bind *All the World* now."

'"You!" we gasped.

'"Our girls—down at Whitechapel. We took over the shop some time ago. Five girls are at work in it now. . . ."

'Now we knew, in a sort of way, that *All the World* was bound at

105

some mysterious place called "Florence's",* down in Whitechapel. And we had heard vaguely, something about bookbinding as a trade for the rescue girls. . . .'[19] And yet another article fresh from the mint of Susie Swift's mind is on its way to the printers.

The beginning of 1888 saw also a boom in the rescue work's knitting machine business: 'Men's socks, of medium thickness and size, in various heather mixtures, grey, speckled grey, navy blue, brown and cardinal, 1s. 4d. a pair, carriage of parcel in addition. . . .' Four months later there was a 'Great reduction in price' to 1s. 1d. Doubtless such speckled socks were among 'A small parcel of goods . . . sent . . . to the Aberdeen Woodside Industry and Art Exhibition and . . . awarded a diploma of honour.'[20] They certainly headed the list in a turn of century appeal for warm clothing to be sent to men at the South African front. The War Office considered the following items absolutely essential: Knitted socks, worsted nightcaps or Tam O'Shanters, cardigan jackets, flannel shirts, woollen drawers and vests, cholera belts, and neck mufflers—all of which could be ordered through the Army's knitting factory and dispatched direct to the docks, and all of which carried the added incentive of encouraging 'those who are endeavouring to work their way back to good and useful lives'.[21]

Statedly employing the poor was well under way by 1888 as far as the rescue homes were concerned. By the following February 10 knitting machines were in operation at Grove House, Upper Clapton, 'washing texts' (presumably 'washable') and under-clothing could be ordered from 183 Amhurst Road, Hackney,[22] and shirt finishing employed the Belfast girls.[23] Mrs Bramwell Booth's June advertisement for an efficient upholstress to teach the trade, was eventually met by one with 16 years' West End experience, and within 18 months the following advertisement was appearing: 'New work, alterations, repairs, mattress and bed dressing, blind and carpet making undertaken; also dry cleaning in all its branches.'[24] Skirt-making is added to the rescue skills in 1891[25] (although, since it is not heard of again, this could well be a misprint for *shirt*-making), and the same year, despite Mrs Bramwell's five years of determination to keep *off* the laundry work,[26] a laundry was taken over—'Our first customers doubtless will be Commissioner Cadman's sixpenny lodgers in the "Ark".'[27] Twenty-three women were initially employed in the

*This is not a reference to Mrs Bramwell Booth, but to the manager, Mr Florence.

106

Stoke Newington laundry, coming from the slums, the shelter, the rescue homes, 'and stray workless who apply on their own account'.[28] Concerning this admixture Florence Booth wrote: 'One feature of the new arrangements, and it is a very pleasant one to me, is that the customary particular classification of the women we have been compelled to make hitherto, will be almost entirely avoided, and those who come to us for help will be grouped together according to their capacity for work, and without reference to the peculiar kind of sin or misfortune which may have brought them to need our assistance.'[29]

Before passing from this account of the Army's earliest employment opportunities for women to examine its dealings with unemployed men, we pause to assimilate the opening paragraph of an 1891 *Deliverer* article by Clara Ozanne on the subject of 'Woman's Side of the Labour Question', which, she claims, until then had been afforded very little notice. 'When speaking to a gentleman the other day on this subject, he replied, "Let the women remain at home and look after their houses and see to their husbands' comforts." Very good advice, no doubt, where there is a house-band. That is to say, a partner who is able to keep a house over his wife's head, and provide her with means to obtain comforts for himself and family, but there are too often exceptional cases, and Eve's daughters find themselves compelled to take a large share of the curse pronounced upon "the grand old gardener and his wife", and this frequently without the ameliorating result promised to our first parents—they "sweat" 'tis true, straining every nerve to keep the wolf from the door, and yet they fail to earn their daily bread. It is to help such as these that *another seam has been let into The Salvation Army's big umbrella,* and already has the Social Scheme brought hope and food to women who were "ready to perish".'[30]

BUT now to that other member of 'the worshipful company of out-of-works' (to use Major Swift's descriptive phrase): the unemployed man. Of him Bramwell Booth was to write in the 1890s: 'The workless man is the whole social problem in concrete. He is the coming pauper; he is the potential criminal; he is the would-be suicide. And more than this he is the scion of a miserable house, he and his children after him even to the third generation, which under existing conditions eat the bread which has been earned by the sweat of somebody else's brow, and he will die 20

107

years before he ought to die, leaving behind him a legacy of misery and shame in the children who will follow his example, and do their part to impoverish the world they might have done something to enrich and improve. . . . From the beginning of our social work we have been to the utmost of our opportunity grappling with this problem and either finding temporary labour or permanent employment for large numbers of men.'[31]

By way of confirming this claim, a glance at William Booth's December 1888 'memorial' to the Home Secretary will discover a résumé of the first year's work at the Limehouse food and shelter depot, in which he reports: 'We are happy to say that during these months we have been able to exert an immense amount of influence for good upon these characters, and have raised 127 men, who came in abject poverty, into a position of decency and comfort, as they are now earning a good livelihood in situations that have been found for them.'[32]

With the opening of more and more shelters it became imperative that something be done on an organised scale for the swelling numbers of the worshipful company of out-of-works congregating nightly under The Salvation Army's big umbrella. Though not in this instance the originator, Major Swift was certainly the articulator of two ideas which sought to alleviate the unemployment problem. In an *All the World* article on 'Sociology and Salvation' she wrote: 'We hold far more strongly than Bismarck, that every man has an inalienable right to demand honest work and its wage from his fellow men, quite aside from the divine interposition which we believe we constantly see. Beside the comparatively few of an immaculate moral stamp . . . plenty of men pass through our shelters with characters as good as those of the average workman. One of our officers is eager to form a *labour bureau* for the benefit of such.

'A brigade of men for painting, whitewashing, and renovating generally, has been formed by Captain Keates. The "boss" is an ex-clerk, who is glad to get this employment.

'Several men from St John's shelter assisted in the moving of our printing apparatus from Southwark Street to Clerkenwell Road. Our foreman praised their industry and care very highly.

'For the characterless men, the opening of an *industrial home* is almost a necessity. *We* can believe in "Wunny", and "Dublin

Bill", and "Old Archie", and the rest. A ticket-of-leave man and a titled gambler are alike to us. But we can hardly expect people who are shaky on the "new birth", and not clear on the work wrought by God in sanctification to feel as we are inclined to do—surer of many of these than of the "ninety and nine just men who need no repentance".'[33]

The labour bureau idea was reiterated by the General at an April 1890 meeting celebrating two years of shelter work. Together with first mention of a farm, the labour bureau was to be a feature of 'the General's new scheme'.[34] (The book of the scheme was not to appear until towards the end of the year.) The industrial home concept emerged in the opening of the first factory in June 1890.[35]

Meanwhile a new name had burst upon the Army's social scene: articles from the flamboyant pen of Commissioner Frank Smith began to appear in its papers. From command of the American troops he had been given oversight of men's food and shelter depots, and was now appointed to take charge of the newly established Social Reform Wing. Writing in July 1890 of the week-old labour bureau, Commissioner Smith reveals that of the 200 applications made, between 40 and 50 had already been placed in employment. Foundation stone of the yet-to-be-named City Colony though it was, from its inception the bureau held strong rural implications. 'Already in the hay-fields are being heard the happy songs of shelter hay-makers, and to our country friends we would say, if you are in need of workers when strawberries have to be picked, and the pears, hops, and apples have to be pulled, remember the labour bureau!' Hallelujah workshops, he intimated, were in course of preparation, and the salvation bakery was already in full swing.[36]

Enlarging upon the role of the labour bureau in the following month's *Deliverer,* Smith writes: 'The plan of operation consists—
(1) In the opening of a central registry office, in which registers will be kept *free of charge,* wherein the wants of both employers and workers will be recorded, the registers being open for consultation by all interested.
(2) In the institution of public waiting-rooms for men and women, to which the unemployed may come, for the purpose of scanning the newspapers, and inserting advertisements for employment at lowest possible rates; writing-tables, etc., being provided for their use. These rooms will also act as "houses of call", where employers can meet and enter into engagements with workers of all kinds, by

appointment or otherwise, thus doing away with the snare that awaits many of the unemployed, who have no place to wait other than the public-house, which at present is almost the only "house of call" for out-of-work men.

(3) In the making known to the public in general the wants of the unemployed, by means of advertisements, circulars, and direct application to employers.

(4) In the issue of labour statistics, with information as to the number of unemployed who are anxious for work, the various trades and occupations they represent, etc.

(5) The opening of branches of the labour bureau, as fast as funds and opportunities permit, in all the large towns and centres of industry throughout Great Britain.'

'There is no free Labour Bureau except that of the Salvation Army,'[37] declared *The Star* the following year. Nor was there to be in the immediate future, although the opening of two labour bureaux at Canning Town and Stratford in 1893 by the West Ham Town Council[38] (in Keir Hardie's parliamentary constituency)[39] was reported in *The Darkest England Gazette,* together with a description of what was probably the earliest job creation scheme: tree-planting in some of the principal public roads, and roadwork in outlying hamlets.[38] That same year the Army expressed 'great interest . . . in the formation of a Government Labour Department, which will gather statistics and information with an ease and—it is to be hoped—scatter it abroad with a prodigality not possible to private enterprise'.[40] Not until 1909, however, did Parliament take steps to provide for the establishing of nationalised labour exchanges.[41]

Back at the Army's earliest bureau: 'At first employers held severely aloof', reported *The War Cry,* 'sceptical, no doubt, as to the success of our efforts, and although as yet our supply of labour greatly exceeds the demand, there are many hopeful signs. . . . Some friends have been to a slight extent uneasy as to the possibility of the bureau being used as a convenience by employers who are having differences with their employees, and fearful that we might inadvertently be led into supplying labour in places where strikes, etc., exist. . . . Our friends have no need to fear on this point. We shall not rob Peter to pay Paul. . . . The bureau will not be made a convenience of by those who wish to cut prices or fight against the requirements of dissatisfied employees.'[42]

By September things were getting interesting: two young

applicants were sent by the bureau to Singapore as missionary teachers in a methodist school which demanded well-saved men who could teach to the seventh standard. A congregational minister came hunting for work, followed some months later by an ex-baptist minister and a workhouse labour master. Elijah Cadman (successor to Frank Smith) unconsciously revealed himself a prophet of 'women's lib' by advising that 'The Social Wing supplies workpeople of all kinds'. In the small type that follows, however, those same workpeople are reduced to 'a large number of men',[43] and it seems clear that employment-seeking women for the most part remained the preserve of Mrs Booth, Mrs Bird and Mrs Pepper—in spite of a labour bureau claim that 'we could usually find six women situations for every one who asks for work. Probably this is because workless women do not stand and walk about the streets all day like their brothers, and do not hear our possibilities discussed'.[44] There is little to suggest that an amalgamation of the rescue work and the Social Reform Wing was ever seriously mooted. Indeed, by the end of 1891 the name 'Women's Social Work' had so overtaken usage of the term rescue work as to make the distinction between the men's and women's spheres even more pronounced.[45]

Nevertheless 'workpeople of all kinds' (but in this case men) continue to be our current pursuit. The first kind is the won't work. 'The won't work always comes to the front when trade is bad; he figures largely in times of special relief distribution, Mansion House committees and unemployed agitations', wrote Bramwell Booth. 'Is it not about time to take some simple way with your work not? Why should he not be brought before a magistrate, invited to prove some sort of employment or active efforts to obtain it, and in default, committed to an agricultural settlement, and made to dig his bread out of the earth! If he objects to dig, cut off his diet. He will soon come to.'[46] Lest this should be seen as a hard-line approach, we balance it with an insight from Superintendent Blandy of the salvation bakery. 'We've to grapple with two difficulties—the mental indolence of the gentleman and the physical indolence of the loafer. Both classes are not only undeveloped, but deficient, and the grace of God won't supply physical tissue, be it of brain or muscle. But it will vitalise what is there and often it will draw out what you never dreamed was there.'[47]

Another of the 'workpeople of all kinds' is 'the man without a backbone'. Of him Bramwell Booth writes: 'The man without

111

moral stamina is, perhaps, the most disappointing of all the denizens of Darkest England. Without force of character, power of will, or tenacity of purpose, he floats helplessly down with the tide; and even when you throw him a rope . . . he lacks the energy and enterprise to take hold of it. . . .

'Now what does our experience prove? . . . That the spiritual reformation, of which our Lord Jesus Christ is the mainspring, is the first great hope for this human flotsam and jetsam. It is not enough to change his environment, to rekindle his hope for better days, or awaken again the respect and confidence in himself that he used to feel in times long since gone for ever; it is not enough even to find him work and keep him at it, and pay him for it; he must find some force outside his own poor ruined nature which will fortify him first against himself, and then against the strong tides running the wrong way all round him. To him, therefore, with a special patience, we preach Jesus, the carpenter of Nazareth, the Saviour of earth's broken and weakest things; and in a large number of instances, we do it to blessed purpose.'[48]

Yet the won't works and the man without a backbone were by no means all the story. Questioned on the composition of the out-of-works in 1893, Commissioner Cadman replied: 'Mainly unskilled labourers. Only about 10 per cent are mechanics, who are "up" in their respective trade, the rest are bricklayers' or carpenters' labourers, and men of that stamp; many of them dock-labourers, now crowded out by the "regimenting" system that is in vogue.'[49] Other men only needed to be set on their feet—like the town councillor from Huddersfield who had failed in business and fallen as far as the shelter door. ' "Looked like an old horse on its way to the tanyard. . . . He used to address envelopes for a shilling a day, living at the shelter, and then acted as our labour clerk, till he managed to get himself a little respectable, and then he got this place as secretary . . . at £250 a year. He is re-united to his wife, whom he has not been able to support, and gave a donation for our work the other day." ' An ex-jockey, a physician, an ex-wesleyan minister, a master builder—all were bound in the massive bundle of 'workpeople of all kinds' flocking to the Army's labour bureau, and mostly housed in its shelters.

In March 1891 *The War Cry* reported Commissioner Cadman as being 'in great feather. He has invented a new name for the shelters and the factories. The shelter he calls the "dredge", and the factory the "elevator". By means of the dredge, he said, we pick the submerged up from the depths, and then we get them on the elevator, which lifts them up and up until they get on the top with a red jersey on and a flag in their hand, shouting "Glory to God!"' Three hundred men were by this time at work in the three elevators at Hanbury, Fieldgate and Old Streets.[43] The object of statedly employing the poor in this fashion being 'to make it unnecessary for the homeless or workless to be compelled to go to the workhouse or casual ward, food and shelter being provided them in exchange for work done, until they can procure work for themselves, or it can be found for them elsewhere'.[50] 'Every man who enters an elevator comes . . . on the understanding that he receives only food and shelter for the first four weeks, and must, so long as he stays, if unmarried, live under our oversight at the Lighthouse, or at the Ark. He is paid at first in twopenny tickets. Four of these entitle him to three full meals and a bunk at the Lighthouse. . . . As soon as his sectional foreman announces that his labour is worth more, he is out on "full-value tickets", viz., breakfast and supper, threepence; dinner, fourpence; and a dormitory ticket, valued at twopence, fourpence, or sixpence, according to circumstances. This last will depend partly upon his deportment and cleanliness.

'The newcomer goes into the first-floor dormitory of the Lighthouse as a "third-class man". His accommodation is like that at the shelters—a coffin-like wooden bunk, a seaweed-stuffed mattress, and a skin covering. The second-class men have the same, in a rather better lighted, cheerier-looking room on the floor above, while a first-class man rejoices in spring-mattress, sheets and blankets.

'All this visible, tangible reward of industry is part of the process of moral education which the majority of the Lighthouse inmates must undergo before they can be of much use to themselves or the world. Usually, the broken-down man who gets a berth in the factory and a bunk in the Lighthouse feels that he is fairly on the second round of the ladder. Bitter was the protest made by the first-class men when one tender-hearted captain prepared to fill some empty bunks in their dormitory with "transient lodgers". "Going to let dossers in here, captain?" they wailed; "you're never going to let dirty chaps from anywhere in with us elevator men!" And at the initial stage of their moral and spiritual elevation, this feeling is a healthy one. Did not the apostle warn his young converts from heathenrie to be "*first* pure, then peaceable"? Separation from evil and dirt is the first instinct of a man struggling into a better life. Later on, he may be able to walk through the one unharmed and to endure the other in effort for his fellows. But part of our work is to create ambition. Some men seem as if they would never be able to earn much more than their lodging and their two-penny food tickets, and never care to try.'[51]

Writing in *In Darkest England and the Way Out* William Booth explained: 'When we have got the homeless, penniless tramp washed, and housed, and fed at the shelter, and have secured him the means of earning his fourpence by chopping firewood, or making mats or cobbling the shoes of his fellow-labourers at the factory, we have next to seriously address ourselves to the problem of how to help him back into the regular ranks of industry. The shelter and the factory are but stepping-stones, which have this advantage—they give us time to look round and to see what there is in a man that we can make of him.'[52] At this stage in a man's elevation the labour bureau and the reserve fund come into play. The one to find him work, the other to help set him up in it. 'The reserve fund . . . consists of one-third of whatever money grant a man is allowed. This reserve is banked to his credit, and he is not at liberty to draw it until he signifies his wish to leave the factory. Then, if he goes to a situation, it is laid out in tools and clothes. He has his railway fare to his destination and usually a few shillings to start with. The other two-thirds of his grant he may spend as he likes.'[53]

Meanwhile, back at the elevators, men not yet ready to be processed by the labour bureau were learning new skills—the most novel of which was the manufacture of 'Booth's Beer'. A paragraph in *The War Cry* for 29 August 1891 ran: 'An editor, who was not a lineal descendant of the boy who never told a lie, inferred that Booth's Beer only existed in the General's mind. We should like everyone to know that as well as being in his mind, it is also contained in the General's barrels and bottles, and it is made on the premises of historic Limehouse shelter. The captain in charge of this department will be glad to receive orders for any quantity from a dozen bottles to a butt, and will send it to your mansion on our salvation brewer's dray. There is one thing certain, that by purchasing our elevator beer, or social invigorator, as it is called, you will be helping to stop the flow of intoxicants and help us to save the drunkard.'[54] Human turtles (sandwich-board men) and circular deliverers advertised Salvation Army meetings, while the contents of 789,000 self-denial parcels were folded and packed,[55] and a bootblack brigade trudged into action.[56]

By the end of 1894 seven elevators were employing 1,000 men in such varied industries as firewood chopping, carpentry and joinery, cabinet making, sack making, mat making, carpet weaving, tambourine making ('Commissioner Eva Booth was delighted with these, and had a tambourine sent to Scotland to use on her tour; also a drum for little Jhai'), brush making, mattress making, painting, engineering, wheelwrighting, saw mills, tin working, paper and rag sorting, tailoring, shoemaking, match making, cardboard box making, bakery, clerks in the offices; in addition to which were those who, after a trial term, were employed as cooks, watchmen, gatekeepers and scrubbers in Social Wing premises.[57] From this list two industries deserved to be explored in their own right, so significant were they to become.

IN March 1891 *The War Cry* carried the following politely worded appeal from one of the men on The Bridge: 'Gentlemen's cast-off clothing is much needed; also a sack of potatoes; little fish &c., are very acceptable; fragments from gentlemen's tables, hotels, restaurants, &c., will be thankfully received and much appreciated. For this purpose we have now a little "red maria", which Capt. Hopkins, on receipt of a post-card, will be only too glad to send round to receive whatever kind friends feel disposed to give.' Six months later the mists (not to mention the aroma) surrounding the little red maria crammed with gentlemen's cast-off clothing, little fish, the fragments from gentlemen's tables, began to clear with a *War Cry* report that 'Commissioner Cadman has just issued an official announcement concerning the commencement of the Salvage Brigade, one of the most important items in the "Way Out" of "Darkest England". A commodious wharf has been secured at Battersea, and may expect shortly to see a fleet of salvation barges on the Thames, plying between Battersea and Hadleigh, carrying salvage material down and bringing produce up.'[58] '"The day is coming,"' declared that already well-proven priest and prophet, Cadman, '"when this nation will have to give an account even of its waste, which could, if used properly, support the whole of the unemployed. . . . I want to bring together waste materials and waste individuals, so that by putting the two wastes together, just as we turn old paper into new, fit for the Royal Family's use, or for government offices, so we make homeless and despairing men and women into new creatures, and fit them to occupy parallel positions in life."'[49]

Describing the salvage work as 'unquestionably destined to be the most sensitive and the best supplied with active and passive nerve-fibres of all the ganglia of our social nervous system', Major Swift took time out to review the actual salvage. '30,000 old helmets, interesting relics of the Egyptian War, are, so far, the only reward bestowed upon us by a grateful government. . . . The Social Wing proposes to put some of its small boys to work stripping off the linen coverings, with a view to sending them to the paper mill . . . for that same inscrutable power called government has decreed that we may not sell or wear them in their present condition.'[59] Fortunately there was plenty else—paper ('"Girls are the best paper hands"'), rags ('every lot of rags means at least 30 sortings'), old metal, umbrellas, pianos, baskets, mattresses, hats (hats feminine and masculine, hats trimmed and untrimmed, hats old and new'[59]), old books ('doctors of divinity by the dozen'),[60] and no doubt a little fish or two. The honesty of Salvation Army paper-sorters became proverbial, postal orders, cheques and articles of value frequently being found among the waste and 'returned to sender'.[61]

The wide-awake corps officer of Chiswick held an old clothes harvest festival which resulted in a large wagon-load of clothes, boots, hats, etc., being handed over to Colonel Thurman, Salvage Corps brigade officer. 'Houndsditch and Petticoat Lane were not in it' apparently. *The Social News* of 9 January 1892 took up the theme in imaginative fashion and American spelling: 'In this ever-increasing life-saving fleet there is to be found a little craft, storm-tossed and weather-beaten. No trumpet heralded it forth on its life-saving work. No kindly pen noted its birth or recorded its successful launch. It is true it was but a poor, ungainly, ill-looking, none too sweet-smelling craft at best, and seemed to promise but little credit to anyone. None cared to harbor it. It might with truth have been christened "Nobody's Child".

'The prison-gate home gave it shelter for a time, but its stay was brief. Headquarters would have none of it. Even the shelters shook their skirts when it came near, and for a time a resting-place could only be found for it under the sheltering wing of that last refuge of the workless and hopeless, the labour bureau. Yet there its peace was disturbed, until at last there arose a "Joseph" who knew it, one of its own kindred and tribe.

'The Salvage Brigade came into existence, stretched forth its welcoming arms, and in its bosom the "old clothes shop" found a happy, restful, abiding place. . . .

'When a man or woman first feels the pinch of poverty they naturally rush to the pawn-shop with their decent articles, to keep the wolf from the door. This goes on until the looking for work becomes an impossibility—they have lost the appearance of the worker, and take their places amongst the "submerged". Ask the clerk, the mechanic or the laboring man what is the main cause of their inability to find employment. In nine cases out of 10 you will get the same reply: "No employer would look at me as I am." . . . Within the past few months we have clothed 1,710 men and women . . . nor does this include the numerous little ones who have been made happy.' Perhaps the most unlikely of City Colony provisions to have survived the passage of the years, as many as 10 family service stores are nevertheless listed in the 1983 *Year Book* as operating in inner-city areas around the United Kingdom—each proving to be a valued successor of that old clothes shop of 1892.

MAY 1888 found a Special Committee of the House of Lords inquiring into the 'sweating' system rampant in certain areas of industry. Contrary to accepted modern usage, the 'sweater' was not the exhausted exploited worker, but the sub-contractor or middleman who obtained unfinished work from factories and farmed it out to workers in their homes for the proverbial meagre pittance.[62] *War Cry* reports at this time show slum officers encountering families who subsisted on a shilling a day from rabbit fur pulling, or five shillings a week from pickle bottling, ninepence per dozen for brush making, 3d for chopping 100 bundles of wood, six shillings a week for paper sorting.[63]

Before the House of Lords Special Committee appeared one William Adamson, vicar of Old Ford, East London, bearing sworn evidence to the effect that some years previously poor people in his parish made matchboxes in their homes at twopence three farthings a gross, finding their own paste. The Salvation Army, however, came into competition with these folk by offering to do the work for twopence halfpenny. The result was, reported the reverend gentleman, that the large firms lowered their price to twopence farthing. '"Are these individual members of The Salvation Army?"' questioned Lord Dunraven.

'"No, my lord, the organization itself—at headquarters. None of the members of the Army are permitted to do work without the sanction of the General. The male and female members live in barracks, and for years have competed for laundry work, and laundry work came down accordingly.''' [64] (This during Mrs Bramwell Booth's five years of keeping *off* the laundry work!)

'The ridiculously untruthful character of these statements' [64] was refuted by Bramwell Booth in a letter to *The Times* in which he declared: '(1) The Salvation Army never offered to make match-boxes at any price; (2) no firm, large or small, could therefore have come down in price through our competition; (3) there is no barracks of the Army in the world where male and female members of the Army live; the Army never has competed for laundry work, and does not and never did do laundry work at any price.' [65] He gave identical evidence before the 'Sweating Commission', as it had come to be known. [66] That other purveyor of evidence, the vicar of Old Ford, had 'heard', while sitting on the Charity Organisation Committee, the things he swore to, and had, needless to say, absolutely no personal knowledge of the facts. [67]

Nor was it only the home worker who was exploited. Factory hands suffered sordid conditions and woefully inadequate wages— particularly in the match industry. Indeed, within weeks of the Army's alleged sweating scandal, the girls of Bryant and May's London match factory were on strike, gaining immense public support, and forcing the firm to improve wages and conditions. [68] The Salvation Army lent support by donating 5s to the London Trades Council Match Girls' Strike Fund, [69] and by mocking up 'four sweaters' victims' dens' (with real 'victims') in a corner of the Crystal Palace exhibition hall, during the Army's 25th anniversary celebrations two years later. [70] That was the summer of Commissioner Frank Smith, it will be remembered, and in the wake of a deal of bad and grossly inaccurate publicity regarding the Army's supposed role in the match industry, he showed of what fighting stuff the movement was made by inserting the following paragraph in *The War Cry*: '*Matchmaking*—will any of our soldiers and comrades, who thoroughly understand the manufacture of matches in all its branches, kindly communicate at once with Commissioner Frank Smith, 36 Upper Thames Street, London E.C.?' [71] At about the same time the Founder would have been drafting into his soon-to-be-published social scheme the paragraph which reads: 'The labour shops will enable us to work out our anti-sweating experiments. For instance, we propose at once to commence manufacturing matchboxes, for which we shall aim at giving nearly treble the amount at present paid to the poor starving creatures engaged in this work.'[72] Clearly, although matchbox making was in Booth's mind at this stage as part of the Darkest England scheme, a match factory as such was not. Frank Smith evidently had other ideas. Nevertheless, to be planning to press any part of that scandal-occasioning industry into Salvation Army service at a moment when the scandal had scarce died down would seem foolhardily incautious to the conservative-minded salvationist a century on. The same charge could be levelled at the laundry work, which, despite all previous 'hands off' policies, and denials before the 'Sweating Commission', had nonetheless come into being by March 1891.[27] Foolhardiness was it? Should we not rather judge it as an enviable ability to see life steadily and see it whole; an ability to recognise priorities; a refusal to be deflected by ill-informed criticism? Above all, should we not see it as a determination 'to know nothing among men, save Jesus Christ and Him crucified'?[73]

As if this spate of foolhardiness were not enough, coals of fire were heaped on the unfortunate head of the vicar of Old Ford by the Army's decision to locate its match factory in an erstwhile confectionery premises[69] in that part of his parish known as Lamprell Street.[74] Opened by the General in May 1891,[75] the factory employed 100 workers[76]—either unconnected with the Army's social scheme, or already 'elevated' by it.[77] There the vicar (should he have felt so inclined) would have had every opportunity of seeing matchbox makers working under pleasant conditions to the tune of 4d per gross[78]—a far cry from the 2½d of his accusation, or the 2¼d of the middlemen. Many of the actual match makers themselves, like their methodist manager, George Nunn,[79] had worked in the industry all their lives, routinely contracting necrosis from the phosphorus used in the match heads, and though escaping the lingeringly painful deaths of scores of their fellows, they lived (as did Nunn) with the resultant loss of most of their teeth and a substantial part of the jaw bone.[80] Now that new light was dawning in Darkest England, however, phossy jaw's days were numbered. 'Carry salvation into every detail of your life' War Cry readers were enjoined, 'and buy these "lights", and if your grocer has not yet got a supply, give him no rest till he does.'[81]

Although few match factories were at first willing to follow The Salvation Army's lead in abandoning the deadly phosphorus, by 1900 public opinion (roused by the Army's intensive advertising campaign) had forced the larger factories to adapt their methods. A year later the Lamprell Street factory was taken over by the British Match Company,[69] the use of phosphorus in match making being rendered illegal after 1910 by a 1908 Act of Parliament.[82]

Not for the first time in its short history, in setting out to alleviate a specific human misery, The Salvation Army had proved itself a highly effective stimulus to social reform—in this instance, all in the cause of statedly employing the poor.

10
New coats for a drunkard's stomach

THE brief manufacturing life of Booth's Beer in 1891-2 was by no means the first Salvation Army programme aimed at the reform of the drunkard. As early as April 1867, in an article in *The Nonconformist* entitled 'Irregular Religious Agencies', the objects of the embryo Salvation Army—then known as The East London Christian Mission—were set out as:

(1) Central hall.

(2) To open theatres, halls, shops and rooms in prominent situations all through the East End.

(3) To establish a drunkards' mission. To include a drunkards' refuge.

The kind of social conditions contributing to the need for this third objective can be glimpsed in a *Christian Mission Magazine* report from Whitechapel, describing Christmas 1871: 'Dec. 25th. . . . The weather being very severe, we found it difficult to work in the open air; the streets also being strewn with drunken men and women, added to our difficulties. . . . Monday 26th. Feeling deeply moved by the drunkenness existing among the people, a few of us ventured to beard the lion in his own den; and in the midst of great opposition, and with the snow falling fast around us, we preached Jesus to the people. Some few appeared deeply moved. After which we repaired to the hall, where tea was provided for a large number who attended.'[1]

By the end of 1873 a temperance society formed one of the activities of the Hackney Mission Station,[2] and two months into the new year Mrs William Booth was writing: 'Those of our readers who have seen our last year's report, "The Masses Reached", must have been struck with the fact that a very large proportion of those brought to God through the instrumentality of this Mission were formerly drunkards. Only those who are intimately acquainted with our people know, however, what fearfully sunken moral

121

wrecks many of them were when our measures first arrested their attention.'[3] The following month she was outlining plans for the Drunkards' Rescue Society: 'The plan of working which seems to promise most success is, to mark a drunkard as he reels along the street, or is hurled out of a public-house door, or as he ambles up to an open-air service; try to win him by a few words of sympathy and interest, which is far more easily done than would be imagined by those who have never made the experiment. Then get to know from himself, or those around him, where he lives, and promise to visit him the next morning, which must be done whether he is willing or not. Once find him at home, and a great point is gained. Being sober, and under no temptation to put himself on the defensive, he will listen to your remonstrances. Surrounded, as he generally is, by the emblems of his folly and wickedness, in the dilapidation of his home, the scared aspect of his children, and the tears of his wife, he is open to assault, and will frequently join in his own condemnation. As you proceed to tell him of a Saviour's love, and the possibility of reformation and salvation, instancing others who were once such as he, but who "are washed—who are sanctified", he listens with a look of hopeless astonishment; but the tear in his poor, bleared eye, tells you that his conscience is not quite seared, nor his heart so much harder than that of other sinners. When you propose to kneel and ask God to help and save him, he shuffles on to his knees—knees which, perchance, never bowed in prayer before; and as you pray he sobs, and in spite of his despair, begins to hope. This is no fancied picture of a first visit to a drunkard's home; such scenes are familiar to some of us as blessed facts of personal experience. . . . True, this is but the first step; many visits have to be paid, and perhaps much labour bestowed, before the poor victim is fully rescued from the thraldom of his fatal habit; but shall the task be abandoned because it is difficult?'[4]

After more in the same vein, there follows the inevitable appeal for labourers and finance in this new undertaking, and, as if to strengthen that appeal (and certainly in the above-mentioned tradition of 'instancing others'), there appears later in the same issue the story of one of the first such 'volunteers': 'A little while ago a Christian young lady offered herself to the Lord, through us, for any labour in the vineyard that might be possible to her. We immediately set before her this open door, and urged its importance. She shrunk from what appeared so difficult a task, and so tremendous a responsibility. We urged her to pray about it. She did, and soon afterwards we received a communication stating that, in humble dependence on the Lord, she was willing to un-

122

dertake the task.' The October magazine carried a Drunkards' Rescue Society report by Miss Agnes Pollett, this same young lady, which not only describes the work, but also gives a vivid picture of that East London spot where the Mission had its beginnings some nine years earlier. 'With "Man and Crossman's Tap" on the one hand, and two other flaming gin-palaces on the other, in the very heart of the East of London, is a public house known as "The Blind Beggar". Its gilded taps, and brilliantly-painted front, contrasting strangely with the bruised and bloated faces of the poor creatures who find therein the means to drown for a time at least the sorrow and remorse of which they are the wretched victims. On the side of the pavement opposite these decorated man-traps of the devil, is an open space, a sort of no-man's ground, before the wide highway is reached, on which we hold a service every Sabbath from one to three o'clock. As they pass in and as they come out of this group of drinking-houses, they pause to hear our message of hope and deliverance.'

At the Mission's annual conference three months earlier, two of the principal resolutions had centred upon this very subject:

'3. That this conference is thankful that a special agency for the rescue of drunkards has been established in connection with the Mission, and desires that some extra effort of the same kind be made at every station of the Mission.

'5. (4) That a special effort for the rescue of drunkards should be organised at each station, into which drunkards who are converted should at once be enlisted.' [5]

Temperance meetings rapidly became the order of the day—a typical report of the many appearing in the magazine being this from Limehouse: 'The drunkards' rescue band are still at work here with great success. Thirteen signed the pledge on Saturday night. Some who have been a terror to the neighbourhood in which they lived are now sober and respectable. *We hope soon to see them converted to God.*' [6] Amazingly enough it took William Booth almost another three years, if not to recognise this dual standard, then at least to deal with it. In the opening address of the 1877 conference he declared: 'As to the temperance question . . . our opinions upon the question, as it affects our societies, differ. Let us wait till we can arrive at something with unanimity: until we have made up our minds to some definite plan it will be useless to talk. But in the meantime let us *make all our people abstainers,* and then jump on all temperance-meetings without God in them. We will

123

have no song-singing or recitations. I cannot express my disgust at any entertainment of that sort. We will have no mere teetotalism. We will have godly meetings, and we will teach our people never to drink or touch the stuff for Christ's sake.'[7] Neither the jumping on 'all temperance-meetings without God in them', nor the teaching of 'all our people never to drink or touch the stuff for Christ's sake', was a new decree. An extract from the minutes of the very first Christian Mission conference in 1870 reads: 'Temperance societies and meetings . . . 3. Every meeting shall be commenced and concluded by singing and prayer, and shall be conducted throughout in a Christian spirit. 4. Only such melodies shall be sung as are of good moral tone; no foolish or frivolous singing or speaking shall be allowed on any account whatever. . . .' Nevertheless, there were those meetings, seven years later, that needed jumping on. Regarding total abstinence, the same conference moved that: 'All our members shall be urged to abstain from the use of all intoxicating drinks except in cases of absolute sickness, and also from smoking and all other evil and offensive habits.' That there should be no prevarication on this principle, a later minute of the same conference reads that in connection with the administering of the Lord's supper 'unfermented wine shall on all occasions be used'. The first cash book for the Channel Isles corps of St Peter Port throws light on what form this 'unfermented wine' took. An entry for 1 November 1881 shows an expenditure of 1s 6d on 'blackcurrant jelly for wine for the sacrament'—this outward and visible sign of an inward spiritual grace presumably being administered by Captain Charlotte Jackson, the officer commanding. In passing we pause to observe that in this entry lie focussed two of the several reasons for the Army abandoning this sacrament. Writing more than 40 years later of his father's decision, Bramwell Booth explained: '. . . little by little he came to believe that there was danger in the continuance of this practice amongst us. Its chief danger, in his eyes, lay in its divisiveness. It involved many questions. To begin with, it was unthinkable that we should use fermented liquors. Many of our people, both men and women, were rescued drunkards, and already some of our converts, who had been sent to the churches, if they had not broken down immediately, had at least been placed in grievous temptation owing to the cup which they were offered. This may seem to be a minor question, but it was persistently troublesome. On the other hand, many of our people did not like the idea of "diluted jellies", and unfermented wine was then unknown, at any rate in this country; others, again, preferred that the element should be water. . . .

'A further and more acute difficulty was that many of the evangelists were women, as had been the case from the early years of the Mission, and the idea of women administering sacraments was at that time almost unthinkable to many good people, in spite of our stand, from the beginning, on the perfect equality of men and women in the Kingdom of Christ.'[8]

The *Daily News* had its own observations to make on the Army's temperance stand. Under the caption 'Great Battles at Coventry Fair' on Tuesday 17 June 1879 it reported: 'Perhaps the abandonment of idleness, blasphemy and drink all together proves too severe a trial for many; for temperance is a strong article of faith with The Salvation Army. "It must continue a strong article," said one of the leading spirits' [*sic*] who happened to be Elijah Cadman. '"It is impossible to improve them as long as they drink. We take their drink away, and that puts clothes on their backs and money in their pockets, and, mark me, we find them amusement— or, at least, enjoyment of a new kind by awakening their intelligence and giving them employment for it."'

'A Great Demonstration of Saved Drunkards' was held in the Strand's Exeter Hall in May 1884, to be followed the next week by a special 'Don't Drink' number of *The War Cry*. The following January William Booth told 'A Great Demonstration of Foreign Officers' in the same hall that 'They had just started a drunkards' rescue brigade, which . . . prowled about the streets and took drunkards home, administering a preparation of coffee, the coffee being carried in a pouch. The drunkard and his wife would be got to the Barracks next day and saved.'[9] Since all of 11 years had elapsed from the launching of the Drunkards' Rescue Society, we may well question the General's use of the words 'just started' in the above report. What *had* just started was a new method of organising this particular work. 'A gentleman solved the problem last week,' explained *All the World*. 'Up and down from head to foot he scanned the men who were proffering him help and counsel, until the truth broke through his drink-clouded mind, "My God! they must be Christians!" So they are. The name by which they are especially known at the training homes, however, is the "Drunkards' Rescue Brigade", and their work corresponds to that done by the girls from the Women's Training Home [the Cellar, Gutter and Garrett Brigade] in similar localities. Four lads, under the direction of an officer, live constantly in this Whitechapel district, devoting their nights to scouring the streets for the souls which they could win in no other way. They wear no uniform, and are not known as belonging to The Salvation Army. . . . From 12 to two every afternoon the brigade follow up the cases of the night before. . . . "Aside from what they are doing directly for the men they come in contact with," says the Commandant of the Men's Training Home' (the third Booth son, Herbert), 'the tact and experience my men gain in this work, they could get in no other way."' [10]

Not every drunkard with whom the Army came in contact was below the poverty line by any means. The rescue receiving house girls' statements book for 1886, for instance, records the case of Mrs H.—wife of Major General H., sister of Sir Eustace P., who asked Bramwell Booth if he could do anything for her, she being a slave to laudanum and drink. Bramwell sent her to Mrs Frost at 52 Blenheim Street, Chelsea—which was, it will be recalled, the first mother and baby home.

'The Salvation Army has opened a house for gentlemen inebriates' declared *The War Cry* for 24 September 1887, but it looks to have been a non-starter, since no details are given, and nothing more is heard of the venture until nearly three years later, when, at the annual slum and shelter anniversary meeting, the General lists an inebriates' home as part of his soon-to-come-to-birth social scheme. [11] Five months pass before 'our women's inebriate home' is featured in the paper. 'The tales we have heard of the effects of the spirit grocer's licence, especially on women, are simply appalling. Female servants, artisans' wives, ladies, &c., are rapidly becoming slaves to the drink fever. Most of them are otherwise respectable.'

'What is the cure? Semi-imprisonment, deprivation of the drink for a time? Yes, these are helps, but not, alas! alas! cures, or else the prisons would be grand inebriate homes. No, no, moral reformation can only be properly gained by a heart-change. We depend upon the saving power of Jesus Christ. The General has now given us instructions to start a home for inebriate women immediately.

'Our Proposed Plan.

1. We will take a large house with a garden in or near London, to accommodate 20 women and five officers.

2. Our patients shall only be women, whose great besetment is drink, and who want to escape from it.

126

3. We shall charge from 5s. to 15s. a week for each patient, according to the means of those who send them.

4. We will put everyone who comes to our home to some light work, so as to keep their minds occupied, and at the same time lighten the expenses.

'. . . We should like a piano or harmonium very much. We also want a good motherly, active, thoughtful woman to be housekeeper.'

Surprisingly this communication did not come from the pen of Mrs Bramwell Booth of the rescue work, but from Major J. J. Cooke of the slum work.[12] However, a year later, 'Mrs Bramwell Booth is anxious to hear of one or two *salvationist* or *thoroughly Christian families,* into which inebriate cases could be received as members of the home circle. Care, tact and kindness indispensable. An opportunity here presents itself for one whose circumstances make it impossible to take up more active service, yet, having a God-given love for the suffering and the captives, desires to take up some special soul-saving work.' This appeal appears under the caption *'All Expense Defrayed'.*

Meanwhile, Major Susie Swift's mind and pen were busy with the subject. In her *Brief Review of the First Year's Work of the Darkest England Social Scheme,* published at the end of 1891, she records: 'The General has distinctly stated that nine-tenths of all the power of this social work has to be expended in off-setting the results of England's annual drink bill of £130,000,000. . . .

'Men have come to the elevator and begged the officers to keep every penny they earned and let them have none, for fear they should drink again. And yet in no case where the man has not definitely accepted the converting grace of God, has any reformation proved permanent. . . .

'This work requires superhuman love and patience. No one need fancy simple *human* kindness and good fellowship can ever be sufficient for the work of a social reform officer.

'"They swing this way and they swing that way before they settle," said an officer to us the other day. "Our men take a long time to settle. I'll think one is all right and off my hands, and put him off my mind, and the first I know I get a letter—'Dear Adjutant, I am in trouble; can you kindly come and see me,' and

127

off I go, saying to myself, 'So *he's* not settled yet! Hallelujah! Never mind. Look at Z. Wasn't he off and on for a year or so, and now he's all right. So will this fellow be yet.'"

'What if he falls when he finally goes out into the world? Then he may come back again, if he will, and begin over again. Through the discipline of hunger and cold and misery, which brought him to factory and Lighthouse in the first place, up through the discipline of seaweed mattresses and twopenny meals, and steady, cheery work, he will come at last, by the grace of God. While, on the other hand, when a man does break a rule, or fail to give entire satisfaction generally, our factory officers do not treat with him on the lines that they are representing a large trading concern in any sense of the word, but they bear and forbear—show him the folly of a foolish act, explain to him how much more it is to his advantage and always will be for him to be a man, refer him to somebody he works with, as showing an exemplary character, and so on, as long as patience lasts; and when that is exhausted, they go to their knees and get a fresh supply, and struggle for his soul again and again.'

By 1893 she was coming to grips, whether consciously or unconsciously, with Superintendent Blandy's remark that 'the grace of God won't supply physical tissue, be it of brain or muscle' (see page 111). In one of two *Deliverer* articles entitled 'Papers for Social Toilers' she declares: '*You must have a real, practical belief in God's power and will to do all that is necessary to make people good.* Otherwise you will always be saying with a spasm of false charity: "Poor fellow! He can't break off drinking all at once! The coats of his stomach are inflamed. At least, he must expect an awful battle!" . . .

'"But do you think God *will* make new coats to a drunkard's stomach?" somebody asks. Certainly, if that is essential to making a sober man of him! I believe that God is willing to remove all those physical consequences of sin, which, if left, must necessarily prove a future temptation to sin. We salvationists, with files of *The War Cry* before us and our memories filled with the testimonies of comrades steeped in drink and vice for years, who maintain that the desire for drink has been removed from them instantly, cannot doubt this. But we may forget it. Or we may give place to the devil by shrinking from pressing the idea of *deliverance* upon a man who finds it difficult to grasp, and stopping short at the truth that God will enable him to *overcome*. We may be so afraid of "expecting too much" from people that we promise too little to them!

'And if God deals with the drunkard's stomach and nervous system, why not with a man's brain-matter? Habitual deceit and dishonesty mean, after a while, certain changes in brain-matter. So must any habit of mind.'[13]

We have no record of what became of Major Cooke's proposed plan to start a home for inebriate women, but at the end of 1893 *The Darkest England Gazette* was announcing: 'Frequent applications have been made to us from time to time with reference to taking charge of persons of that unfortunate and degraded class—women inebriates. Up till now we have had no opportunity of dealing with them. Fortunately, Mrs Bramwell Booth has now been enabled, by the kindness of our friend, Mrs Newberry, to utilise some very suitable premises, beautifully situated in the midst of a charming countryside. We trust to give in our next issue an illustrated description of this the latest of the many homes now connected with Mrs Bramwell Booth's rapidly-extending rescue organisation.'[14]

The promised 'illustrated description' the following week located the home as being in lovely country between Reading and Didcot and whilst admitting that 'very little had been accomplished hitherto for that difficult class', Mrs Bramwell asserted that 'the measure of success that we have met with in the past, and the number of those who when brought to us were considered almost hopelessly enslaved, but who are now walking at liberty, lead me to believe for great things in the future'. What then became of Mrs Newberry and her offer remains shrouded in mystery. No more is heard of the project until an 1896 *Deliverer* reference to Mrs Major Reynolds: 'still waiting the opening of the door of our inebriates' home with expectation and high hopes. We have had considerable difficulty in finding premises in which to begin this all-important work. Perhaps some of our friends could give us information of any old family house in the suburbs of London which they think might do.'[15] Temporary premises described as 'our first inebriates' home' were recorded as being actually opened in April, although no further detail is given.[16] With the moving of the nursery home to Lanark House, Lower Clapton, in June of that year, Grove House, Upper Clapton, became a home for women inebriates,[17] being transferred to Hillsboro' House, Stamford Hill, at the end of

June 1901.[18] That same year an inebriates' retreat for men was opened in an old mansion, formerly known as Hadleigh Great House, on land adjacent to the Farm Colony[19] (see chapter 12). Victoria House, as it was known, was listed in *The Salvation Army Year Books* for 1907-8 as coming under the direction of Mrs Bramwell Booth, even though it was a home for men. Its last *Year Book* listing was in 1910, whereas a home for women inebriates was listed as late as 1943. Indeed, for many years there were two such homes for women, and when one of them, Springfield Lodge at Denmark Hill, became a home for the mentally defective in 1915, another inebriates' home was opened in East London.[20]

For 20 years during the '40s and '50s a ministry to inebriates was absorbed into regular hostel work in the United Kingdom, and it was not until 1962 that *The Year Book* announced briefly: 'A centre for alcoholics has been opened in the provinces.' By 1963 this had been amplified to describe the centre (in good North American fashion) as The Harbour Light Residential Home, at Highworth, Wiltshire. Since those days a highly specialised programme of treatment has been built up for the alcoholic, giving concentrated attention to medical, psychological and spiritual needs. The salvationist of the 20th century meanwhile maintains the total abstinence stand of his pioneering forebears, believing that the 'consistent example of caring people in a world where . . . self-indulgence often results in lasting hurt to others'[21] continues to be what is required of him by his Lord.

11
The great machine

'WE are a great machine, and we go about in bits—I'm one of the smallest of them,' declared evangelist Elijah Cadman in describing The Christian Mission's function to a Whitby police inspector in 1878.[1]

'The Scheme, in its entirety, may aptly be compared to A Great Machine,' declared William Booth, unabashedly borrowing Cadman's quaint quote without acknowledgement, when, 12 years later, he came to write page 93 of his massive social scheme, *In Darkest England and the Way Out.*

To the uninitiated, still labouring under the popular fallacy that all Salvation Army social work stemmed from the 1890 scheme, it should perhaps at this stage be pointed out that all but three of the facets of social service dealt with in the previous 10 chapters of the current book found their genesis *before* 1890 (some of them, indeed, before that 1878 landmark which designated The Christian Mission a Salvation Army). Even boy-mending machinery, set in motion in 1891 and finally brought to pass in 1910, came into being *alongside* the Darkest England scheme, not as a direct part of it. There were, of course, still other aspects of social service which did arise directly out of the scheme, and which will be dealt with in the remaining chapter. However, to state that a goodly proportion of the great machine's functions were already in gear before 1890 is not to denigrate Booth; it is simply to emphasise that the impact of his blueprint was all the greater for being well tried.

First hint of the scheme came in the April 1890 slum and shelter anniversary meeting at Exeter Hall, when the General told the gathering that 'at the present moment he . . . was turning over a scheme in his mind which he hoped to fully explain at a future meeting'. Having outlined much with which we are now familiar from earlier chapters of this book, he told his audience that they 'could at once begin by contributing five and twenty thousand pounds for a start'.[2]

131

Two months later an extract from the June number of *The Review of Reviews* is quoted in *The War Cry,* in which W. T. Stead says: 'I have seen in rough outline the scheme that is fermenting in the minds of the leaders of the Army; and I say without hesitation, that it is the most hopeful and the most daring of the kind that has been promulgated in my time. The launching of the great scheme may be expected in the autumn. It is too vast and far-reaching to be produced for months to come. But it is there, and no one can say whither its development may lead.'

Stead undoubtedly was closely involved with Booth during the writing of the book. Undoubtedly too he was the 'great light of present-day journalism' whom *The War Cry* quotes as writing in the *Pall Mall Gazette* on the subject of the Social Reform Wing and its workers: 'They are close enough to all the worst forms of our social evils to understand them, and the General has got sufficient hold upon a sufficient number of men and women to justify an attempt to grapple with them in serious earnest. What the Social Wing means to do before it has completed its ultimate development, no one can say; but those who visited the social reform settlement at the Crystal Palace and heard the voices of the General and Commissioner Smith and saw the dossers and the ex-convicts and all the human *debris* that is being built up again into the fabric of civilisation and humanity, could see as in a glass darkly, that here is the beginning of an enterprise greater than any we have witnessed in our own time.'[3] Two months later *The War Cry* intimates that the October *Review of Reviews* is to contain 'a lengthy article, fully illustrated, on The Salvation Army, from the pen of Mr W. T. Stead'.

Only days before *In Darkest England and the Way Out* was published, Catherine, William Booth's 'continual comrade' of 35 years, was taken from him. 'Although the book was nearly completed, I had only read to her one or two of the opening chapters, reserving to myself the pleasure of going through the whole with her when finished. But, alas! just as the volume was passing to the printers the angels came and took her home! Still, what a heralding it was of the effort! Her passing bell called the attention of the world to the scheme which was about to be launched, 16 days after she had been laid in the grave.'[4] W. T. Stead paid his own tribute to Catherine Booth. 'She has not been allowed to see the formal publication of the great manifesto . . . but she was no stranger to its contents. She was the prophetess of the new movement—she saw it afar off, was glad she was a socialist of the heart, full of passionate sympathy with the poor and the oppressed of every land and clime; full, too, of fierce indignation against all who did them wrong. . . .

'That The Salvation Army is entering upon a new development is probably due more to her than any single human being, and in its new social work we see the best and most enduring monument to the memory of a saintly woman who has been released from her sufferings. But that may also be said to be true of The Salvation Army itself. The Army could no more have come into existence without Mrs Booth than could the family of sons and daughters who are now carrying on the movement. No one outside can ever know how much all that is most distinctive of the Army is due directly to the shaping and inspiring impulse of Mrs Booth. But even outsiders like myself can see that but for her it would either never have been, or else it would have been merely one more of the many small but narrow sects which carry on mission work in nooks and corners of the land.'[5]

From a letter Stead wrote to *The Star,* published on 2 January 1891, it is clear that what Booth described as 'the attention of the world' was by no means totally uncritical. 'According to the theory favoured by those who are eager to clutch at every stick with which to beat the General,' wrote Stead, 'his Darkest England Scheme is not his scheme at all, but Smith's and mine. Smith conceived the scheme, and I wrote the book—so the story runs—and the General is a mere man of straw or a puppet in the hands of Frank Smith and W. T. Stead. What arrant nonsense all this is! They little know the General who indulge in such speculation. Everyone knows perfectly well that two years ago, nay, even one year ago, General Booth did not see his way to the utilisation of The Salvation Army as an instrument of social reform. Smith wanted it to be so employed three years ago. So did many other people. But it is one thing to press for action and another thing to know how and when to act. When Smith was in America attending to his own business the Army, largely under the direction of Mr Bramwell Booth, was making tentative efforts towards social work by the establishment of the slum brigade, the food depot and the night shelter. When Smith came back and submitted himself to his old commanding officer he was placed in charge of the Social Wing and while there he developed the factory—the realisation of an idea first mooted at an officers' council at which Smith was not present, but which unquestionably he did much to help into practical shape. The

experience gained by the Social Wing encouraged the General to take up a decided step in advance. He decided upon writing "In Darkest England" and propounding "the way out", which has since attained so world-wide a fame. . . .

'The General asked me to find him a literary hack to help him to lick the huge and growing mass of material into shape. I volunteered to hack. I served as scribe temporarily under his orders, and I succeeded with the aid of three zealous and competent stenographers in getting through my journeyman work up to time. But it revolts me to hear people who profess to be friends of mine talking as if the help which I was proud to render to General Booth in any way detracts from his claim to be considered author of the whole scheme.'

In his book *Mrs Booth of The Salvation Army*, published in 1900, Stead again emphasises his secondary role in the production of *In Darkest England*: 'I saw her several times during these last weeks at Clacton. I was down there helping General Booth as a kind of voluntary secretary and amanuensis in getting the mss. of "Darkest England" into shape.'

If Stead's references to Frank Smith in *The Star* letter of early 1891 seem somewhat caustic, it must be remembered that the lately created leader of the Social Reform Wing was at that very moment causing his own stir in the press, having tendered his resignation but two months after publication of *In Darkest England*. Being the dramatic kind of character he was, it was perhaps inevitable that some kind of power struggle would ensue from his having necessarily to work in such close proximity to William and Bramwell Booth. He was probably not the first Army leader (and certainly not the last) to have found his style cramped by 'London', after the comparative freedom of command in an overseas territory. His short career as Social Wing leader appears as flamboyant as his penmanship. *The War Cry* for 4 October 1890 gives three-column coverage to events surrounding 'The Extraordinary Action of the Police' in bringing Smith and other salvationists to trial as the result of a clash between the police and an Army procession heading towards Exeter Hall in the Strand. 'It was one of those cases in which the testimony of opposite sides was so much in dispute that it was most difficult to put your finger down and say, "Here is the truth",' asserted the magistrate, fining Smith and another officer 40s each or 21 days. In spite of many sympathetic offers to meet the fines, they chose imprisonment, 'our dear commissioner in the yellow uniform of Her Majesty's mistaken subjects, in a cage with thick bars'. To a friend sent to pay his fine Smith said he would rather stay where he was. 'Perhaps it might have been a good thing in some ways if he had, as we should have got a faithful report of how short-sentence prisoners are treated. He may, however, get run in again at a more convenient time.' The General intervened, and the upshot was that 'poor commissioner had to deny himself the pleasure (?) of serving his 21 days and come out.'

Close on two months later a letter appeared in the same paper from 'A London physician: Dear Sir,—The other day I was walking along Upper Thames Street and saw a man vainly trying to lift a heavy box, when along came Commissioner Smith, whom I knew from having seen his likeness in *The Star.* He saw the difficulty and at once went to the man's help, and the box was put in position. I could not hear what he said, but he smiled at the man with a smile that lit up his face and then went on.

'I looked at the man and there were tears in his eyes.

'Surely here is an example to follow. I am not a member of the Army, but I think it well to let both the Army and the outside public know what I saw.'

On 4 December Smith was explaining the Scheme at Toynbee Hall, where 'every shade and grade of East End thought was present. . . . Although in an environment to which he was in a great measure totally unused, the commissioner came out with more than ordinary brilliancy, and the kindly spirit of consideration that ran through his reply, the singularly happy and good-humoured sharpness of his repartee, and, above all, the earnest eloquence with which he pressed home his cause, the needs of those he sought to benefit, and the sorrows of the nation, the social life of which it sought to cleanse and purify, won all hearts and swept away as a morning cloud the mists of prejudice and mis-understanding.'

On 2 January 1891 (the day W. T. Stead's letter on the authorship of *In Darkest England* appeared in *The Star*), one from Frank Smith appeared in *The Times,* explaining the reasons for his resignation, which had already been announced in that paper on 26 December. On 3 January *The War Cry* went into print on his resignation, reiterating what William Booth had written in *The*

Times of 29 December. The grounds given by the Boxing Day issue of *The Times* had been: 'Mr Smith has always been of the opinion that it was before all things necessary to keep the social working of the scheme as distinct as possible from the religious work of the Salvation Army.' The grounds given by William Booth were: 'that he [Smith] has not been left so free and independent in his action as he wished.' This was countered by the explanation: 'It will be evident that in the formation of a new section of our operations—in the working out of a great deal of which we had only limited experience—it was absolutely necessary that things should be moulded and fashioned according to the judgment of the General. Especially will this be seen, when it is remembered that this department would have to work in harmony with the divisional commands throughout the country. . . .

'The resignation of Commissioner Smith is a matter of very great regret, and we need scarcely say that it has been a great disappointment to the General, who very highly esteemed him, and the following extract from Mr Smith's last letter to the General shows, we think that there has been no unfriendliness on either side: "You need fear no alarm as to my intentions. I do not contemplate anything on the lines of opposition. While I just as earnestly as ever agree to the end desired, we differ as to the methods of working. Anything I can do outside to bring about the object in view, you can reckon on me."'

Frank Smith was re-accepted as a Salvation Army officer in 1901, with a lesser rank, but left again some years later, eventually becoming Member of Parliament for Nuneaton.[6]

'For my part I do not believe the Salvation Army contains a man capable of taking his place,' declared a *Times* Special Correspondent on 2 January, notwithstanding the fact that Cadman's promotion to commissioner and appointment to the charge of the Social Wing had already been announced by that paper on 27 December. His resilience would not make heavy weather of such a limited assessment. A supposed descendant of the Saxon herdsman Caedmon,[7] who, though illiterate, became the earliest English Christian poet,[8] Elijah Cadman was himself illiterate until at the age of 22 he was taught to read by his new bride.[7] Not that he was without earlier opportunity. Sent to a dame's school for twopence a week, he soon disgraced himself by kicking her shins, and was consequently deposited in the coal-cellar. Seeing the mouth of an unused chimney, he climbed through it, and, at not yet six years of age, 'settled his trade' and became a sweep's boy, climbing chimneys legally until he was 13, and thereafter illegally.[7] "Cadman had become an excellent sweep, quick, ready, thorough, punctual, shrewd, thrifty. Once he began to earn he was never without money. There was strong, long life in his body, he brimmed with the vitality that had carried him safely through hardships; he was eager, adventurous, pugnacious, and a nuisance to the police. His only recreations were fighting, racing, bathing in river or stream, jumping, blowing up wasps' nests, bird catching, and imitating bird-calls. Whistling he practised into an accomplishment . . . and he earned a reputation for fighting like a devil and drinking like a fish."[7] Incapable of taking Smith's place though *The Times* may have considered him, he was certainly a force to be reckoned with, and never more so than when, an instant conversion to teetotalism behind him, many months of struggling gave place to the transforming power of a spiritual conversion. Having become a Christian Mission evangelist in 1876, by 1890 'Elijah Cadman was apparent in Colonel Cadman, but with extensive alterations'. His turn-of-the-year promotion and appointment to leadership of the Social Wing he accepted 'joyfully'.[7] It was an attitude of heart sorely needed. Not only were the pages of the nation's foremost newspapers seething with acrimony towards William Booth on the subject of Frank Smith's resignation, they were also both full of doubt as to his personal ability to write *In Darkest England*, and, paradoxically, full of criticism as to what he *had* written.

What he *had* written was, in the words of *The Daily Graphic*, a 'work dealing with the crying social evils of the time. He has taken Mr Stanley's account of the African forest regions as the groundwork for the allegorical treatment of a state of social darkness and despair which is ever present side by side with the civilisation and philanthropy of the present time. This allegorical allusion is in keeping with all the methods of The Salvation Army, and these methods, ridiculous as they may seem to those who are not brought face to face with the problems which The Salvation Army endeavours to solve, have a value which has been established long before the days of Mr Booth. . . .

'The most striking feature of the General's book to those who are accustomed chiefly to the noisy and aggressive side of The Salvation Army's proceedings, is the moderation and restraint which, on the whole, characterises all that he says. He endeavours, he tells us, throughout to understate rather than to overstate the difficulties of the case. . . .

'General Booth does not mince matters as to the condition and prospects of what he calls the "submerged tenth". His facts and conclusions, appalling as they are every time they are brought to the notice of the happier world, have not been waiting for the publication of this book to assert their claim to notice and prompt remedial action. Unfortunately, in this respect, he tells us nothing new; perhaps there is nothing new in this respect to tell. But General Booth's title to an exceptionally attentive hearing is twofold. The Salvation Army has worked more consistently, and on a larger scale in darkest England, than any other organisation of mercy; its forces are not seldom recruited from the "submerged tenth", and it gains power for further efforts by using its proselytes of the slums to approach the shy ferocity of the abandoned and hardened for lack of hope. In addition to this claim from the present and the past, General Booth puts forth a scheme for the healing and prevention of the scandalous miseries of the poorest classes, which, whatever the ultimate judgment upon its feasibility or its propriety, at least makes a fairly practical show upon paper, and has been tried already on a small scale by The Salvation Army. . . .

'It must not be thought that this very remarkable work is all statistical. It abounds with wonderful stories of real life and slum experiences, and is full of shrewd observations and telling truths. One need be no adherent of salvationist methods in religion generally to see the immense power for good possessed by this single-hearted organisation. In times when the masses are supposed to be socialistically and atheistically inclined, it is something to find an army, however its familiarity with sacred names and subjects may shock the well-protected and refined, which goes boldly and tackles the vilest in their vileness and sets its face as a flint against persecution and scorn.

'Love of God, shown in love to man, is the test of all Christianity . . . but The Salvation Army, with its quaint allegorical methods, has got far more forward than any other body just now, and though General Booth's scheme may not meet with universal approbation, it would be well if he, experienced in the matter with which he professes to deal, were enabled by the public generally to alleviate those patent miseries upon which he so forcibly dwells.'[9]

'The denizens in darkest England, for whom I appeal,' wrote Booth, 'are (1) those who, having no capital or income of their own, would in a month be dead from sheer starvation were they exclusively dependent upon the money earned by their own work; and (2) those who by their utmost exertions are unable to attain the regular allowance of food which the law prescribes as indispensable even for the worst criminals in our gaols. . . .

'When, in the streets of London, a cab horse, weary or careless or stupid, trips and falls and lies stretched out in the midst of the traffic, there is no question of debating how he came to stumble before we try to get him on his legs again. The cab horse is a very real illustration of poor, broken-down humanity; he usually falls down because of overwork and underfeeding. If you put him on his feet without altering his conditions, it would only be to give him another dose of agony; but first of all you'll have to pick him up again. It may have been through overwork or underfeeding, or it may have been all his own fault that he has broken his knees and smashed the shafts, but that does not matter. If not for his own sake, then merely in order to prevent an obstruction of the traffic, all attention is concentrated upon the question of how we are to get him on his legs again. The load is taken off, the harness is unbuckled, or, if need be, cut, and everything is done to help him up. Then he is put in the shafts again and once more restored to his regular round of work. That is the first point. The second is that every cab horse in London has three things: a shelter for the night, food for its stomach, and work allotted to it by which it can earn its corn.

'These are the two points of the cab horse's charter. When he is down he is helped up, and while he lives he has food, shelter and work. That, although a humble standard, is at present absolutely unattainable by millions . . . of our fellow-men and women in this country. . . .

'The difference between the method which seeks to regenerate the man by ameliorating his circumstances and that which ameliorates his circumstances in order to get at the regeneration of his heart, is the difference between the method of the gardener who grafts a Ribstone Pippin on a crab-apple tree and one who merely ties apples with string upon the branches of the crab. To change the nature of the individual, to get at the heart, to save his soul, is the only real, lasting method of doing him any good. In many modern schemes of social regeneration it is forgotten that "it takes a soul to

140

move a body, e'en to a cleaner sty", and at the risk of being misunderstood and misrepresented, I must assert in the most
unqualified way that it is primarily and mainly for the sake of
saving the soul that I seek the salvation of the body.'[10]

Having outlined in the first part of the book the plight of the
submerged tenth, the General gives over the second part to a
description of the threefold scheme with which he means to solve
the problem. 'The scheme I have to offer consists in the formation
of these people into self-helping and self-sustaining communities,
each being a kind of co-operative society, or patriarchal family,
governed and disciplined on the principles which have already
proved so effective in The Salvation Army. These communities we
will call, for want of a better term, colonies. There will be—

(1) The city colony

(2) The farm colony

(3) The oversea colony.'[11]

The main features of the city colony have already emerged in
earlier chapters of the present book. The farm and oversea colonies
will be dealt with in the final chapter, since these two aspects arose
out of the scheme, rather than being part of the in-put which led to
it.

The 'being misunderstood and misrepresented' which Booth
foresaw when he asserted so strongly that it was primarily for the
sake of the soul's salvation that he sought to save the body, was
spearheaded by T. H. Huxley, whose spate of letters to *The Times*
eventually found publication in book form under the title *Social
Diseases and Worse Remedies.* We content ourselves with but one
excerpt: 'Mr Booth tells us with commendable frankness, that "it is
primarily and mainly for the sake of saving the soul that I seek the
salvation of the body", which language, being interpreted, means
that the propagation of the special salvationist creed comes first,
and the promotion of the physical, intellectual, and purely moral
welfare of mankind second in his estimation. Men are to be made
sober and industrious, mainly that, as washed, shorn, and docile
sheep, they may be driven into the narrow theological fold which
Mr Booth patronises. If they refuse to enter, for all their moral
cleanliness, they will have to take their place among the goats as
sinners, only less dirty than the rest.'[12]

(' "Don't some of them dislike your religion altogether?" ' asked a journalist of General Booth some years later. ' "Yes, they come in thinking they do. And we bide our time. They may get saved in the end; and they may not. But meantime—"

' "Yes, meantime?"

' "It cheers them up. They may laugh at it, but it makes the thing go. The music and the emotion stir them." ' [13])

There were other opinions than Huxley's, of course. Canon Farrar was announced to preach upon the subject of the General's book in Westminster Abbey on a Sunday afternoon in November. 'In his best judgment he believed the scheme to be full of promise if the necessary funds were provided, and he merely regarded it as his humble duty to render the undertaking such aid as he could.' [14] Lady Henry Somerset was described by *The War Cry* as being 'With the "upper tenth"—an audience of wealth and influence' crowding out Kensington Town Hall—where her ladyship expressed the view that 'the General's book breathes out hope from one cover to the other.' On the same occasion the chairman, Walter McLaren, MP, declared he had 'every confidence in the Army financially, and no sympathy with those who declined to subscribe to this fund because it would be controlled solely by General Booth. The accounts of The Salvation Army were kept with the same regularity and strictness as any great mercantile concern in this country, and audited by the same firm of accountants as audited the books of the Midland Railway Company.' [15] Unlike the now extinct Midland Railway Company, The Salvation Army can make the 1980s' claim that its second-century financial affairs continue to come under the scrutiny of the same firm.

The raising of the necessary million pounds in 1890 must have called for all the ingenuity of an ingenious mind, and all the faith of Miss Sapsworth's Abraham. If an initial £100,000 were donated immediately, it would see the scheme launched, provided there was guarantee of interest on the remaining £900,000 (ie £30,000) for future years. [16] By 30 January 1891 the amount subscribed and promised had reached £102,559 1s. 2d. and William Booth signed the Darkest England Trust Deed at a public meeting in St James's Hall, thus securing the funds entirely for the purpose intended. [17] Meanwhile *The Accountant,* a newspaper devoted to the interests of actuaries, assured its readers: 'The Salvation Army accounts are clear, and undoubtedly well kept. Very creditable specimens, and

142

we only wish that the accounts of all charitable institutions were as carefully and clearly kept.'[18] To the constant insinuations that Booth was purloining for his own purposes money donated to the scheme came the patiently reiterated reply that not a penny of it went into a Booth pocket, a generous settlement providing for the family's support having been made in Christian Mission days by Henry Reed, a Tasmanian sheep farmer.[19] If similar charges were to be laid at the doors of his social work officers, a glance at the *Orders and Regulations for Rescue Homes* (1892) shows that a clear pattern was early established.

Page 14: *Chapter* 3, *Section* 5—Allowances:

1. When officers reside in the homes no salary is given, and any officer, either in them or in the rescue headquarters, who is able, wholly or in part, to pay her own expenses, is expected to do so, and to count it a special privilege thus to have it in her power to give her services to the Lord and to work, free of charge. As, however, very many cannot do this, a small allowance is made for the purchase of clothing and petty personal expenses. For captains, this is at the rate of 5s., and for lieutenants, 4s. per week. It is not guaranteed, but whenever possible, will always be made. Cadets do not receive allowances.
2. When married couples with families are employed they must have their own fixed salary and quarters outside the home.'

By November 1891 a 200,000 fifth edition of *In Darkest England* was in print, and on the 14th of that month an eight-page Social Wing supplement appeared in *The War Cry* as forerunner of *The Darkest England Gazette* and the later *Social Gazette*. This first issue included articles on 'Village Sociology', 'A Night with the Destitute Workless', 'The Wharf and Salvage Brigade' and an interview with Commissioner Cadman—he who, earlier in the year, was reported as 'having the first pair of shoes made on the premises, and says he shall feel proud to wear them, especially if they are easy in fit.' (This at The Bridge prison gate home, where *boot*making had been the order of the day since 1886. Now 'the old order changeth', and in the footsteps of the hand-sewn boot came the hand-sewn shoe.) Booted or shoed, Cadman was proving to be just such a leader as *The Times* special correspondent had doubted The Salvation Army of containing. By the end of 1892 *The War Cry* was reporting: 'Commissioner Cadman has lost none of the "cunning" which in days of yore packed his halls with curious thousands. In one of our workshops a huge canvas was being decorated with the following legend: "Salvation Army Social Wing. Commissioner Cadman, the notorious explorer, direct from Darkest England jungles, will relate some thrilling episodes in his conquering conflicts with our national curses—drunkenness, poverty and crime. Come in your thousands.'''

Cadman's relating of 'some thrilling episodes in his conquering conflicts with our national curses', was all part of the great 'Social Boom' launched in November 1892 to raise the £65,000 needful for continuing the extensive operations already commenced. 'This money I must have,' declared Booth, 'or I shall be involved in circumstances of great difficulty, and the further development of the scheme in its present proportions will be impossible.'[20] It was a continuing cry. At the opening of the Lamprell Street match factory in 1891, 'Much enthusiasm was evoked when the General announced that the legacy, of which so much had been said in the press, was really bequeathed to us, and that in a straightforward way. Her Majesty's Government would take out something like £14,000. . . . He thought we ought to have some little alteration in our legacy laws, especially when a sum of money was left for religious purposes.'[21] Then in June 1892 *The Times, The Daily Telegraph* and other newspapers had published an 'Important Appeal for Help' over the signatures of 19 prominent personages of the House of Lords, the House of Commons, the Church and social reform. 'From personal witness, or credible report, of what General Booth has done with the funds entrusted to him for the social scheme which he laid before the country 18 months ago, we think that it would be a serious evil if the great task which he has undertaken should be crippled by lack of help during the next few years. We therefore venture to recommend his work to the generous support of all who feel the necessity for some serious and concentrated effort to grapple with the needs of the most wretched and destitute who have so long been the despair of our legislation and our philanthropy.' Now, five months later, came the 'Social Boom'. November 27 was designated Social Sunday, 'when all above the average collections shall be given towards the scheme.'

Continued the General:

'2. I shall ask for the fullest assistance of every officer and soldier in the work of organising and conducting meetings in the churches, chapels, and halls around you. . . .

3. I shall ask and expect that all officers and soldiers will give all the time they can spare from other duties to collect from friends and strangers, at railway stations, in market places, in the streets, and from house to house.

4. I shall ask that from the hour of the publication of this appeal the whole Army will pray for the divine blessing on it.

Friends Outside Our Ranks.

1. From friends outside our ranks I shall ask a generous co-operation. Among other things I shall ask every editor of every newspaper in the country to write an editorial on the scheme, and to ask their readers to assist me in completing the experiment.

2. I propose at once to form a "Social League", the senior members of which shall engage to give or collect at least £5 per annum, and the young people £1. Books, cards and all information will be furnished to help secure at least three thousand members during the coming year.

3. I shall ask all clergymen and ministers to say a good word on behalf of the effort, and every Christian to join the salvationists in praying for the divine blessing, and every man or woman who has the means to do something large or small to help in the rescuing of these perishing crowds.'[20]

Three weeks later *The War Cry* published several columns of closely printed 'Engagements', giving details of which prominent officers would be campaigning where, on behalf of the social scheme, and when. The planning and publicity attached to the 'Boom' reveal strong similarities to the 'For God's Sake Care' campaign which was to take the nation by storm in the late 1960s.

That 'every editor of every newspaper in the country' wrote an editorial on the scheme at Booth's behest is unlikely. Far more likely it is that those who *did* were not necessarily writing in support of the scheme. A year or two later Bramwell Booth was to write: 'English journalism, with occasional exceptions, has a keen scent for pure animus. . . . But just as surely as wilful misrepresentation is rendered difficult of circulation, good-natured lying finds every facility ready to its hand. Your easy-going, gossipy news-collector picks up the most unlikely story, knows by instinct that there is copy in it, waits for no vestige of inquiry or examination, trims it up, and passes it on in the form of a spicy paragraph which will be welcomed in the average newspaper office more kindly than if it was a profoundly thoughtful leader or a rattling review. It is known that we do not strike back, that our friends among those whose advertisements virtually keep the newspaper press of this country alive are but few, that from the very nature of our work the mass of

145

readers cannot investigate a story, and so it goes on. Every conceivable form of exaggeration and imagination is concerned in the manufacture of intelligence about The Salvation Army.'[22] True, The Salvation Army does not 'strike back' in the face of calumny, but against the background of continual suspicion surrounding his use of Darkest England funds the General most wisely called for a committee of inquiry to be set up, 'composed of men of such character and influence as would command due respect for their verdict from friend and foe alike. . . . The Earl of Onslow very kindly offered his services for this purpose, and on him has largely devolved the work of selection.'[20] Grudgingly conceding that 'although that body is not perhaps the strongest that might have been got together for such a purpose, it undeniably consists of persons whose judgment will rightly have weight with the community', *The Times* went on: 'The public will be quite satisfied if the authorities of the Army can establish that its funds are invested in such a manner as the funds of a charity ought to be invested, that its affairs are conducted in a businesslike way, that the results hitherto yielded by the Darkest England Scheme promise a reasonable measure of success. If the General can prove this, he need have no anxiety about the state of his balance-sheet for the future, and the public will very sincerely rejoice should he succeed in doing so.'[23]

On 19 December 1892 the 'Printers in Ordinary to Her Majesty' published the *Report of the Committee of Inquiry*, which thoroughly examined each aspect of the scheme—including the Women's Social Work—and published appropriate balance sheets as part of the report. Regarding the use of Darkest England funds, 'they have been devoted only to the objects and expended in the methods set out in that appeal, and to and in no others'. Furthermore, 'it appears that the methods employed in the expenditure of such monies have been and are of a businesslike, economical, and prudent character', and that 'the accounts of such expenditure have been and are kept in a proper and clear manner.' A section is given over to '*Personal Expenditure of Mr Booth and his Family*. In examining the accounts, the committee were careful to inquire whether any portion of the travelling expenses of the members of The Salvation Army had been borne by the "Darkest England" Fund, and whether Mr Booth or any of his family have drawn any sums for their personal use therefrom. No such expenditure appears to have been incurred. There is no reason to think that Mr Booth or any member of his family derive, or ever have derived, benefit of any kind from any of the properties or

146

money raised for the "Darkest England" Scheme. Some members of Mr Booth's family draw salaries from the spiritual wing of The Salvation Army, and a list was put in from which it appears that Mr Booth himself has received nothing from either side of The Salvation Army. He has a small income partly settled on him by a personal friend and partly derived from the sale of his literary works, the amount and nature of which he explained to the committee, and which seemed to them commensurate with the maintenance of his personal establishment.' The £7,383 profit from the sale of *In Darkest England and the Way Out,* however, was ploughed back into the scheme.[24]

Publicly exonerated, Booth could give his mind more fully to raising the £65,000 he had looked to the 'boom' to bring in. Had the report been issued at an earlier date, he felt, a larger response could have been hoped for. As it was, by the second week of January 1893 £15,250 of the £65,000 had been received. More was expected to materialise. Meanwhile a permanent annual income must be secured for the social work. To the idea of the Social League was added that of the Light Brigade, the membership of which 'shall simply engage to place at least one halfpenny per week in a box which shall be provided for that purpose, and which box will be collected by our agents regularly every quarter'. These boxes were to be known as 'Grace Before Meat' boxes, and leaguers were encouraged to stand them upon their dining tables 'so that when you and your friends sit down to the comfortable repast which providence sets before you, you may be reminded of those not thus favoured, and have the opportunity to send a mite to alleviate—nay, to assist—in saving them from further destitution.'[25] The practice is still continued into the 1980s.

The Darkest England Gazette for 14 October 1893 announced that the whole of the money raised by the Social Department during the forthcoming self-denial week would be devoted entirely to the furtherance of the Darkest England Scheme. Indeed, the reader discovers, 'during last self-denial week, the love and sympathy of those submerged classes in the elevators and shelters towards their fellows resulted in the raising of £73. . . . Again we ask every reader individually, "What will you do?"' A couple of years later The Ark men collected 5s. towards the cost of farthing breakfasts for the children of Bermondsey, and within the month the following insertion appeared in *The Social Gazette*: 'Sergeant-Major Barton, of Kennington Lane, desires to thank his shopmates at Messrs Rabbits and Sons for the great kindness they have shown to the poor children during the recent severe weather, and to inform them that the money collected has reached the sum of £4 4s. 4½d.'[26] Edward Rabbits, it will be remembered, was the methodist bootmaker who, back in 1852, provided the young William Booth with 20 shillings a week that he might break with the wretched pawnbroking trade and take steps towards becoming a minister.[27] Booth's boots had journeyed far since then!

But we digress from the Darkest England Fund itself, which, in the same year (1895), had a total turnover of £151,000—including the sale of goods manufactured in the various institutions. Of this, £9,000 was contributed in 'Grace Before Meat' box halfpennies by 'poor people', and £18,000 was received in subscriptions and donations from 'the charitable'. The outgoings for rent, rates and taxes on the buildings used by the scheme were £8,000, and £4,000 was expended in salaries of people connected with the scheme—including legal, medical and other professional charges.[28] The Women's Social Work was included in these figures, and Mrs Bramwell Booth was constantly devising new ways of raising funds. Rescue auxiliaries were created in 1894—they being friends of the Army who could help:

'1. By seeking to arouse interest in, and spread information concerning the Salvation Army rescue work.

2. By receiving and forwarding to Rescue Headquarters . . . gifts of clothing, boots, etc. . . .

3. By securing annual subscribers; also monthly collectors who would undertake to collect small sums monthly, in each case providing gratis a copy of the current number of *The Deliverer.* . . .

4. To arrange for drawing-room and other meetings where possible, to which representatives from headquarters will be sent to speak of the work.'[29]

By 1898 most Women's Social Work homes had a pedlar attached. These were officers whose entire time was spent in hawking from door to door articles made in the various women's homes and factories. This made for a valuable source of income if it *was* hard on the feet. 'I am one of the privileged pedlars', wrote such an officer, 'because I drive a donkey and cart.'

Writing upon the state of the scheme in 1896 the Founder said: 'True, we have not yet done everything promised at the onset; but, if we have not done some of the things named, we have, I think, amply made up by doing some not named. If we have not accomplished all expected from us in this dark England of ours, we have gone beyond all expectations in other dark corners of the earth, and, to a salvationist, one man is as good as another, seeing that he equally enjoys pulling a fellow-creature out of the gutter, whether he be perishing in India, Australasia, or in the land that he describes as home.'[30]

Seventeen years into the scheme, he listed for public interest his original proposals and their actual outcome. In 1890 the following ideas were mooted (those marked with an asterisk were actually carried out):

*Food depots	Travelling hospital
*Night shelters	*Inebriate homes
*Workshops and labour yards	*Rescue homes
*Labour bureaux	*Preventive homes
The household salvage brigade	*Inquiry office
*The farm colony	Refuges for street children
The industrial village	*Industrial schools
*Agricultural villages	Asylums for moral lunatics
The oversea colony	*Improved lodgings
*Universal emigration	Workmen's cottages
*The salvation ship	*The poor man's bank
*Slum visitation and nursing	*The poor man's lawyer
*Prison-gate brigade and ex-	*The intelligence department
criminals homes	Matrimonial bureaux
Whitechapel-by-the-Sea	

By 1906 the following branches of work, not named in the original proposals, had been added to the scheme:

Wood yards	Midnight soup kitchens
Shoe blacking brigades	Midnight work amongst women
Street cleaning brigades	Special training home for social officers
Express brigades	Maternity homes
Knitting and needle workrooms	Farthing breakfasts for children
Laundries	Hospitals
Police-court visitation	Servants' homes.[31]

Not that Booth's spectacles were rose-tinted. His eagle eye quickly marked any deficiency, and his tongue was not slow in pointing it out. Giving an historical sketch of the social work to officer-delegates gathered for the International Social Council of 1911, he declared: 'In the history of the Social Work, nevertheless, there have been, as you will know, any number of shortcomings. We have not realised all our expectations, nor fulfilled all our dreams. It was not to be expected that we should. This is an imperfect world; the movement has been imperfect, and the people who have carried it on have been imperfect also. Consequently, it is only natural that we have had imperfect results.

'(a) Many things have been calculated to cause these shortcomings. For example:

'i—There has been a great lack of direct aim at the true goal of our Social Work on the part of some officers who have been engaged in its direction.

'Some of our comrades have been content with a "soup-and-blanket" regime. That is to say, they have too often been satisfied with the alleviation of the miseries of the hour, and have stopped short of the removal of the evils that have caused the poverty, vice, and agony from which the sufferings sprang.

'Consequently the work, being superficial, has in some cases only had superficial and temporary results.

'You get out of a thing as much as you put in—and no more, and that, not only in quantity, but in quality. If you go in for root-and-branch efforts, you will get root-and-branch results.

'ii—Another cause of our shortcomings has been the lamentable fact that some of our officers have been deficient in personal religion.

'Our Social Work is essentially a religious business. It can neither be contemplated, commenced, nor carried on, with any great success, without a heart full of pity, and love, and endued with the power of the Holy Ghost.

'iii—Another of our difficulties has been the scarcity of suitable people for carrying the work on. This was also to be expected. If we had been content with hirelings, and had sought them out from among the philanthropies and churches, we should have found plenty in number, but it is equally certain we should have had considerably more doleful failures than those we have experienced.

'We are not only making but are now training the social officers, and we shall doubtless improve in this respect, whilst the work they turn out will be bound to improve proportionately.

'iv—Then again a further reason for our shortcomings has been our shortness of money. This need unfortunately is not passing away, as you will all well know. . . .

'(b) Nevertheless, and notwithstanding all our shortcomings, the position now occupied by our social operations, and the influence exercised by them on the great and small of the earth, is in evidence in every continent and on every hand.

'There is no doubt that the world, as a whole, feels much of the admiration and gratitude which the press lavished upon me on my recent birthday [his 82nd]—admiration which was assuredly intended not only for myself, but for the Army as a whole, and not only for the Army as a whole, but for its social workers in particular. . . .

'Truly our future chroniclers will have to record the fact that our social operations . . . imparted a divine dignity to the struggles of the early years of The Salvation Army's history.'[32] And that this chronicler gladly does.

IT would be no small oversight to conclude a chapter on 'The Great Machine' without giving passing glance to the type of subject featured week-by-week in its newspaper—known successively as *The Darkest England Gazette* and *The Social Gazette*.

An outstanding theme over a number of years was 'Women's Rights'. Not that this paper had a monopoly on the subject as far as Salvation Army publications were concerned. As early as 1876 *The Christian Mission Magazine* went into print on the issue: 'They say it is quite impossible for women to preach the gospel. What *is* it proper for women to do? Is it proper to stand before the public for many hours daily in a shop? The universal practice says that it is. We are thankful that "Mr Frederick Smith, of Leeston, Weston-Super-Mare," and other excellent people with him, are urging upon the public attention that these poor shopwomen should at least have seats to sit upon when not waiting upon their customers. We wish the agitation every success, and cannot imagine any real objection to it.

151

'But has woman no better destiny than to stand or sit in waiting upon man's bodily needs? Will anyone find out a reason why women should not stand before the public to offer them the bread of life, the wine and milk of the gospel, and the robes of righteousness?

'Thank God, our columns bear witness monthly to the fact that God has poured his Spirit in these days upon his handmaids as well as upon his sons, and that women, guided and supported by his hand, can accomplish everything in spiritual work that man can do.'[33] The 23 November 1895 issue was designated 'The Shop Assistants' Number', and on 13 January 1900 *The Gazette* reported: 'With the New Year came into force a new law which, we are sure, will confer a great boon to a much-suffering portion of the community: we refer to the Shop Assistants Act, which compels every shopkeeper who employs female assistants, to provide seats behind the counter, or in such other position as may be suitable, in the proportion of not less than one seat to every three female assistants employed in each room. The great weariness experienced by female shop assistants, who for 10 to 12 hours per day have been obliged to keep standing, cannot be realised by those who have not passed through the experience. The heartlessness also manifested by shopwalkers in the matter of girls sitting down has been little short of brutal.' Two months later, however: 'The recent Shop Assistants Act does not seem to be working well . . . the wily shopkeeper has found that, like most other Acts of Parliament, it can be evaded. It is true that when one in authority calls to enquire into the matter, he finds nothing to which he can take exception. But yet no one ever sees the girls sitting down. The explanation is simple. Seats are provided, but no one is allowed to sit on them. The Act only says that seats must be provided. It does not say that assistants must be given an opportunity of sitting on them.'

Related issues crop up from time-to-time. 'A society has been formed in China, called the "Heavenly Foot Society", which is attempting a crusade against the inhuman practice of binding the feet of women,'[34] we read in 1893. On the facing page of the same paper 'A shop assistant has been communicating her experiences of tight-lacing at a "fashionable West End establishment" to a contemporary. She says:

'It was continually being dinned into our ears by the manager that still tighter lacing was desirable, and it was even suggested that we should sleep in the corset. As soon as our whalebone prisons

152

were observed to stretch, new and narrower ones were provided. One girl, a niece of a partner in the firm, who had the "show" figure of us all, had a corset fitted with a metal belt secured by a tiny lock. She could loosen the top of her stays at night, but her waist could never expand without the knowledge of her aunt, in whose possession the key remained.' Added *The Gazette* cryptically: 'Such charges . . . ought to be supplemented with the name of the firm. If they have foundation we may be certain tight-lacing is not the only evil that springs from that "fashionable establishment".'

'Should Married Women with Families Go Out to Work?' formed banner headlines in 1900, with 'Our Special Commissioner says—"No!"' as its riposte. Promising 'startling facts on the moral and financial aspects of the question', page one treatment is given to the subject.[35] The following month *'Wanted: The Abolition of Barmaids'* was the provocative front page headline, whilst one need turn no further than the first issue of the paper to find 'The Servant Girls' Charter', the eight points of which were: 'Proper training, considerate treatment, decent sleeping accommodation, sufficient food, reasonable hours and vacations, religious liberty, the employment of sufficient servants, no compulsory beer-fetching.'[36]

'The Poor Man's Lawyer' provided a very real service in the columns of *The Gazette,* no charge being made, and confidence being rigidly maintained. Such answers as 'The fowl would be trespassing, but you would be liable if your dog killed it, especially as you are aware of the propensity of the dog', evoke much curiosity regarding the unpublished query.

'How I earned sixpence a day and lived on it'; cartoons about children under 16 not being allowed to 'buy booze'; and constant rumblings about 'the antiquated, cumbrous, costly, and totally inefficient system of poor relief', filled *The Gazette*'s columns. Five months of publishing behind it, it took stock of its 'aims and objects. . . . The *Gazette* has revealed an almost unoccupied field of journalism. It has rallied to the cause of social regeneration a steadily increasing following of benevolent, energetic and Christian men and women, who, with us, consider all attempts at the deliverance of the lower orders of society utterly utopian, unless they are framed and managed so as to bring down the constant inspiration of the Spirit of God. The *Gazette* has articulated the needs and views of the workers and friends of the great scheme with

153

which it is identified, and gives promise of becoming one of the most useful newspapers for keeping Great Britain awake to the social dangers which threaten it at every turn, by indicating how these dangers may be averted and their causes removed.'[37] Such, then, was the role of *The Social Gazette*.

WE make pause here to consider another of Susie Swift's skilfully sown seeds. Within two months of *In Darkest England and the Way Out* being published, and while all the world seemed agog over Frank Smith's resignation, an article from her pen, entitled 'Trotter Granny', appeared in *The Deliverer*. The old soul's gripping story is told with drama and determination, and it is evident by the penultimate paragraph that the good major has studied her General's scheme and found it wanting—in one respect at least: 'Is there going to be no corner in the Social Scheme for such as Trotter Granny? What about our thrifty, hard-working, *old* people? Must the day come when . . . Granny's old eyes dim and fade with only the dull blue wash of a workhouse ward before them? When rheumatism ties her sinewy arms into such knots that she can no longer carry her basket of trotters; when the little bottle of tea is no longer potent against the long shivering fits which end in a wearing, wearying cough; must she wear the remains of her old life out tending the fretful workhouse babies which are never thought too heavy or too wriggling for an old woman's arms, till she drops them on the floor in self-defence?'

'Oh, for a salvation almshouse! Will no one add *that* to the scheme?'[38] Silence.

Four years later, a leader in *The Darkest England Gazette*: 'A satisfactory evidence of the growth of the principles of the Darkest England Scheme has just been afforded by the proceedings of the Poor Law Conference. They would seem to indicate that a new era is dawning for the pauper. "Rattle his bones over the stones, he's only a pauper whom nobody owns," will, we may now hope, soon be a dirge of bygone days.

'Old-age pensions, though to our mind conferring a benefit at the latter, instead of, as the money should be applied, at the beginning of a man's career, show, nevertheless, a symptom of the new spirit to which we refer.'[39]

Another four years pass before Bramwell Booth writes thus: 'For a thousand years gone by, England had made some kind of

154

provision for her poor out of the funds of the community. The history of the laws for dealing with the aged, the imbecile, the vagrant, and the pauper in this country would make a thrilling story—and a laughable one as well. If anything was needed to prove to the world the uselessness of law without love to reform men, that history would make it clear! . . . The existing poor-laws have a most demoralising effect on the people. . . .

'Mr John Morley refers to only one aspect of the difficulty in the following from an address to the Eighty Club in 1889: "There is something very terrible in a system by which, when a man who has laboured and toiled all his life, grows old and infirm, and can toil no more, he is to be treated as if he had done something wrong, his home broken up, his children taken away from his control, and he, who would work but cannot, is to be bundled off to the workhouse with ne'er-do-wells, who could work but will not."'[40]

In 1909 state old-age pensions of 5s a week were first introduced for those over 70 whose income did not exceed 8s. Those who did receive 8s but less than 12s from other sources, had their state pension trimmed accordingly, whilst those whose private income soared beyond 12s a week received no state aid at all.[41]

Then, in *The Social Gazette* of 17 August 1912, Susie Swift's long dormant seed finally comes to fruition with mention of 'our eventide home, opened two years ago at Walthamstow'. Enlarging upon this, the Women's Social Work report for 1913 explains: 'The homes for the aged are our latest additions to the Women's Social Work, and have so far been managed by slum sisters who have extricated the dear old people from conditions of poverty and loneliness, as they have journeyed here and there in the dismal haunts of back streets, even of cellars and garrets.

'What can be more pathetic than to think of aged women, who have been respectable and trusted servants, yet have often outlived master and mistress, and who, being without the necessary means, have had to seriously face the time when the workhouse must receive them. . . . Of course, the old-age pension is a help, but there are women who are aged before 70, and what is to become of them? To solve a very small part of the difficulty, we have opened two eventide homes, where we receive women who are already 70, and others who, though they may not have quite reached that age, yet often, very often, need the care which they can obtain in these homes.' These first two, at Hampstead Garden Suburb and

Highams Park[42] (probably the previously mentioned Walthamstow home), were structured on the Norwegian sunset home idea.[43] Thirty years and several real estate legacies later, the Army in the United Kingdom was running 19 eventide homes for women, five for men and a 'retreat for aged couples'.[44]

Writing in the 1927 report of the Women's Social Work, Commissioner Catherine Bramwell-Booth confessed that during the year: 'Cases came to my notice that made me wonder whether I want to grow old.' Having no choice in the matter, she approached her 100th birthday 56 years later continuing to evidence this same concern for the elderly—most of whom were considerably younger than she! By that time (1983) increasing longevity had raised the total number of eventide homes to 39, an analysis of which strongly reflected sociological trends in that 16 catered for women, three for men, and 20 for both men and women.[45] The sheltered housing concept which has become so intrinsic a part of the Army's care facilities for the elderly in the second half of the 20th century seems a long way from Susie Swift's plea for a salvation almshouse. Nevertheless it is in this guise that the Trotter Grannies of the 1890s have finally found their vindication.

12
Where angels might be glad to find employment

WHEN the Founders' eldest grandchild (later to become Commissioner Catherine Bramwell-Booth) was but 10 years old, she wrote in exquisite copperplate to Mrs Major Stitt of Hadleigh Farm Colony:

April 11th 1894

Dear Mrs Sitt, [sic]

I don't know how to thank you for sending me such lovely flowers! it is so kind of you! Miriam and Mary both ask to have some put in their gardens; we shall go and plant them this morning when our lessons are over.

We are so fond of plants and animals, that we should like to live at the farm colony all together.

I hope your little baby is quite well! We were at the 'Two Days with God' on Monday! we enjoyed it very much. I hear there were 500 saved.

The dear General must be very tired.

Thanking you again,

Your loving little friend,

Catherine Booth[1]

Her 'dear General' would have approved. 'God didn't put Adam and Eve into a factory; he put them into a garden,'[2] he declared, pointing out the scriptural basis for his theory that one outcome of all his elevating and bridging must be to get men and women back to the land. To that end, the second part of his scheme for the reclamation of the 'submerged tenth' of Darkest England was the setting up the aforementioned farm colony at Hadleigh in Essex, 'past the cockle-beds and across the marshes' of the Thames estuary, three miles from Leigh, and five from Southend.

157

Consisting of an initial 800 acres at the time of its March 1891 purchase,[3] by the end of the year it had expanded to 1,000 acres of arable and grass land, with an additional 200 acres of waste land or 'saltings' giving promise of future recovery[4]—not to mention needful employ. Later expansion led to a 3,200 acreage.[5] The three-farms-become-one held within their boundaries the ruins of a castle constructed in 1231 by Hubert de Burgh, Earl of Kent,[3] a right of way to which brought the sightseeing public into close contact with the work of the colony from its inception.[6] The fact that the London, Tilbury and Southend Railway cut through these farm lands and that the Thames river and main London road bordered it south and north, meant that excellent transport facilities were to hand both for marketing produce and bringing in supplies. Salvation barges, operated by that part of the city colony known as the salvage brigade, now plied their way between Battersea wharf and Hadleigh, whilst tramlines were laid to connect the farm colony wharf with its three farms.[6] A random check shows that 300 barge trips were made, for instance, in 1894, containing among other things some 9,000 tons of manure and ashes, 1,500 tons of coal and coke, lime, chalk, sand, etc, while over a million colony-made bricks were sent away by river.[7]

By the end of 1891 cow-houses, sheepfolds, piggeries and stables were under construction, together with a dairy, a mill, factories to deal with farm produce, offices, stores and so on. 'Besides the old farmhouses on the estate, there have been erected, since May 2nd, five lofty and well-appointed dormitories . . . for the colonists, which will accommodate about 50 each. There is a dining-room to seat 300, with kitchen, pantries and store-rooms complete; also a wash-house, a laundry, a bathroom . . . and a commodious reading-room. . . . A nicely sheltered hospital' had, as its orderly-in-charge, *a duly qualified medical practitioner . . . one of the rescued.* He is under the supervision of a physician from Leigh, who attends twice a week. All these buildings, together with eight houses almost completed, for the use of officers, are built upon concrete foundations, the materials for which have been obtained from the gravel pits by the "unskilled" labourers.'[3]

These last are described in the *Orders and Regulations for the First Farm Colony* as 'men and women who, having from misfortune or any other cause lost their positions in life, are without employment, and desire to labour for their maintenance, and to be trained in habits of industry and honesty, in the hope that they will be able again to earn their own livelihood. . . .

'Colonists will generally be received from the elevators and shelters of the Army in London. . . . Each man or party of men will be accompanied with a return showing (a) his name, age, trade, and other personal particulars; (b) the nature of his conduct during his stay in the elevators; and (c) a medical certificate as to the condition of his health.'[3]

The elevating system, familiar to those coming from the Army's shelters, was early brought into operation at the farm. An agreement, signed by each colonist, bore on its reverse side the following information:

'The Colony is intended only for those who cannot obtain occupation elsewhere, and who are prepared to work, having shelter and maintenance only provided in exchange for their labour. Though the managers thus do not offer any wages, in order to encourage good workmen who will benefit the colony to a greater extent than the cost of their maintenance, in every case *after the first month* upon the colony, and in some cases before the end of the month, certain grants will be made under the following conditions:

'(1) All colonists, unless qualified for a special position at the end of the trial period named will be placed in one of three divisions: third class, who will be allowed 1s. per week; second class, who will be allowed 1s. 6d. per week; and first class, who will be allowed 2s.6d. per week.

'(2) The class in which any colonist will be placed will be settled by his superintendent before the end of the first month's trial.

'(3) From the first class will usually be selected, as required from time to time, special men for special positions as orderlies and foremen, who will have grants of special amounts.

'(4) If any colonist on arrival on the Colony is found to have special training for a particular position, the superintendent may offer him at once such special position without waiting for the end of the period of trial. Usually, however, the colonist will be placed either in the second or third class at the end of the trial period, his subsequent progress being entirely dependent upon his conduct and work.

'(5) The grants named are used first for the payment of any clothes or articles supplied to the colonists by the managers.

159

'(6) If the colonist owes nothing to the colony for clothes, &c., he may draw one third of his grant in cash, the remainder being left as a reserve fund, as provided in the rules. In cases where the superintendent thinks proper, he can allow the one-third in cash, even if the colonist owes something to the colony.

'(7) Each colonist will be provided with a card, which will show at the end of each week the amount of reserve to which he is entitled.

'(8) For any infringement of the rules, or negligence in work, a portion or the whole of the weekly grant may be stopped by order of the Director of the Colony and for more serious misconduct a colonist may be reduced to a lower class of grant or be discharged from the colony.'

Reported *The War Cry* of 26 September 1891: 'From the 15th September the whole of the colonists on the Hadleigh Farm Estate have been total abstainers. As it was not insisted that the dossers should be necessarily salvationists, so at first it was not made obligatory that they should become total abstainers. The latter condition, however, has been found essential to the well-being of the colony, and recently it was put to the 60 non-abstainers on the farm. The result was that only one declined the pledge, the remainder, 59, electing to remain under the new conditions. This self-denial shows well for the general satisfaction of the men.' As *The Social News* puts it a couple of months later: 'A brown field and a heavy lane are the best kind of inebriate asylums. They will prove far more effectual than even the watch and penalty by which liquor will undoubtedly be kept far from our colony.'

Susie Swift, who, on an earlier visit to the colony, had found herself accomplishing the last lap of the journey in the company of four travelling bags, a cornet case, one or two parcels, a bundle of boots, three or four milk-pans and a couple of fenders, felt herself obliged, in September 1892, to correct an impression which had appeared under her editorship in December 1891's *Brief Review of the First Year's Work* of the Darkest England Scheme. In it had been reprinted part of an article written for one of the leading reviews by the farm's consulting director, Harold E. Moore, FSI, MRAS,[3] which Major Swift prefaced by saying: 'Mr Moore is not a salvationist, and came to the colony unbiased by any theories born of previous experience in philanthropic or religious work. His opinions are certainly free from prejudice in our favour.' We here reproduce passages from the article, which, with hindsight, Major

160

Swift found it necessary if not to countermand, then at least to counterbalance. 'Those who have now learnt something of the operation and organisation of the colony will be asking to what extent does the experience . . . show that it will accomplish the objects for which it was acquired. At present it has not effected much, but on the other hand much can scarcely be expected from such an organisation within the first few months of starting, and before the necessary sufficient competent officers are appointed, or the necessary buildings erected. Some things, however, have been accomplished. Some of the colonists have been restored to the position in life for which they had received training. . . . Others are now on the colony gaining experience in their respective business, which they may have left long since, but which, through the assistance afforded them, they may be able to start again. Clerks of many years' experience are doing the work in the colony offices, in order that they may get back into training again, while a landscape painter is provided with materials, and gradually getting back the practice necessary for his work. In other cases, men with no training are being taught indoor trades . . . and in order to encourage them to get outside work, piece work is offered them on the terms of outside men as soon as they are competent. . . . Some few who have come on the colony have an ambition to work a small allotment farm, others wish to become gardeners, others wish to emigrate. All these are being assisted to attain the objects they have in view.

'The greater number, however, of the men are those who are well conducted, who perform satisfactorily all the work which is given them to do, but who have no ambition, no desire for the future, and no persons dependent upon them. These, though they perform willingly the work given them on the colony, even if their work would be worth a few shillings a week more outside, would yet prefer to remain where, as long as they work and are of good behaviour, they are provided for without difficulty on their part, and are free from the temptations of ordinary life and the risks of temporarily getting out of employment. . . .' Little here of the 'training school for emigrants'[8] material which Booth had envisaged when propounding his scheme; rather was it fuel for the fires of his critics.

Unabashed, Susie Swift sought to shed further enlightenment upon her reading public in a nine months later *All the World* article. 'One can quite understand that this may have appeared to be the temper of the first set of men brought down to the colony—

162

men whose spirits had been broken by privation, often the result of pure misfortune, or whose brain and nerve-power had been weakened by lack of nourishment or superabundance of stimulant. But when pure air and good food raised the tone of those men, they created round about themselves a more bracing moral atmosphere which had its effect from the very beginning upon after-comers; and the present governor emphatically confirms the conclusion to which our own observations had led us—i.e., that to say now that the "greater number" of our men would gladly settle down as social parasites, would be to libel our present colonists.

'Constantly, our malleable human clay is being moulded and hardened into fresh brick for the foundation of the oversea colony. Not *all* clay will make bricks. Not all men will make backboned oversea colonists. But with men as with bricks, there is much in the baking! And, curiously enough, brick-making seems to be one of the very best kinds of training for these men. It is immensely popular work. . . . When you hoe a hill of potatoes, somebody else digs them out next summer, and you don't *see* the result of your backache. But good, solid, hard work as brick-making is, you have, out of it, the satisfaction of flopping your finished article down by your side and reflecting till it is wheeled away, that you did it yourself. This alone is a pleasant sensation, if you have been, for several months, carrying sandwich boards on which you did not even paste the "ads".' And Susie Swift is off on a graphic description of the Hadleigh brick-making industry.

Benefits to the general public abounded at the farm colony: 'Upon receipt of a postal order for 10s. a splendid goose, weighing from 11 to 12 lb, will be sent direct, carriage paid, to any address. Write to "*The Governor,* Farm Colony" . . .', advised *The War Cry* as Christmas approached. 'So many friends have wished to come and view the operations of the colony, that the Park Farmhouse has been wholly set apart for their accommodation. . . . Guests are received here—always by previous arrangement—for single nights or by the week. Separate meals can be obtained at a very moderate tariff. . . .

'The refreshment-room, down near the castle, has grown up to meet the needs of the excursionists. . . . The colony bakery and kitchen do their part towards furnishing forth refreshments. . . .

'The Field Commissioner's excursion party of London soldiers last month proved that the colony is a splendid resort for large parties. The 2,500 whom the railway tickets showed must be somewhere about, found such ample space that there was no crush and no crowd.'⁶ Doubtless the aforesaid excursion party gladly availed themselves of the 'photographic studio' attached to the 'refreshment department, where portraits, groups, &c., may be taken at popular prices, and views of the Social Work and farm colony be obtained. A *dark room* for the use of amateurs upon application' was a further draw, and all this was stamped with the assurance 'All profits go to the benefit of the colony.'⁹

Announced *The Darkest England Gazette* for 20 January 1894: 'An important step has been taken by the Camberwell Board of Guardians, and one which has, perhaps, the most direct bearing on anything done, since the social scheme was launched, upon the practical question, "What shall we do with our able-bodied paupers?" The Local Government Board has sanctioned the Guardians . . . transferring able-bodied male inmates of the workhouse to our farm colony. Out of 50 who volunteered, 24 were selected by Major Stitt last week, and have since been appointed to the various branches of industry at Hadleigh. It is, of course, too early to speak of results. Meantime, we are glad to report that the arrangements, so far, have given mutual satisfaction.

'The colony receives from the Guardians five shillings per week per man, and the men, in addition to being provided with full subsistence, get a small weekly money grant, which is banked to their credit, so that on leaving they may have it to assist them in a new start. Many of the men may prefer to remain on the farm, take plots of land, and wait until the oversea colony is ready to receive them. The departure . . . carries, of course, its own interpretation— that the social scheme is rapidly coming to be recognised as having the main essentials for immediately relieving the distressed and preparing them to regain lost positions without demoralising either the helped or the general public.'

Faced with accusations by a Local Government Board inspector that out of 70 workhouse men sent to the colony 57 had left, and of these 30 had found their way back to the workhouse, 'Candle-ends' Stitt¹⁰ (so named because of his propensity for economy) 'expressed surprise. . . . If Mr Lockwood looked into the matter carefully . . . he would see reason for congratulation in the very figures that he finds fault with. The workhouse sent out 70 men, for which it was paying between 5s. and 8s. a week, according to the returns of the Local Government Board. . . . They sent them to us and agreed to pay us 5s. a week each for their support—the minimum sum, you will notice—and a few weeks after they are rid of over 50 per cent of them. I think the ratepayers in all the parishes would be pleased to see the cost of keeping their paupers cut down one-half every few weeks like that. . . .

'Then just think . . . what we do for these poor fellows. You mustn't suppose that it is an unalloyed pleasure to deal with them. If we take 40 out of 70 cases and either make them do well on our farm or put them out to other employment, or in any way make them self-supporting, the Local Government Board and Boards of Guardians are the last who ought to complain.'[11] And complain, for the most part, they did not. September 1895 marked the visit of Henry Chaplin, President of the Local Government Board, to the farm,[12] and although it needed the vigour of a W. T. Stead to bring the president's politely non-committal comments to life, he was certainly not critical. In an interview with *London* (described by the *Gazette* as 'That cleverly-managed, but rather vinegary weekly'[13]) Stead observed: 'I see that Mr Chaplin has at last taken Sir John Gorst's advice and gone to Hadleigh himself. That is the right thing to do. I wish that more people would go to Hadleigh and see what is being done. Few people could have been more prejudiced against the farm than Sir John Gorst. But I remember him telling me with great emphasis that all his prejudices melted before the facts which he saw. When he came back, he told Mr Chaplin he had seen a miracle. 'For', said he, 'I have seen casuals picked off London streets, converting Essex clay and Essex farms into a market garden,' and years ago he begged Mr Chaplin, interested as he has always been in agriculture, to go and see the experiment for himself. Now that Mr Chaplin is President of the Local Government Board, he has followed Sir John Gorst's example, and I cannot but hope that good results will follow.'[12]

In the colony visitors' book, Mr Chaplin, good visitor that he was, recorded that he was 'much indebted to the officers for the courtesy and kindness'[12] shown to him there. It was a courtesy and kindness not perhaps immediately evident in Colonel Stitt's previously reported reply to the critical Local Government Board inspector. Yet when a colonist from the professional classes was asked his opinion of the officers after nine months at Hadleigh, he confirmed Chaplin's view. 'Taken as a whole, they are a splendid lot of fellows, sympathetic and kind-hearted, and ever ready to do each and every man a good turn, and if I am allowed to make distinctions, I might mention the governor as a man with as kind a

165

heart as I ever met, ever ready to forgive; and although this was my first estimation of him, the longer I am brought into direct personal contact with him, the more I am convinced of its truth. He is frank, and maybe blunt, and rubs you hard at times, but that is what a sturdy man likes.'[14] Major Swift had already made her own assessment of the situation, recorded not in the visitors' book but in *All the World*: 'Softening, mellowing, ripening, expanding— that is what these poor fellows' cramped, sin-hardened, misery- shrivelled natures need. Good food, pure air, kind words, healthy moral tone in the actions of their officers, will do much toward this. The grace of God can do—*is* doing—more and most; and we never turn away from any bit of our social machinery, feeling so convinced that therein its dynamic power is comparatively unimpeded, as at the farm. Its only need is more officers, intelligent and devoted, loving God truly and deeply enough to love the colonists and to love one another; for friction among those who are over them means simply spiritual murder to these men, who must be taught their duty to their neighbour in syllables!'[15] As to the overtly 'religious' operations of the colony, our informant from the professional classes adjudged them as 'Religious freedom all round. Each man's religious principles are respected, if sincere and honestly acted out, and the greatest credit is due to the governor for the great tact he often displays, even when his own religious predilections are at stake. The one object and aim of the officers is to endeavour to make men "good", and here I am one with them, for I am convinced that unless a man has within him "grace", define it as you will, there is no sure guarantee for the future, and no sure hope for his ultimate recovery.'[14]

Five shillings per week per man from the Camberwell Board of Guardians and their imitators notwithstanding, the total deficit for the farm's year in 1895 was £5,900. Writing to the Army's Chancellor of the Exchequer, Commissioner George Pollard, Bramwell Booth analysed the situation. 'There is no doubt the seasons have been by far the worst we have ever had. The terrible frosts in the winter not only destroyed some of the crops, but lasted so long that the time for sowing and cultivation of others was lost. Then the drought in the summer lasted practically all the summer, that is to say, we were three months without rain, and a large part of it without water except for cattle and hardly that. . . .

'Agriculture generally is said to have had the very worst year ever known in this country. Bird told me that there were more farmers going through the court and being put into their homesteads as caretakers this Michaelmas than in any previous year since the Crimea War. . . . Calamity has followed calamity, and we have not escaped.

'Nevertheless, I am thoroughly dissatisfied with the result. If we cannot do better than others, then we ought to sell out, and when misfortunes multiply as they have done at Hadleigh in 1895, I consider the General is justified in saying that they have ceased to be misfortunes, that they have become mismanagements and mistakes. Still, you know how we have all toiled, and even if we have gone down, we have died hard.'[16]

Something had to be done, and done it was the following month in the guise of 'an important development of the Social Work of the Army', which, a *War Cry* editorial claimed, had been mooted 18 months previously at an international council. 'It has for some time been evident to Headquarters that great advantages would flow from the union under one commanding officer of two of the great sections of the Darkest England Scheme, namely, the city colony in London, and the industrial farm colony at Hadleigh. . . . The General has decided upon doing so under the command of Commissioner Cadman. The commissioner will take up his official residence on the farm colony and an assistant-governor will be appointed for the city colony, who will be second in command there, and who will, of course, reside in London. . . .

'Very few . . . have any idea of the extent of the business at Headquarters associated with the social work of the Army. In addition to the vast enterprise in this country, kindred work is springing up all over the world. . . .

'For some time it has been apparent a department specially to deal with this growing feature of Salvation Army operations ought to be created at Headquarters, under the direction of an experienced, capable officer. That department the General has now ordered to be set up at once and to its development he has appointed Colonel Stitt.'[17]

Remarked an Army journalist: 'When Commissioner Cadman, many years ago, had "his character told" by a phrenologist, he was informed that he would do well as an engineer, make a mark as a popular preacher, or excel in the capacity of relieving-officer!

'Could that phrenologist see him today in charge of Hadleigh

Farm Colony, he would find that his youthful subject had succeeded in combining the offices of all three!'[18]

Four years later, when Cadman 'farewelled' from the Men's Social Work after almost 10 years as its leader, reflections on the work appeared in the *Century Magazine*. Written by Sir Walter Besant (before his death that same year), it said of the colony: 'Every one of these men, if left to himself and his promptings, would cost the country (including his maintenance, without counting the loss of his labour, and including the expenses of prisons and police to take care of him) at least £100 a year. We have therefore a very simple sum: How much can the colony afford to lose every year and yet remain an economical gain to the country? On a roll of 250 there is the gain to the community of £25,000 a year. If, therefore, the Colony shows a deficit of £3,000 a year, the country is still a gainer by £22,000. Anyone may carry on this little calculation. Or suppose that 50 per cent of the cases prove failures, the remaining fifty still save the country £5,000 a year. And what is much more, they, being honest themselves, bring up their children to ways of honesty—their children and those who follow after. Who can calculate the gain thereby?'[19]

Another gain, some would claim, was that the farm colony was becoming 'respectable'. The Hon Cecil Rhodes and Lord Henry Loch, late High Commissioner for Africa, were among visitors in 1898.[20] 'Her Majesty the Queen has just bought three pens of cockerels and pullets from the poultry section of our farm colony', reported the *Gazette* in 1899. '*Hairdresser wanted* to take charge of the farm colony hairdressing saloon', advertised Colonel Lamb in 1901—and what could be more 'respectable' than that? His wife, however, had her feet firmly on the ground when, the same year, she advised: 'Mrs Colonel Lamb of the Industrial and Land Colony, Essex, also begs for old clothes and *large* boots and shoes for the poor fellows there.' By 1903 a school had been opened for the children of the colony and its surrounding district—a staff-captain having been given charge of proceedings. 'The attendances have gone steadily up, so much so that the Board of Education has agreed to the erection of another building, which will be built as quickly as possible to meet the need.'[21]

In the spring of 1905 *All the World* reported four classes of men to be working on the colony. 'First of all there are the men sent there by the Mansion House Committee, which has compassion on the London unemployed, their wives, and little ones. Then there is a contingent of men "planted out" by the *Daily Telegraph* readers for the purpose of preparing for emigration to Canada. Next come the men sent down by various workhouse authorities in the hope that they will acquire enough manliness and knowledge of manual labour to take themselves off the rates; and, finally, the colonists. . . . The first three classes are looked upon more or less as visitors, and although good influences are all around them they are not so closely linked up with Salvation Army effort as the colonists, who have nearly all come through the social institutions.'

By the time its coming of age was celebrated in 1912, this place 'where the angels might be glad to find employment' had received 6,870 men, of whom 4,297 had subsequently been sent to situations, 'thus showing that about 90 per cent regain their place as decent and useful members of society'.[22] The colony was to play an important role in the Army's emigration scheme, and over the years thousands of previously unemployed young men were successfully settled in British colonies, having learnt new skills at Hadleigh. During the First World War it catered for convalescing Belgian troops, and after the Second World War youngsters on probation were employed at the farm. In recent years small numbers of alcoholics have undergone rehabilitation there, as have prisoners and offenders on parole. In 1982 the function of the colony had come full circle: through the Manpower Services Commission a squad of 12 unemployed, supervised by conservationists, undertook a hedge-laying and planting project, enhancing the area and providing much-needed habitat for wild life.[23]

'A GREAT scheme of home colonisation, by which 200 of the workless poor and their families can be placed upon five-acre holdings and provided with cottages, seed, and stock, and supported until the holding provides enough to support the settlers and their families, is announced in a letter which the General, on Tuesday, December 19th, addressed to the King.' Whether or not this announcement brought an overplus of joy to the Royal Family's Christmas festivities *The Social Gazette* for 30 December 1905 does not record. The terms of the experiment, however, doubtless did. 'By the generosity of Mr George Herring a fund has been placed at my service which . . . amounts to £100,000, and is ultimately to be paid by us in annual instalments of £4,000 to Your Majesty's Hospital Fund.'

By the summer of 1910 Mr Herring had died,[24] but the scheme was provided for, and the Boxted Settlement (two-and-a-half miles out of Colchester) was formally opened in July by Earl Carrington, President of the Board of Agriculture.[25] 'The smallholders are all drawn from the working class. Very few of them have ever earned more than £1 per week. They are, of course, men of proven character, and enthusiastic for the success of the venture they have undertaken. . . . While the system of production is individualistic, the smallholders are getting the full benefit of co-operation both in the purchase of their supplies—seeds, manures, etc.—and also in the disposal of the produce grown. . . . Practical tuition is given not only in growing, but in grading and packing the produce, and in the adaptation of the best marketing methods. In the selection of men to whom this opportunity of self-establishment has been given, no regard has been paid to creed, but it has been insisted that every man shall be an abstainer.'[24]

But in spite of such stringent selection procedures, by the end of 1911 things had evidently—perhaps predictably—gone badly awry. 'Owing to their failure to observe the terms of their agreement upon which they were received at Boxted, and to the neglect of their smallholdings, several of the settlers were informed that they could not be accepted as permanent tenants.

'On hearing this a small number of them began to speak evil of the Army and of those who had tried in every possible way to advise and help them. They also refused to give up their cottages, and in some cases openly announced their intention to remain in them, neither cultivating their land, paying rent, nor keeping the rules of the scheme.

'As a consequence it became necessary, in order to protect the property of the undertaking and to fulfil the General's legal responsibilities to the fund, to commence proceedings to obtain possession of the holdings.'

The Charity Commissioners were invited by Bramwell Booth to make full inquiries into such complaints as were made against the Army by the recalcitrant tenants. This done, the Chief received a letter which read in part: 'The Commissioners recognize that the duty placed upon "the Director" to determine and superintend the operations of a charity so special in its objects involves very considerable labour and responsibility upon him and other officers

170

of The Salvation Army, and they desire me to express their appreciation of the manner in which that duty is being discharged.'

Continued *All the World*: 'As every thoughtful person knows who has any knowledge of such problems as the settlement of families on the land, it was not to be expected that all those who were placed on trial at Boxted would succeed or would be happy there; and it is obvious that those who prove unsuitable for the work and life of a smallholder should remove and make way for others who are more suitable.

'It was not until after two seasons, when the position of those who were not doing well was made apparent by the state of their ground, the absence of money, stock, or visible means of support, or by their own dissatisfaction or depression, that the General ordered the facts in each case to be fully considered. As a result . . . we made to some of them an offer of employment as labourers so as to give a further chance of training, still with the prospect of a holding later on, but with, in the meantime, a fixed income of 14s. per week and five-roomed cottage, piggery, and garden free. . . . Some accepted, but eight or 10 promptly rejected the offer of employment, and joined with the eight or nine whom we considered hopeless, to resist our efforts. Some outside agitators then appeared on the scene, and in response to our offers of generous treatment, money to get them back to friends, full value in cash for the little crops they had, introductions to work, and other helpful proposals, the men replied, rejecting it all, and saying *that they did not intend to give up the property of the charity.*'[26] What followed was described by an independent eye-witness in a letter to the national press as '. . . a demonstration of sham resistance and stage-managed "pathetic scenes".'

'There were five or six men present . . . who had nothing whatever to do with the differences between the settlers and the authorities, who were nothing but agitators and without whom there would have been no trouble at all.

'But what I want to tell the public is that . . . most of the "pathetic scenes" were faked . . . for the express purpose of the cinematograph machine which was on the spot.

'Take the case of the first house which was cleared. The man opened the door and was ready to go out. I was told he had another place ready to go to, and Colonel Iliffe offered him a lorry to remove his goods in, but this he refused, and insisted on his goods being put out on the highway, where he was photographed with all his goods and chattels round him, and a placard provided by one of the agitators for the purpose—a "pathetic picture" to order. This same man had walked out of his holding, but had forgotten his part and had to be reminded by the agitators that he must be "carried" out, and he accordingly laughingly returned, and was kindly carried out like a baby by a laughing constable, while the camera buzzed away, and another "pathetic scene" was recorded.'[27]

Pathetic scenes notwithstanding, 27 other families were at this time 'happily working towards a successful issue',[28] aided greatly, no doubt, by a weekly *Social Gazette* column 'For Smallholders', which featured such helpful articles as: 'Nettle Tea for Chickens', 'Sluggish Livers in Poultry', 'Goats' Winter Fodder', 'Cheese Shrinkage', and 'Trapping Wireworms'. By 1914, when Colonel Stitt was appointed to oversight the scheme,[29] 67 holdings—varying in size from four-and-a-half to seven acres—were operating in the 400-acre area. 'The scheme is being given a good trial, and in so far as reasonable success can be achieved, it is already deserved,' recorded the *Year Book*. Settlement of £65,000 having been paid over to the King Edward's Hospital Fund (as provided for by the terms of the original Herring agreement with William Booth), the scheme was eventually taken over by Smallholders Limited,[30] and the weekly *Gazette* column was no more.

THE third and final stage of William Booth's regenerative scheme was the oversea colony. 'To mention oversea is sufficient with some people to damn the scheme,' recognised its originator. Yet: 'The constant travelling of the colonists backwards and forwards to England makes it absurd to speak of the colonies as if they were a foreign land. They are simply pieces of Britain distributed about the world, enabling the Britisher to have access to the richest parts of the earth.'[31] Arrogant that may seem, but this was the age of 'Rule Britannia!' and upon such attitudes a nation with an area of 120,000 square miles and a population of 33 millions founded an empire covering eight million square miles of the globe's surface and 200 millions of the world's inhabitants.[32] No surprise should be occasioned therefore by the fact that Booth envisaged 'the transfer of the entire surplus population of this country . . . with enormous advantage to the people themselves, to this country, and the country of their adoption'.[33] As we shall see, the already settled inhabitants of Britain's colonies felt otherwise.

Compared with Booth's emigrants the Pilgrim Fathers, who sailed to America aboard *The Mayflower,* paled into insignificance: 'In the Salvation ship we shall export them all—father, mother, and children. The individuals will be grouped in families, and the families will, on the farm colony, have been for some months past more or less near neighbours, meeting each other in the field, in the workshops, and in the religious services. It will resemble nothing so much as the unmooring of a little piece of England, and towing it across the sea to find a safe anchorage in a sunnier clime. The ship which takes out emigrants will bring back the produce of the farms, and constant travelling to and fro will lead more than ever to the feeling that we and our ocean-sundered brethren are members of one family.'[34]

Where the salvation ship was to sail to was another matter. *The War Cry* for 17 September 1892 reported that Major Clibborn had lately landed at Plymouth, having been absent for three months inspecting farm and other suitable properties in Cape Colony, East Griqualand, Orange Free State and the Transvaal. In August of the following year *The Darkest England Gazette* featured a page one picture of 'Overcrowded England and England Over the Sea,' with the comment: 'It is well known that the over-the-sea colony of the social scheme has not been started, but equally well known, we hope, that the General is prepared to do so whenever he is provided with the necessary funds. If three years ago the magnitude of the need was felt, how much more must it be today? Wave after wave of commercial depression has forced into the great submerged sea thousands of able-bodied erstwhile bread-winners. What with tariff wars on the Continent and industrial wars at home, the shadow of the winter of '93 looks terribly dark. The general effect will be an augmentation of human misery in the great cities. . . . There is still neither time nor inclination in our legislative councils to consider a national remedy. Other topics hold the field.

'The monstrosity of this national neglect of what is beyond all question the most important social problem, is heightened by the fact that a remedy is to be found; a remedy that does not necessitate economical disturbance; a remedy that can be immediately applied, and a remedy that is both cheap and convenient. . . . It is the careful and systematic transfer of the people to the land'[35]—more specifically, to the colony-over-the-sea. This glorious enterprise the Army was willing to embark upon at once, the *Gazette* assured its readers, if substantial help was forthcoming.

Pointed out an East London Poor Law Guardian: 'The General

173

stated that if his scheme were adopted, in five years there would not be a pauper in London; but to-day there are more paupers than ever.' Pointed out the *Gazette*: 'The speaker, had he read the General's book, or the latest report upon the social scheme, never could have made such a reckless assertion. If the scheme, with its capital of one million pounds sterling, had been adopted, by this time, we venture to say, the London unemployed question would be within measurable distance of solution; but instead of one million—and what is that sum to a nation like ours?—only one-tenth was contributed, and because of the failure of the British public to subscribe the annual contribution of £30,000, the oversea section of the scheme could not be started. That section of the scheme was emphatically described as the arch-key to the whole. The grand success, so confidently predicted at the time, was plainly and repeatedly declared to be conditional upon the starting of the oversea colony.'[36]

Four months later the columns of the same paper manifested a slight shift in emphasis. 'A contemporary seems to think . . . that the want of funds has been the main hindrance to its realisation. While it is true that that fact has prevented the acquirement of several large tracts of land, the chief difficulty, and one which can only be appreciated by those who have tried colonisation schemes, has been fixing upon all-round suitable land.'[37] This, in spite of the fact that two weeks earlier a list of 38 countries and states had been printed, all of which had offered the Army land—'from the modest 10-acre plot up to millions of acres'.

By mid-January 1894 this slight shift of emphasis had come out into the open as a fully-fledged problem. What was holding up the oversea colony was not the lack of money, or the lack of suitable land, but a reluctance on the part of the colonies to yield up such suitable land to receive 'the residuum' of London's slumland. Under the heading 'Over-Sea Fears', the *Gazette* disclosed: 'A very sympathetic note appears in the *West Australian Mining Register* regarding our oversea colony proposals. This influential colonial journal considers our intentions to be wise, and wishes the scheme hearty success. Reverting to some observations passed by the *Pall Mall Gazette,* our contemporary, however, re-echoes the hope that in the event of Western Australia or any other British colony being finally selected, "the sweepings of the London slums" will not be flung into it. This really is unnecessary. The fears of the colonies are based upon the bitter experiences of convict "settlements", beside which our colonies will be as different as a prison is to a

174

happy home. . . . When the safeguards promised by the General are carried out, we venture to say that the men who will be sent to a better land will be among the worthiest that ever left these shores with similar aims in view. Moreover, as the *Pall Mall* stated, the General would be, indeed, ill-advised if he did not select good sound bone and sinew for his oversea colony.'[38]

The *West Australian* (presumably a different publication) vigorously asserted that 'when people are required to develop and cultivate Western Australia's vast areas of waste lands, more particularly in the South-East and South-West Divisions, where a large population is essential, it is not to be supposed that she will refuse attention to a scheme for the condemnation of which, if well conceived and managed, no sufficient grounds have been proved to exist. . . . If General Booth can give us men trained, and capable of being trained, to agricultural work it would be folly not to accept the offer. They are just the sort of colonists we need.'[39] Even so, little more is heard of the suggestion.

In February 1895 Reuter's Press Agency felt the subject newsworthy enough to flash round the world the fact that 'General Booth, of The Salvation Army, was entertained last night at a dinner given at the residence of the Earl of Aberdeen, the Governor-General of Canada, at which the cabinet ministers were also present.

'The General asked that a grant might be made to him of a large section of land in the north-west on which he might settle graduates of the Salvation Army farm in England.

'Sir Mackenzie Bowell, the Premier, in reply, expressed himself in favour of the scheme. He saw that there were difficulties in the way, but said that they might be overcome.'[40] They *might,* but they *weren't*—in spite of the fact that an announcement was made in June to the effect that 'Colonel Stitt and Brigadier Clibborn, two able and experienced officers, assisted by Mr Lawford, a true and tried friend as well as an expert in everything that pertains to agriculture, will proceed almost immediately to inspect certain sites in Canada. . . . I understand that the appointment of this committee of enquiry does not signify the committal of the General to Canada, although it is to be hoped that it will be successful by its report in ultimately doing so. God speed the trio!'[41] It remains a moot point whether God chose not to, or whether he was prevented from so doing by the Canadian authorities.

By the end of 1896 exasperation was setting in. In his *Notes on the Darkest England Scheme* Booth revealed: 'I have . . . still one bold generous offer awaiting further inquiry which is not likely to be defeated by selfish and ignorant prejudice. This, at the moment, appears to be my last hope of realising my purpose as it regards the oversea colony under the British flag, to which I have hitherto so tenaciously clung. Should that prove another disappointment, I must reconsider some of the generous offers that have been made elsewhere.'

The remaining stages in the saga of William Booth's quest to found an oversea colony are outlined by Frederick Coutts in *Bread For My Neighbour* (Hodder and Stoughton, 1978), which also gives a fuller treatment of both the farm colony and the emigration scheme. Sufficient is it for our present purposes to note that though the idea of the oversea colony as such came to naught, the emigration scheme which was to have fed it prospered over many years.

We have already marked the fact that in an early 1885 *War Cry* Mrs Bramwell Booth appealed for information as to how she could assist those of her rescue girls who wished to emigrate to do so (chapter 2). In April of that year *All the World* reported that Hanbury Street Refuge was 'jubilant . . . over a letter from the very first girl who ever came into the refuge. After having earned a good character in a situation, she was, by the kindness of some friends in Whitechapel, enabled to emigrate, and writes from her situation in Canada. She says she realised when crossing the ocean that "the past was under the blood", and that, if the ship went down, Heaven's gates were open for her.' That emigration was a subject surrounded by fears at this time comes over very clearly in a series of interviews with unemployed Black Country iron workers which *The War Cry* featured the following year. '"Why not emigrate?" was the question I repeated as I went from house to house. "Why sit still and starve when you might be doing well in another country?" . . .'

'"No, no, it's safe for we to stop at home, where coal is to be had cheap and the landlord trusts we for the rent, than turn out these times!" . . .'

'Remarked another, "What sort o' work is to be got abroad? Folks do say it's awful bad everywhere. Best stop where there's a roof-tree, and an oven to bake the bread when a bit of flour's to be got, than go abroad and die under the bushes.''' [42]

A month later the Devonshire House prison gate home reported, 'One of the youngest members of our family circle . . . has left us this week for Manitoba', [43] his passage being paid for by friends of the Army.

Writing from his Canadian command in May 1887, Commissioner Coombs requested: 'Will all soldiers intending or wishing to emigrate to Canada this summer, please inform us beforehand. Commissioner Coombs undertakes to find any number of situations for servant girls, with characters from employers and captains, who can have every liberty to attend Army meetings, wear uniform, etc., with higher wages than in this country.

'He also undertakes to arrange for settling soldiers capable of farm labour on government land out west, if sufficiently large companies can be arranged for.'

No sooner did Elijah Cadman find himself in command of the Social Wing four years later, than he inserted the following intimation in *The War Cry*:

Emigration

'Soldiers of the Army, and others, who desire to emigrate to the colonies or elsewhere, should communicate at once with Commissioner Cadman, International Headquarters, from whom they will receive fullest information as to the best countries to go to, cost of passage and outfit, the trades most in demand, and fullest particulars as to the course they should take.

'It is intended that the Social Wing should give the fullest attention to this subject. A great deal of valuable information has already been obtained, not only from the various governments and shipping companies, but also from our own officers in all parts of the world.' [44]

In November 1891 it was announced under the same heading: 'In the nine months of this department's existence we have dealt with some 700 applicants for abroad. Advice has been given in each case, and many letters of introduction to our officers and friends abroad. Some 95 emigrants have booked through our office, and we have received nearly £900 on account of passage-money. In a

177

goodly number of cases situations have been arranged beforehand, and many who were living in distress, and almost in a state of destitution here, are now doing well and prospering in the land of their adoption.'[45] Furthermore, 'farm labourers, single or married, can earn about three times the wages they are getting in this country, in Western Australia. The agent-general will pay half-passage money to all accepted parties.'[46]

Major Swift's *Brief Review of the First Year's Work of the Darkest England Scheme* points out that: 'These emigrants should not be confounded with our own proposed colonists. These 98' (three more had added themselves to the number since the November statistics were published) 'have gone on their own account, to settle in places of their own choice, and will be entirely independent of the Army, although we have, in nearly every case, given letters of introduction to our officers abroad'. In most cases their passages would have been booked through The Salvation Army Shipping Department, whose advertisements jostled those of the Emigration Department for *War Cry* space.[47]

Ten years later *Friends of the Poor,* the annual social report for 1901, showed in its statement of accounts an expenditure of £167 15s. 5d. for 'passages to Canada, &c.' This ties up with word in the Army's official history that the first batch of men to emigrate from Hadleigh had left in 1901.[48] *Precipices,* the report for 1904, advised readers that '£42,000 is needed during 1904-5 for the maintenance of the social operations. . . . For assisting suitable men and women to emigrate—£3,000 is needed.' Three years after this the *Year Book* reported: 'Many of the applicants were without the means to pay the cost of their transfer to the colonies where work waited them; but fortunately, we were in a position to assist by way of loan some of the most urgent and promising applicants, and during the past three years over 15,000 people have emigrated through our agency. The proportion of the repayments already made is a most gratifying feature of the work, and some of the loans of 1904 have been repaid, and are again in circulation in 1906.'

By 1904 a weekly 'Emigration Advice Bureau' had begun to appear on the back page of *The Social Gazette,* earlier pages often featuring 'before' and 'after' stories of farm colonists or complete salvationist families who had been helped to emigrate to Canada, as well as reports of fresh consignments being dispatched. Hints for such as these appeared also in *Emigration Gazette,* an occasional paper published by the department. 'Do not forget that, although you are at sea, you are still in Christian waters. Grace before and after each meal should never be forgotten.'

'Put your cap in your pocket when you land, and don your best hat. Also discard your leggings until you want them at work, which will be soon enough to wear them.'

'Don't brag and tell the Canadians that the country belongs to *you*. You will find them remarkably nice people, and very easy to get on with. Don't tell them how to do their work! They have their own methods.'[49]

With the passage of time it became evident that advice on the subject needed to be handed out to more than the emigrant. An article in *The Field Officer* by Commissioner David Lamb, head of the Emigration Department, rounded upon those corps officers who bemoaned the fact that so many of their soldiery were taking advantage of the Army's scheme and emigrating. 'I remember enquiring into a complaint about a band which had been seriously crippled by the emigration of a number of its members. What did I find? This simple fact—that six out of the eight emigrants had been out of work for weeks and saw no prospect of work being found for them in their town. And yet the FO (and the DC!) complained because the Emigration Department . . . found work for these comrades and helped them to get to it!

'I heard of another band which had "gone to pieces" because of the Emigration Department—two thirds of the band having emigrated at one time! Investigation here showed that the band originally consisted of three members—that one, a married man, had been out of work for some time—saw no prospects at home— emigrated, taking with him his son—the second "third" of the band—and there is the whole story!'[50]

When it is discovered, however, that as early as 1904 Lamb was offering to send not only the 25 bandsmen requested by a job-providing North American bandmaster, but 100 of the same,[51] one cannot help feeling some slight twinge of sympathy for the beleaguered British FO (corps officer).

Salvationists were by no means the only folk emigrating under the auspices of The Salvation Army, and consequently it was a problem that perplexed far more than the field officer. By 1905 the

Army had chartered its first steamship,[52] filling it with over 1,000 emigrants, 600 of whom were wage-earners. The setting up of a labour bureau on board by Canadian salvationists meant that all 600 had secured employment before disembarking. The following year the Army secured four voyages by chartered ship, a full complement of 1,250 passengers on each trip.[53] By 1910 some 50,000 had been helped to emigrate by them. That same year H. Rider Haggard wrote of 'the sorrow that I felt at seeing so many men in the prime of life leaving the shores of their country for ever, especially as most of them were not married. This meant, amongst other things, that an equal number of women who remained behind were deprived of the possibility of obtaining a husband in a country in which the females already outnumbered the males by more than a million. . . .'

'"Give us your best," say the colonies. "Give us your adult, healthy men and women whom you have paid to rear and educate, but don't bother us with families of children whom we have to house. Above all send us no damaged articles. You are welcome to keep those at home.". . .

'Can we afford to go on parting with the good and retaining the less desirable? On this subject I had a long argument with Colonel Lamb, and his answer to the question was in the affirmative, although I must admit that his reasons did not at all convince me. He seemed to believe that we could send out 250,000 people, chosen people, per annum for the next 10 years without harm to ourselves. Well, it may be so.'[54] Three years later Lamb went on record as saying: 'There are 45,000 widows, with 120,000 dependent children, in the British Isles in receipt of Poor Law relief, and there are probably an equal number just as deserving, struggling on without Poor Law assistance. . . .

'It is well known that in the British Isles there is an excess of nearly two million women over men; that the average weekly wage of the working woman is about 7s.—factors which must, as the world is at present run, tell against the working woman who is also a widow, in her struggles. It is also well known that in the King's dominions overseas there is an excess of men over women, and thus—quite apart from the fact, which is frankly, if not publicly, accepted, that re-marriage will frequently be found a satisfactory and happy 'way out'—there will at once be open to her and her children in the new lands opportunities which the Old Land would never have presented.

'Then there is that great army of children—estimated at over 200,000—who are mostly 'unwanted' in the sense that they are for one reason or another, and in various ways, maintained by the state or the charitable public. The cost to the community, including the children of the widows referred to above, is at least 10 million pounds per annum.

'Under these circumstances it is not to be wondered at that many of the boys pass quickly into 'blind-alley' occupations, and the girls, growing up without a mother's care and love, frequently become a further source of anxiety and expense as the years go by.

'It is to meet this sad condition of affairs that the latest development of the Army's emigration operations has been devised.'[55]

The 1922 Empire Settlement Act[56] added further impetus to emigration schemes such as the Army's, and although it would probably prove impossible to estimate the number in erstwhile British colonies who owe today's 'good life' to the fact that once upon a time, in desperation, their 'Old Country' forebears answered the advertisements inviting them to communicate with Coombs, or Cadman, or Lamb, or Bullard, of The Salvation Army, from time to time a story is pieced together which helps to place in perspective the well-being of many generations. Take the story of Tom Nash, for instance.

On 15 October 1971 this jeweller from Brisbane, Australia, called at the Army's International Headquarters during a brief visit to London. It was important to him that he included The Salvation Army in his itinerary for that day because he wanted to express his thanks for the good start given him on 15 October 1927, when, as one of 700 emigrants, he sailed for Australia on a ship chartered by the Army. As 44-year-old evidence, he produced the Bible given him by General Bramwell Booth on that occasion. Now, an alderman, a justice of the peace, and a patron of all manner of good causes (including the Army's Boothville hospital), Tom Nash found himself shaking hands with the manager of the Migration and Travel Department, Lieut-Colonel Ronald Topley, who, as a teenaged employee of the Emigration Department, had played a not inconsequential part in helping another teenager towards his brave new world.[57]

In a strange way Tom Nash's story is linked with that of

Commissioner Leslie Pindred (R), well-known Canadian salvationist. Mrs Major Miriam Evenden, Director of Historical Research at the George Scott Railton Heritage Centre in Toronto, takes up the story: 'Leslie Pindred was born in June of 1911 in Inverness, in the highlands of Scotland, to Salvation Army officer parents. Two brothers and a sister were added to the family by the time he was nine years old. His mother's death, at 40 years of age, precipitated his father's resignation from officership and a temporary break-up of the family. . . . Once a month Mr Pindred visited the boys' home where Leslie lived for two years, and on those occasions father and son attended The Salvation Army. It was during a service conducted by the Chief of the Staff, Commissioner Edward Higgins, that Leslie was gloriously converted.

'Reunited with the father he idolised, Leslie became an enthusiastic and ardent salvationist. At 12 years of age he was record sergeant in the corps originally begun in his father's home. At 14 he was happily immersed in a multitude of young people's activities at the corps and thoroughly enjoying the challenges of grammar school. Change, however, was on the horizon.

'Leslie's father decided to emigrate to Australia. As eldest son it was to be his responsibility to precede the family to the land of opportunity and pave the way for them. Arrangements were made for him to travel to London and then on to The Salvation Army's land colony at Hadleigh. Unnerved by the unexpected turn of events, Leslie's anxiety was tempered by the cheerful efficient staff, the crash course on mixed farming, and the companionship of high-spirited young men who, like himself, were embarked on a great adventure.

'At the end of five weeks he was devastated to discover that the Australian Government had turned him down because he did not measure up to their physical requirements . . . by seven pounds. His father could not be speedily contacted and pride would not allow him to return home to family and friends. He decided to accept the other option open to him and emigrate to Canada.

'During the summer of 1926 Leslie Pindred arrived in Smith Falls, Ontario, and proceeded to a farm near Stittsville. The Dawsons, for whom he worked, were Plymouth Brethren. They nurtured his faith and encouraged him to finish his education. In

1932 Leslie Pindred entered The Salvation Army training college, from Smith Falls.

'Exactly 40 years from the day "his plans were altered", he received marching orders from General Frederick Coutts, appointing him as Chief Secretary to the Australia Eastern Territory'[58] where that other erstwhile boy emigrant, Tom Nash, was now a prosperous business man and a staunch supporter of The Salvation Army.

What was it William Booth had said in 1889? 'You don't need novels if you come to The Salvation Army. There is nothing in any of them so romantic as the things that are happening every day among us.'[59] And upon such a claim we make so bold as to rest our case.

End piece

THE tale of the beginnings of The Salvation Army's social services is far from being told. On the threshold of its second century new departures are still coming to pass, while much that was pioneered in Christian Mission days is yet fulfilling a vital role in the welfare state of which it was the forerunner. The years between have their own tale to tell—which must be left for another occasion. Through all those years, however, the staff of the Army's Social Services have sought, in their Founder's words, 'to observe continually the sacrament of the Good Samaritan'.

On 1 April 1978 the Men's and Women's Social Services were for the first time amalgamated under one administration. Although the Army's Social Work is a direct offshoot of its evangelism, as we have seen, in the United Kingdom it was made a separate operation by virtue of a deed executed by the Founder at a public meeting on 30 January 1891. Originally called the Darkest England Scheme, it is now referred to as the Social Trust Deed.

'For the poor shall never cease out of the land: therefore I command thee, saying, Thou shalt open thine hand unto thy brother, to thy poor, and to thy needy, in thy land' (Deuteronomy 15:11).

Leaders

1884 Mrs Florence Booth

1912 Commissioner Adelaide Cox

1926 Colonel (later Commissioner)
Catherine Booth

1930 Lieut-Commissioner Mrs
Agnes Povlsen

1932 Commissioner Catherine
Bramwell-Booth

1940 Mrs Commissioner Edith
Cunningham
(Joint leader with
Colonel Mrs Phillis Taylor)

1942 Lieut-Commissioner (later
Commissioner) Mrs Phillis Taylor

1947 Colonel (later Lieut-
Commissioner) Janet Allan

Governors

(Men's Social Work)

1890 Commissioner Frank Smith

1890 Commissioner Elijah Cadman

1900 Commissioner Randolph Sturgess

1914 Colonel John B. Laurie

1920 Colonel (later Lieut-
Commissioner) William Iliffe

1924 Colonel (later Lieut-
Commissioner) George Jolliffe

1930 Commissioner Charles Sowton

1930 Lieut-Commissioner (later
Commissioner) George Langdon

1936 Commissioner George Jolliffe

1939 Lieut-Commissioner (later
Commissioner) John F. Lewis

1942 Lieut-Commissioner (later
Commissioner) Ranulph Astbury

1944 Commissioner Alfred Barnett

185

1947 Lieut-Commissioner (later Commissioner) H. George Bowyer

1951 Mrs General Phillis Orsborn

1952 Lieut-Commissioner (later Commissioner) Emma Davies

1953 Lieut-Commissioner (later Commissioner) M. Owen Culshaw

1959 Lieut-Commissioner (later Commissioner Dorothy Muirhead

1960 Lieut-Commissioner (later Commissioner) William F. Cooper

1964 Lieut-Commissioner (later Commissioner) Herbert Westcott

1968 Lieut-Commissioner (later Commissioner) Julia Tickner

1968 Commissioner Albert E. Mingay

1969 Commissioner Ernest Fewster

1973 Colonel (Dr) William McAllister

1975 Colonel Eva Burrows

1977 Colonel Anna Hannevik

1978 amalgamation

Leaders

Salvation Army Social Services (GB)

1978 Colonel (later Commissioner) Anna Hannevik

1982 Colonel Roy Lovatt

1987 Colonel Frank Fullarton

1991 Colonel Margaret White

1995 Lieut-Colonel Trevor Tribble

1997 Amalgamation with The UK Territory Programme Service

186

Sources

AUTHOR and publisher are listed at the first appearance of each book. Thereafter only the title is given.

CHAPTER ONE: The destitute poor and the suffering saints

1 *All the World,* Dec 1893, p 477.
2 *The History of The Salvation Army,* Sandall, vol 1, p 48 (Nelson, 1947).
3 *Twenty-one Years Salvation Army,* Railton (1886), pp 37-38.
4 *Christian World,* 15 Feb 1867.
5 *The Christian Mission Magazine,* Feb 1870, p 25, Mar 1870, p 41.
6 *Heathen England,* Railton (1877), p 107.
7 *The History,* vol 1, p 83.
8 *The Christian Mission Magazine,* Dec 1870, p 182.
9 Ibid, Jan 1871, p 10.
10 Quoted in Ibid, Nov 1874, p 316.
11 *The East London Evangelist,* Dec 1868, p 47.
12 *The History,* vol 1, p 195.
13 *Echoes and Memories,* Bramwell Booth, p 1 (Hodder & Stoughton, 1925).
14 *Work in Darkest England* (1894), p 17.
15 *The War Cry,* 7 Sep 1889, p 9.
16 Quoted in Ibid, 14 Sep 1889, p 7.
17 Quoted in Ibid, 28 Sep 1889, p 2.
18 Ibid, 26 Jan 1889, p 3.
19 Ibid, 16 Feb 1889, p 2.
20 Ibid, 14 Sep 1889, p 7.
21 Ibid, 28 Sep 1889, p 8.
22 Ibid, 7 Sep 1889, p 2.
23 Ibid, p 9.
24 Unpublished letter, 13 Aug 1906.
25 *The History,* vol 1, p 244.
26 *Round the Clock* (1917), p 90.

CHAPTER TWO: Saving a girl for seven pounds

1 *International Social Council Addresses* (1911), p 3.
2 *The History,* vol 1, p 84.
3 *The Deliverer,* May 1921, p 37.
4 *The History,* vol 1, p 243.
5 *Maiden Tribute,* Unsworth, p 4 (SP & S, Ltd, 1949).
6 Note confusion caused by Edmonds back-dating material from 1883 as though happening in 1882. However, his diaries and *The War Cry* confirm an 1883 opening.
7 *The History of The Salvation Army,* Sandall, vol 3, pp 11-12 (Nelson, 1955).

8 *The War Cry,* 1 May 1886, p 13.
9 *Maiden Tribute,* p 7 footnote.
10 *Life of William Booth,* Begbie, vol 2, p 388 (Macmillan, 1920).
11 *Catherine Booth,* C. Bramwell-Booth, p 388 (Hodder & Stoughton, 1970).
12 *All the World,* Feb 1888, p 84.
13 *The Deliverer,* Nov 1928, p 86.
14 *The War Cry,* 29 Jan 1887, p 8.
15 Ibid, 14 Jan 1893, p 9.
16 *Maiden Tribute,* p. 39.
17 *All the World,* Jan 1893, p 5.
18 *Sunday Circle,* 18 Mar 1933.
19 *The Deliverer,* Jul 1904, p 2.
20 *The Salvation War* (1884), p 146.
21 *The War Cry,* 25 Oct 1884, p 4.
22 *All the World,* Feb 1885, p 27.
23 *The War Cry,* 6 Feb 1886, p 2.
24 Rebecca Jarrett's unpublished memoirs.
25 Booth family oral tradition, related by Lieut-Colonel Olive Booth, 17 Jul 1981.
26 See: *Maiden Tribute,* Unsworth (SP & S, Ltd, 1949)
         The Maiden Tribute, Terrot (Muller, 1959)
         The Age of Consent, Stafford (Hodder & Stoughton, 1964)
         The Case of Eliza Armstrong, Plowden (BBC, 1974).
27 *The Case of Eliza Armstrong,* p 16.
28 *The Deliverer,* Apr 1928, p 9.
29 *The War Cry,* 23 Jun 1888, p 8.
30 Ibid, 8 Jun 1889, p 5.
31 *A Brief Review of the First Year's Work* (1891), p 117.
32 *The War Cry,* 17 Jan 1885, p 3.
33 Ibid, 2 Oct 1886, p 9.
34 *The Darkest England Gazette,* 26 Aug 1893, p 6.
35 *Pall Mall Gazette,* quoted in *The War Cry,* 18 Mar 1885, p 3.
36 *The Deliverer,* Jan 1900, p 107.
37 *The Midnight Patrol,* Thompson, pp 55-57 (Hodder & Stoughton, 1974).
38 Ibid, p 109.
39 Interview with Colonel Roy Lovatt, 18 Oct 1982.
40 *The Midnight Patrol,* p 51.
41 *The War Cry,* 26 Jul 1888, p 9.
42 *All the World,* Nov 1889, p 511.
43 *The War Cry,* 28 Jan 1888, p 4.
44 *The Deliverer,* Aug 1891, p 30.
45 Ibid, Oct 1891, p 52.

CHAPTER THREE: The double difficulty

1 *The Salvation War* (1884), p 145.
2 *All the World,* Apr 1885, p 87.
3 *The War Cry,* 28 Jul 1888, p 9.
4 Ibid, 29 Jun 1889, pp 3-4.
5 Unpublished Receiving House Statements, Book 1, p 16a (1886).
6 Ibid, p 61a.
7 Ibid, p 68a.
8 Ibid, p 116a.
9 *The War Cry,* 2 Oct 1886, p 9.

10 Book 1, p 127a.
11 Ibid, p 139a.
12 Book 3, p 27.
13 Ibid, p 102.
14 Book 1, p 295.
15 Nineteenth century street map, City of London Reference Library.
16 Book 1, p 370a.
17 Ibid, p 405.
18 Ibid, p 501.
19 *The Deliverer,* Jul 1889, p 11.
20 Ibid, p 9.
21 Ibid, p 10.
22 Ibid, Jan 1890, p 83.
23 Book 3, p 53.
24 *The History,* vol 3, p 53.
25 Book 3, p 486.
26 Ibid, p 411.
27 Ibid, p 448.
28 *The War Cry,* 29 Mar 1890, p 8.
29 *The Deliverer,* Jan 1890, p 79.
30 *The Christian Mission Magazine,* Sep 1878, pp 231-244.
31 *The Deliverer,* Jun 1896, p 187.
32 Ibid, Aug 1909, p 123.
33 *Rescue Notes,* Jun 1887.
34 *The Deliverer,* Aug 1892, p 23.
35 Nineteenth century street directory, City of London Reference Library.
36 *Work in Darkest England* (1894).
37 *A Brief Review of the First Year's Work* (1891), p 115.
38 *The War Cry,* 23 May 1896, p 4.
39 *Light in Darkest England* (1895), p 109.
40 *All the World,* May 1897, p 216.
41 *The Deliverer,* Jan 1898, p 104.
42 *The War Cry,* 7 Aug 1897, p 8.
43 Ibid, 16 Nov 1918, p 3.

CHAPTER FOUR: **Strictly confidential**

1 *The War Cry,* 9 Mar 1882, p 4.
2 Ibid, 18 Jul 1885, p 1.
3 Ibid, 8 Aug 1885, p 1.
4 Ibid, 8 May 1886, p 6.
5 Book 1, p 21a
6 *The War Cry,* 8 Jun 1889, p 5.
7 *The Deliverer,* Dec 1891, p 89.
8 *The War Cry,* 17 Sep 1892, p 2.
9 *The Salvation Army Year Book* (1910), p 13.
10 *In Darkest England and the Way Out,* William Booth, pp 233-235 (1890).
11 *The Social News Supplement to The War Cry,* 6 Feb 1892, p 4.
12 Ibid, 5 Mar 1892, p 6.
13 *The Social Gazette,* 2 Feb 1895, p 4.
14 *Reconciled* (1927), p 6.
15 *The Salvation Army Year Book* (1951), p 26.
16 Statement: Family Policy in the UK (1979).

CHAPTER FIVE: Emma's orphans

1 *The Christian Mission Magazine,* Jul 1877, p 175.
2 Ibid, Nov 1878, p 305.
3 *The Salvationist,* Jul 1879, p 170.
4 *The War Cry,* 18 Apr 1883, p 2.
5 *Echoes and Memories,* p 157.
6 The 1881 Census shows Harry Andrews as five years old.
7 *THK,* Wiggins, p 22 (SP & S, Ltd, 1956).
8 Unpublished letter, 3 May 1887.
9 Unpublished letter from Ballington Booth to Bramwell Booth, 17 Jun 1890.
10 *The War Cry,* 2 Oct 1886, p 9.
11 *All the World,* Feb 1888, p 66.
12 *The Deliverer,* Dec 1891, p 89.
13 *The Social Gazette,* 18 Nov 1899, p 3.
14 *All the World,* Feb 1888, p 67.
15 *The History,* vol 3, p 217.
16 *The War Cry,* 7 Mar 1885, p 1.
17 Quoted in *The War Cry,* 21 Jan 1885, p 3.
18 Quoted in Ibid, 24 Jan 1885, p 2.
19 *All the World,* Feb 1889, p 82.
20 *The War Cry,* 23 Feb 1889, p 9.
21 Ibid, 11 Jan 1890, p 9.
22 *In Darkest England and the Way Out,* p 201.
23 *The War Cry,* 10 Mar 1888, p 2.
24 *All the World,* Oct 1889, p 480.
25 *The War Cry,* 14 Sep 1889, p 7.
26 *In Darkest England and the Way Out,* p 94.
27 *The Social News,* 5 Dec 1891, p 5.
28 *All the World,* Mar 1892, p 209.
29 *In Darkest England and the Way Out,* p 65.
30 *The War Cry,* 8 Nov 1890, p 5.
31 Ibid, 27 Aug 1892, p 11.
32 *The Deliverer,* Feb 1895, p 124.
33 *The Social Gazette,* 10 Aug 1895, p 2.
34 *Light in Darkest England* (1895), p 66.
35 *The Social Gazette,* 22 Jun 1895, p 1.
36 *Victorian England,* Reader, p 126 (Book Club Associates, 1973).
37 *The Deliverer,* Oct-Nov 1944, p 139.
38 Ibid, Jun 1901, p 195.
39 Ibid, Jul 1901, p 14.
40 Ibid, Mar 1901, p 152.
41 Ibid, Mar 1902, p 131.
42 *The Advantages of Vegetarian Diet,* Bramwell Booth (undated pamphlet).
43 *The Social Gazette,* 18 Jan 1902, p 3.
44 *The International Social Council* (1921), pp 109-134.

CHAPTER SIX: Adequate boy-mending machinery

1 *A Brief Review of the First Year's Work* (1891), p 76.
2 *The Social News Supplement,* 4 Jun 1892, p 5.
3 *All the World,* Dec 1892, p 450.

4 *The War Cry,* 25 Sep 1897, p 3.
5 *The Social Gazette,* 10 Mar 1900, p 3.
6 *The Salvation Army Year Book* (1953), p 43.
7 *Some Aspects of Salvation Army Social Work* (1911), p 146.
8 *The Social Gazette,* 9 Jul 1910, p 2.
9 *Some Aspects of Salvation Army Social Work* (1911), p 149.
10 *The Salvation Army Year Book* (1942-44).
11 Men's Social Work History Book (unpublished).
12 *The Salvation Army Year Book* (1945), p 24.
13 Ibid (1953), p 43.
14 Ibid (1943), p 35.
15 *The Deliverer,* Feb-Mar 1942, p 11.
16 Ibid, Apr-May 1942, p 21.
17 Women's Social Work History Book (unpublished).
18 *The Deliverer,* Feb-Mar 1943, p 59.

CHAPTER SEVEN: **To make us bad 'uns good**

1 *The Christian Mission Magazine,* Jan 1872, p 16.
2 Ibid, May 1872, p 80.
3 *The War Cry,* 16 Mar 1882, p 4.
4 Ibid, 14 Jun 1884, p 4.
5 *Booth's Drum,* Bolton, pp 18-19 (Hodder & Stoughton, 1980).
6 *The War Cry,* 13 Aug 1884, p 4.
7 *All the World,* Apr 1885, p 85.
8 *The Salvation War* (1884), p 150.
9 *The War Cry,* 22 Oct 1884, p 2.
10 Ibid, 30 Jul 1884, p 4.
11 *Daily Chronicle,* 13 Jan 1885, quoted in Ibid, 17 Jan 1885, p 1.
12 *A Brief Review of the First Year's Work* (1891), p 82.
13 *The War Cry,* 12 Apr 1890, p 5.
14 *All the World,* Dec 1891, p 435.
15 *The War Cry,* 7 Feb 1891, p 9.
16 Ibid, 30 Aug 1890, p 8.
17 *A Brief Review of the First Year's Work* (1891), p 79.
18 *The Darkest England Gazette,* 25 Nov 1893, p 7.
19 *Work in Darkest England* (1894), pp 33-34.
20 *In Darkest England and the Way Out,* p 175.
21 *Liverpool Daily Post,* quoted in *The War Cry,* 11 Oct 1890, p 7.
22 *The Deliverer,* Apr 1891, p 154.
23 *The War Cry,* 24 Jan 1891, p 11.
24 Ibid, 28 Nov 1891, pp 6-7.
25 *The Deliverer,* Oct 1894, p 56.
26 *Social Work in Principle and Practice* (1921), p 73.
27 *The Social Gazette,* 25 May 1895, p 2.
28 *Women's Social Work Annual Report* (1898), pp 11-12.
29 *The Good Neighbour,* p 11 (Nat Council of Social Service, 1950).
30 *The War Cry,* 5 Feb 1898, p 3.
31 *Women's Social Work Annual Report* (1906), p 14.
32 *Living Epistles* (1902), p 100.
33 Ibid (unnumbered page).
34 *Sketches of Salvation Army Social Work* (1906).
35 *The Times,* 9 Nov 1971.

CHAPTER EIGHT: **Strange bedfellows**

1 *Light in Darkest England* (1895), p 14.
2 *The Christian Mission Magazine,* Jul 1874, p 197.
3 *The War Cry,* 23 Feb 1884, p 3.
4 Ibid, 17 Jul 1886, p 1.
5 Ibid, 14 Jan 1888, p 6.
6 Ibid, 25 Feb 1888, p 9.
7 Letter from Brigadier Christine Salter to Lieut-Commissioner Arch Wiggins, 27 Feb 1962.
8 *The Social Gazette,* 26 Aug 1899, p 2.
9 *The War Cry,* 3 Mar 1888, p 4.
10 Ibid, 12 May 1888, p 10.
11 Ibid, 3 Mar 1888, p 9.
12 *All the World,* Sep 1889, p 428.
13 *The War Cry,* 10 Mar 1888, p 2.
14 Ibid, 10 Nov 1888, p 8.
15 Ibid, 16 Mar 1889, p 10.
16 Ibid, and 23 Mar 1889, p 10.
17 *The Deliverer,* Aug-Sep 1944, p 133.
18 *All the World,* May 1889, p 231.
19 *The Deliverer,* Mar 1899, p 136.
20 *All the World,* May 1889, p 230.
21 *The Darkest England Gazette,* 8 Aug 1893, p 6.
22 *The Deliverer,* Sep 1891, p 45.
23 Ibid, Jan 1892, p 120.
24 Ibid, Aug 1891, p 24.
25 Ibid, Oct 1891, p 56.
26 Ibid, Dec 1891, p 87.
27 *All the World,* Feb 1891, p 92.
28 *The War Cry,* 26 Jan 1889, p 1.
29 Ibid, 4 Apr 1891, p 9.
30 *Work in Darkest England* (1894), p 67.
31 *The War Cry,* 22 Dec 1888, p 9.
32 *The War Cry,* 5 Jan 1889, p 2.
33 Ibid, 12 Apr 1890, p 5.
34 Ibid, 28 Feb 1891, p 11.
35 Ibid, 24 Oct 1891, p 8.
36 Ibid, 2 Jan 1892, p 7.
37 *In Darkest England and the Way Out,* p 17.
38 *The War Cry,* 8 Feb 1890, p 2.
39 Ibid, 24 May 1890, p 90.
40 Ibid, 28 Nov 1891, p 11.
41 *The Social News,* 5 Dec 1891, p 7.
42 *The Darkest England Gazette,* 4 Nov 1893, p 8.
43 *Westminster Gazette,* 1 Aug 1895, quoted in *The Social Gazette,* 17 Aug 1895, p 3.
44 *The Social Gazette,* 7 Dec 1895, p 2.
45 *Light in Darkest England* (1895), p 26.
46 *The Social Gazette,* 19 Aug 1899, p 4.
47 Ibid, 10 Mar 1900, p 3.
48 Ibid, 26 Sep 1914, p 2.
49 Ibid, 24 Oct 1914, p 1.
50 Ibid, 1 Jan 1916, p 2.

51 Ibid, 12 Feb 1916, p 1.
52 *The Social-Deliverer,* Nov 1917, p 84.
53 *The War Cry,* 9 Nov 1918, p 8.
54 Ibid, 26 Jul 1919, p 3.
55 *Social Problems in Solution* (1921), p 18.
56 Office of Population Censuses and Surveys.

CHAPTER NINE: **The worshipful company of out-of-works**

1 Quoted in *Notes on the Darkest England Scheme* (1896) frontispiece.
2 *The East London Evangelist,* Nov 1868, p 29.
3 Ibid, Jan 1869, p 62.
4 *The Christian Mission Magazine,* Mar 1870, p 46.
5 *The War Cry,* 12 Jan 1882, p 4.
6 Ibid, 19 Nov 1887, p 13.
7 *All the World,* Feb 1889, pp 65-66.
8 *The History,* vol 2, p 61 (Nelson, 1950).
9 *The War Cry,* 9 Jul 1892, p 2.
10 Ibid, 26 May 1888, p 2, and earlier.
11 *The Deliverer,* May 1890, p 145.
12 Ibid, Nov 1890, p 66.
13 Ibid, Dec 1891, p 89.
14 *The Social News,* 5 Mar 1892, p 6.
15 *The War Cry,* 25 Jan 1896, p 6.
16 *The Social News,* 5 Dec 1891, p 5.
17 *The War Cry,* 27 Feb 1892, p 16.
18 *All the World,* Aug 1892, pp 105-108.
19 Ibid, Feb 1888, pp 64-65.
20 *The Deliverer,* Nov 1891, p 72, and corrected version, Dec 1891, p 89.
21 Ibid, Jun 1900, p 191.
22 *The War Cry,* 16 Feb 1889, p 7.
23 Ibid, 16 Mar 1889, p 4.
24 *The Deliverer,* Dec 1890, p 89.
25 Ibid, Apr 1891, p 160.
26 *The War Cry,* 6 Feb 1886, p 2.
27 *The Deliverer,* Mar 1891, p 144.
28 *All the World,* Jul 1891, p 504.
29 *The Deliverer,* Jul 1891, p 8.
30 Ibid, Aug 1891, p 26.
31 *Work in Darkest England* (1894), p 24.
32 *The War Cry,* 22 Dec 1888, p 9.
33 *All the World,* Mar 1890, p 113.
34 *The War Cry,* 12 Apr 1890, p 5.
35 Ibid, 12 Jul 1890, p 4.
36 Ibid, 5 Jul 1890, p 6.
37 Quoted in *A Brief Review of the First Year's Work* (1891), p 22.
38 *The Darkest England Gazette,* 16 Dec 1893, p 6.
39 Ibid, p 4.
40 *All the World,* Mar 1893, p 234.
41 *The History,* vol 3, p 135.
42 *The War Cry,* 2 Aug 1890, p 4.
43 Ibid, 14 Mar 1891, p 7.

44 *All the World,* Oct 1890, p 510.
45 *The War Cry,* 17 Oct 1891, p 3
46 *Work in Darkest England* (1894), p 32.
47 *All the World,* Oct 1890, p 512.
48 *Light in Darkest England* (1895), p 52.
49 *The Darkest England Gazette,* 16 Dec 1893, p 5.
50 *All the World,* Sep 1890, p 480.
51 *A Brief Review of the First Year's Work* (1891), p 33.
52 *In Darkest England and the Way Out,* p 111.
53 *A Brief Review of the First Year's Work* (1891), p 42.
54 *All the World,* Dec 1891, p 25.
55 *The Social News,* 14 Nov 1891, p 3.
56 Ibid, 9 Jul 1892, p 4.
57 *Work in Darkest England* (1894), þ 25.
58 *The War Cry,* 5 Sep 1891, p 8.
59 *A Brief Review of the First Year's Work* (1891), p 72.
60 *The Darkest England Gazette,* 18 Nov 1893, p 10.
61 Ibid, 5 May 1894, p 6.
62 *The Darkest England Match Industry,* Mitchell, vol 1, p 5 (1973 booklet),
     quoting *The Diseases of Occupations,* Hunter (Univ of London Press, 1969).
63 *The War Cry,* 26 Jan 1889, p 2.
64 Ibid, 12 May 1888, p 8.
65 *The Times,* 12 May 1888, quoted in *The War Cry,* 19 May 1888, p 9.
66 *The War Cry,* 4 Aug 1888, p 2.
67 Ibid, 19 May 1888, p 9.
68 *Victorian England,* p 105.
69 *The Darkest England Match Industry,* Mitchell, vol 2, p 3 (1980 booklet).
70 *The War Cry,* 26 Jul 1890, p 7.
71 Ibid, 2 Aug 1890, p 10.
72 *In Darkest England and the Way Out,* p 110.
73 Cadman quoting 1 Corinthians 2:2 in *The War Cry,* 16 May 1891, p 9.
74 *All the World,* Sep 1891, p 214.
75 *The War Cry,* 16 May 1891, p 6.
76 *The History,* vol 3, p 124.
77 *A Brief Review of the First Year's Work* (1891), p 139.
78 *The War Cry,* 25 Apr 1891, p 5.
79 *All the World,* Jun 1891, p 425.
80 *The Darkest England Match Industry,* vol 1, p 9.
81 *The War Cry,* 15 Aug 1891, p 11.
82 *The History,* vol 3, p 12.

CHAPTER TEN: New coats for a drunkard's stomach

1 *The Christian Mission Magazine,* Feb 1871, p 26.
2 Ibid, Jan 1874, p 19.
3 Ibid, Feb 1874, p 33.
4 Ibid, Mar 1874, p 65.
5 Ibid, Aug 1874, p 219.
6 Ibid, Nov 1874, p 308.
7 Ibid, Jul 1877, p 179.
8 *Echoes and Memories,* p 193.
9 *The War Cry,* 17 Jan 1885, p 1.

10 *All the World,* May 1885, p 115.
11 *The War Cry,* 12 Apr 1890, p 5.
12 Ibid, 27 Sep 1890, p 14.
13 *The Deliverer,* Apr 1893, p 150.
14 *The Darkest England Gazette,* 30 Dec 1893, p 6.
15 *The Deliverer,* Feb 1896, p 120.
16 Ibid, Apr 1896, p 152.
17 Ibid, Jun 1896, p 187.
18 Ibid, Jul 1901, p 10.
19 *The Social Gazette,* 5 Oct 1901, p 1.
20 *The Salvation Army Year Book* (1916), p 34.
21 *The Salvationist and Alcohol,* S. Gauntlett, p 8 (SP & S, Ltd, 1982).

CHAPTER ELEVEN: **The great machine**

1 *The Christian Mission Magazine,* Sep 1878, p 232.
2 *The War Cry,* 12 Apr 1890, p 5.
3 Ibid, 26 Jul 1890, p 5.
4 Ibid, 8 Nov 1890, p 9.
5 Ibid, 11 Oct 1890, p 8.
6 *The History,* Wiggins, vol 4, p 372 (Nelson, 1964).
7 *The Happy Warrior,* Wallis (SP & S, Ltd, 1928).
8 *Encyclopaedia Brittanica.*
9 Quoted in *The War Cry,* 1 Nov 1890, p 6.
10 *In Darkest England and the Way Out,* p 18ff.
11 Ibid, p 91.
12 *The Times,* 9 Dec 1890.
13 *The Cape Times,* quoted in *The Social Gazette,* 12 Oct 1893, p 2.
14 *The War Cry,* 15 Nov 1890, p 7.
15 Ibid, 13 Dec 1890, p 6.
16 Ibid, 1 Nov 1890, p 5.
17 *All the World,* Mar 1891, p 238.
18 Quoted in *The War Cry,* 24 Jan 1891, p 9.
19 *The History,* vol 1, p 260.
20 *The War Cry,* 29 Oct 1892, p 9.
21 Ibid, 16 May 1891, p 6.
22 *Light in Darkest England* (1895), p 20.
23 Quoted in *The War Cry,* 5 Nov 1892, p 9.
24 *Bread for My Neighbour,* Coutts, p 82 (Hodder & Stoughton, 1978).
25 *The War Cry,* 14 Jan 1893, p 9.
26 *The Social Gazette,* 30 Mar 1895, p 2.
27 *Life of William Booth,* Begbie, p 111.
28 *Light in Darkest England* (1895), p 101.
29 *The Deliverer,* Nov 1894, p 79.
30 *The Darkest England Scheme* (1896), p vii.
31 *Sketches of Salvation Army Social Work* (1906).
32 *International Social Council Addresses* (1911), p 17.
33 *The Christian Mission Magazine,* Apr 1876, p 84.
34 *The Darkest England Gazette,* 9 Dec 1893, p 8.
35 *The Social Gazette,* 27 Jan 1900, p 1.
36 *The Darkest England Gazette,* 1 Jul 1893, p 2.
37 Ibid, 28 Oct 1893, p 6.

38 *The Deliverer,* Dec 1890, p 90.
39 *The Darkest England Gazette,* 5 May 1894, p 6.
40 *Work for Darkest England* (1898), p 25.
41 *Britain Transformed,* Arkell, p 265 (Penguin Education, 1973).
42 *The Salvation Army Year Book* (1916).
43 *Women's Social Work Annual Report* (1916).
44 *The Salvation Army Year Book* (1943).
45 Ibid (1983).

CHAPTER TWELVE: **Where angels might be glad to find employment**

1   Unpublished letter.
2   *The Social News,* 14 Nov 1891, p 5.
3   *All the World,* Dec 1891, p 404ff.
4   *The Social News,* 14 Nov 1891, p 7.
5   *The History,* vol 3, p 137.
6   *All the World,* Sep 1892, p 171ff.
7   *Work in Darkest England* (1894), p 49.
8   *In Darkest England and the Way Out,* p 134.
9   *The Darkest England Gazette,* 26 Aug 1893, p 11.
10 *Christian World,* 3 Jan 1895.
11 *The Morning,* 22 Sep 1894.
12 *The Social Gazette,* 14 Sep 1895, pp 2-3.
13 Ibid, 21 Sep 1895, p 1.
14 *The Darkest England Gazette,* 5 May 1894, p 12.
15 *All the World,* May 1892, p 387.
16 Unpublished letter, 13 Dec 1895.
17 *The War Cry,* 25 Jan 1896, p 8.
18 *All the World,* Jul 1896, p 291.
19 Quoted in *Friends of the Poor* (1900-1), p 47.
20 *The War Cry,* 28 May 1898, p 7.
21 *All the World,* Aug 1903, p 439.
22 Ibid, Nov 1912, p 590.
23 *The War Cry,* 18 Sep 1982, p 7.
24 *All the World,* Aug 1910, p 407ff.
25 *Regeneration,* Haggard, p 206 (Longmans, 1910).
26 *All the World,* Feb 1912, p 79.
27 Quoted in *The Social Gazette,* 27 Jan 1912, p 3.
28 Ibid, 20 Jan 1912, p 3.
29 Ibid, 15 Aug 1914, p 2.
30 *The History,* vol 3, p 145.
31 *In Darkest England and the Way Out,* pp 143-144.
32 *Nineteenth-Century Opinion,* Goodwin (quoting Dicey), p 259 (Pelican, 1951).
33 *In Darkest England and the Way Out,* p 148.
34 Ibid, p 152.
35 *The Darkest England Gazette,* 12 Aug 1893, p 1.
36 Ibid, 2 Sep 1893, p 6.
37 Ibid, 13 Jan 1894, p 6.
38 Ibid, 20 Jan 1894, p 6.
39 Quoted in Ibid, 14 Apr 1894, p 6.
40 *The Social Gazette,* 23 Feb 1895, p 2.
41 Ibid, 29 Jun 1895, p 2.

42 *The War Cry,* 3 Apr 1886, p 2.
43 Ibid, 8 May 1886, p 10.
44 Ibid, 4 Apr 1891, p 9.
45 *The Social News,* 14 Nov 1891, p 6.
46 *The War Cry,* 28 Nov 1891, p 11.
47 Ibid, 25 Jun 1892, p 16.
48 *The History,* vol 3, p 155.
49 *Emigration Gazette,* Mar 1907, p 54.
50 *The Field Officer,* Feb 1913, p 44.
51 *The Social Gazette,* 9 Apr 1904, p 4.
52 Ibid, 4 Feb 1905, p 1.
53 *The Salvation Army Year Book* (1907), p 46.
54 *Regeneration,* p 80ff.
55 *The Field Officer,* Mar 1913, p 109.
56 *The Salvation Army Year Book* (1938), p 21.
57 *The War Cry,* 6 Nov 1971, p 6.
58 *The Canadian Home Leaguer,* Dec 1982, p 110.
59 *The War Cry,* 8 Jun 1889, p 5.

Social Services in Great Britain and Ireland

as at 1 January 1983

Headquarters: 280 Mare Street, Hackney, London E8 1HE

Departments: Administration; Chaplains; Financial; Investigation; Medical Adviser and Counselling; Personnel and Training; Property; Residential Care.

Complexes: 3; Adolescent Units: 3; Alcoholism Services: Detoxification Units: 3; Rehabilitation Units for Alcoholism: 6; Bail Units: 5; Centres for Men: 39; Centres for Men and Women: 2; Centres for Men, Women and Families: 2; Centres for Mothers with Children: 4; Centres for Women and Girls: 7; Children's Homes: 2; Community Homes (children): 4; Community Homes (senior girls): 4; Conference Centre: 1; Counselling Centre: 1; Day Nursery: 1; Emergency Accommodation Centres: 3; Eventide Homes for Men: 3; Eventide Homes for Men and Women: 20; Eventide Homes for Women: 16; Family Service Stores: 10; Holiday Residences: 3; Investigation Department (missing persons enquiries): 1; Maternity Hospital: 1; Probation Homes: 1; Rehabilitation Centres: 5; Rehabilitation Centre for Mentally Ill/Handicapped: 1; Retired Officers' Residences: 2; Students' Residence: 1; Training Centres: 2; Young Women's Residence: 1.

Index

A

Aberdeen, 82, 106
  Earl of, 175
Adamson, William, 117-118, 119
Adoption, 26, 51, 53, 57
Africa, viii, 138, 168
Alcoholics, 18, chapter 10, 169
Allan, Janet, 185
Andrews, Harry, 49-51
Anti-suicide bureau, 45, 47, 48
Approved homes for boys, 71
  House o' the Trees, 71
  Kilbirnie, 71
Approved homes for girls, 71
  Bristol, 71, 72
  Longton House, 71
Approved hostels for girls, 71
Approved probation hostels, 71
Approved schools for girls, 71
  Woodlands, 72
Asdell, Marianne, 26, 30, 62, 63
Aspinall, Frank, 96
Astbury, Ranulph, 185
Australia, 9, 43, 70, 75, 78, 92, 97, 149, 174, 175, 178, 181-183
Auxiliaries, 148
Ayr, 82

B

Bacon, Francis, 93
Bail units, 79, 82
Barker, James, 46, 68, 75, 78, 80, 81
  Mrs Alice, 32, 45, 75, 78
Barnardo, Dr Thomas, 70
Barnet, 6
Barnett, Alfred, 185
Barton, Sergeant-Major, 147
Battersea wharf, 115, 143, 158
Battle, 73

Bayswater, 23
Belfast, 106
Belgian refugees, 96
    troops, 169
Bermondsey, 96, 147
Besant, Sir Walter, 168
Bethnal Green, 50, 92
Bird, Mrs, 101, 111
Birmingham, 97
Bishopsgate, 10, 96
Bismarck, 108
Blackfriars, 92, 94, 96
Blandy, Superintendent, 111, 128
Blind Beggar, the, 11, 123
Booth, Ballington, 49
    Bramwell, 3, 6, 7, 9, 13-15, 16, 20, 47, 50, 60, 61, 63, 70, 79, 83, 91, 94,
        95, 97, 107, 111, 118, 124, 126, 133, 135, 145, 154, 166, 170, 181
    Mrs Florence, 13, 15-20, 21-22, 24, 25-26, 28-29, 30-31, 33-35, 36, 38,
        43-44, 51, 58-59, 63, 70, 81-82, 87, 89, 101-102, 105-109, 111, 118,
        127, 129-130, 148, 176, 185
    Catherine Bramwell-, 16, 19, 20, 156, 157, 185
    Charles, 83
    Emma, chapter 5
    Evangeline, 57-58, 115, 163
    Georgie, 49-51
    Herbert, 50, 126
    Katie, 49
    Lucy, 50
    Mary, 157
    Miriam 157
    William, throughout
    Mrs Catherine, viii, 3, 10, 11, 13, 17, 49, 50, 51, 53, 100, 121, 132-133,
        135
Booth's beer, 114, 121
Booth-Tucker, Frederick, 50, 59
Borough, the, 18, 56-57
Bow, 70
Bowell, Sir Mackenzie, 175
Bowyer, H. George, 186
Boxted, 170-172
Boys' homes, chapter 6, 131, 149
    Sturge House, 70-71
Boys' shelter, 60
    Fetter Lane, 61-62
Brighton, 12, 44, 99
Brisbane, 181
Bristol, 71, 72, 92
Brown, Arnold, 48

199

Bullard, Henry, 181,
Burrell, William, 11
Burrows, Eva, 186

C

Cab horse charter, 140
Cadman, Elijah, 34, 59, 68, 80, 81, 83, 85, 91, 93, 95, 106, 111, 112, 115,
     125, 131, 137, 138, 143, 144, 167, 168, 177, 181, 185
Caedmon, 137
Canada, 43, 58, 169, 175, 176, 177, 178, 179, 182, 183
Canning Town, 8, 49-51, 110
Cardiff, 12, 81, 90, 96, 102
Carrington, Earl, 170
Castle, Miriam, 38
Cellar, Gutter and Garret Brigade, 24, 56, 125
   Seven Dials, 56
Census (1904) 98
       (1910) 98
       (1913-1921) 98
       (1971) 98
Chaplin, Henry, 165
Chapman, Reginald, 48
Charing Cross, 22, 30
Charity Commissioners, 170
Chatham, 12
Cheap food depots, 7-9, 89, 133, 149
   Canning Town, 8
   Clerkenwell, 8
   Limehouse, 7-9, 58, 84, 108
   Marylebone, 8
   Poplar, 8, 99
   Stepney, 8
   Whitechapel, 8, 89
Chelsea, 29, 30, 126
Chicago, 43
Children Act (1908) 70
Children's Aid Department, 53
Children's homes, 26, 53, 54, 59-66, 75
   The Nest, 62-63
   Lanark House, 62, 63, 129
China, 55, 152
Chiswick, 116
Christian Mission Conference
   (1870) 124
   (1874) 123
   (1877) 49, 123

Christian Mission stations,
  Battle, 73
  Bethnal Green, 50
  Brighton, 99
  Cardiff, 12
  Chatham, 12
  Hackney, 121
  Hammersmith, 3
  Hastings, 6, 11, 73
  Limehouse, 12, 123
  Mexborough, 49
  Newcastle, 12
  Plymouth, 12
  Poplar, 5
  St Leonards, 12
  Shoreditch, 67
  Soho, 12
  Stockton, 3
  Tottenham, 83
  Whitby, 131
  Whitechapel, 3, 11, 121
City Colony, 34, 92, 93, 109, 117, 141, 158, 167
Clacton, 135
Clapton, 6, 15, 24, 38, 54, 63, 75, 88, 106, 129
Clerkenwell, 8, 46-47, 69, 82, 92-93, 108, 134
Clibborn, Percy, 173, 175
Colchester, 170
Common lodging houses, 11, chapter 8
Cooke, James, 57, 127, 129
Coombs, Thomas, 177, 181
Cooper, William, 186
Corbridge, William, 6, 11, 73
Cottrill, Mrs Elizabeth, viii, 11-15, 26
Coutts, Frederick, 176, 183
Coventry, 83, 125
Cox, Adelaide, 26, 39, 82, 185
Crèches, 27, 59, 88
    the Borough, 56-57
    Hanbury Street, 59, 88
Criminal Law Amendment Act (1885) 20, 42, 43
Crystal Palace, 25, 118, 132
Culshaw, M. Owen, 186
Cunningham, Mrs Edith, 185

D

Dalston, 26
Darkest England,
    book, viii, 44, 58, 59, 77, 92, 109, 114, 118, chapter 11, 174

Committee of Inquiry, 36, 146-147
Fund, 142-143, 144-145, 146-148, 170
Scheme, 9, 45, 78, 80, 92, 97, 107, 109, 115, 118-119, 126, 127, chapter
    11, 164, 167, 172, 174, 184
Trust Deed, 142, 184
Davies, Emma, 186
Dawson, Mr and Mrs, 182
Day school, 168
Denmark Hill, 130
Dickens, Charles, 54, 61
Dobson, Captain, 41
Dock strike (1889) 8, 58
Dowdle, James, 12
    Mrs, 12
Drunkards' Brigade, 125
    Rescue Society, 122-123, 125
Dundee, 82
Dunraven, Lord, 117

E

Earls Court, 14
Eastbourne, 95
East Grinstead, 72
Eastern Star, the, 2, 11
Edinburgh, 82
Edmonds, Henry, 12-13
Edward VII, King, 169, 172
Elevators, 113-115, 127-128, 159
    Fieldgate Street, 113
    Hanbury Street, 113
    Old Street, 113
Emigration, 22, 26, 44, 149, 161, 169, 173, 176-183
Empire Settlement Act (1922) 181
Employment, 68, chapter 9
    Bakery, 109, 111, 115, 163
    Bookbinding, 105-106
    Bootblacking, 115, 149
    Bootmaking, 79, 143
    Brickmaking, 158, 163
    Brush making, 115
    Cabinet making, 79, 115
    Cardboard box making, 115, 118
    Carpentry and joinery, 79, 115
    Carpet weaving, 115
    Circular delivering, 114
    Clerking, 115

Cooking, 100, 115, 163
Engineering, 115
Gatekeeping, 115
Keeping watch, 115
Knitting machine operating, 106, 149
Laundry work, 16, 17, 18, 27, 103, 104, 106, 118, 119, 149
Leaflet folding, 115
Mat making, 79, 115
Match making, 46, 115, 119-120, 144
Mattress making, 115
Needlework, 14, 99
Painting, 115
Paper sorting, 115, 116
Parcel packing, 115
Rag sorting, 115, 116
Sack making, 115
Salvage, 80, 115-116, 143, 149, 158
Sandwich board carrying, 114, 163
Saw milling, 115
Scrubbing, 115
Servants' registry, 26, 100-103, 105
Shirt finishing, 106
Shoe making, 115, 143
Tailoring, 79, 115
Tambourine making, 115
Tin working, 115
Underclothes making, 106
Upholstering, 106
Washing, 15
Washing text making, 106
Wheelwrighting, 115
Wood chopping, 74, 79, 115, 149
Evening classes, viii, 69
Evenden, Mrs Miriam, 182-183
Eventide homes, 154-156
Exeter Hall, the Strand, 33, 54, 75, 87, 125, 131, 135

F

Factories, 80, 82, 87, 109, 112, 114, 118, 128, 133, 149, 157
Faith Cottage, 23
Faith House, 23
Family service stores, 117
Farm Colony, Hadleigh, 109, 115, 130, 141, 149, chapter 12
Farrar, Canon, 142
Farthing breakfasts, 52, 58, 147, 149

Fells, Honor, 11
Fewster, Ernest, 186
Financial aid, Government,
    Australia, 92
    UK, 39-40, 91-92
Flawn, James, chapter 1, 58, 81, 84
Florence, Mr, 106
Food-for-the-million shops, 3, 6, 8, 14
'For God's sake care' campaign, 145
France, 43
Free breakfasts, 2
Free teas, 2-3, 58, 121
Frost, Mrs Caroline, 26, 28-30, 31, 32, 35, 38-39, 126
    William, 28-29, 39
Fry, Charles, 100

G

George V, King, 180
Girls' homes, The Nest, 62-63
Gladstone, Herbert, 78
Glasgow, 12-13, 82, 87, 90
Goldsmith, Mrs, 26
Goodwill Department, 71
Gorst, Sir John, 165
'Grace before meat' boxes, 147, 148
Greenock, 82
Guernsey, 28, 29, 124

H

Hackney, 1, 22, 29, 31-33, 33-34, 35-36, 36-37, 38, 50-51, 53, 75, 77, 78,
    101, 103, 105, 106, 121
Hadleigh, 115, 130, chapter 12
Haggard, H. Rider, 180
Hammersmith, 3
Hampstead Garden Suburb, 155
Hanbury Street refuge, 13-14, 16, 17, 19, 27, 62, 88, 176
    women's shelter, 86, 87-90
Hanley, 5
Hannevik, Anna, 186
Harbour Light home, Highworth, 130
Hardie, Keir, 110
Harrison, Captain, 41
Hart, Dr, 34
Hastings, 6, 11, 73

Hayward, Captain A., 74
Headquarters,
  Christian Mission, 188 (now 220) Whitechapel Road, 2, 11
  International, 101 Queen Victoria Street, 54, 100, 167, 177, 181
  Men's Social Work, 272 Whitechapel Road, 9, 68, 116
  Rescue Work, 259 Mare Street, 22, 37, 53, 101, 148
  Social Reform Wing, 36 Upper Thames Street, 118
  Social Services, 280 Mare Street, 29
  Trade,
    96 Southwark Street, 90, 108
    98-102 Clerkenwell Road, 46-47, 102, 108, 134
    79-81 Fortress Road, 63
Herring, George, 169-170, 172
Higgins, Edward, 182
Higham's Park, 156
Highworth, 130
Hoe, Charles, 84, 85, 91
  Edgar, 84
Holborn, 69
Holmes, George, 12
Home for the mentally defective, 130
Hopkins, Captain, 115
Hopkins, Ellice, 17
Hospitals, 33, 34, 36-38, 149
  the London, 19, 38
  the Mothers', 38
  Boothville, 181
Hoxton, 14, 50
Huddersfield, 112
Huntley, Dr Edith, 33, 34
Huxley, T. H., 141, 142

I

Iliffe, William, 171, 185
India, 50, 51, 59, 80, 149
Industrial homes, 26, 71, 82, 108, 109, 149
Industrial Revolution, vii
Inebriates' homes, chapter 10, 149, 160
  Grove House, 129
  Hillsboro' House, 129
  Victoria House, 130
  Springfield Lodge, 130
International Social Council (1911) 10, 71, 150
  (1921) 63, 97
  Inverness, 182

Ireland, 15, 80, 106
Islington, 69

J

Jackson, Charlotte, 124
Jack the Ripper, 88, 96
Jarrett, Rebecca, 18-20
Jolliffe, George, 185
Jones, Susan 'Hawker', 18, 19
Juvenile delinquents, chapter 6, 75

K

Keates, Captain, 108
Kennington Lane, 147
Kensington, 142
Kent, Earl of, 158
Kilbirnie, 71
King's Cross, 23, 67, 68-69, 78, 88, 103, 115, 116, 143
Kitching,
    Theodore, 51
    Wilfred, 51
    Wi'liam, 51
      Mrs Louisa, 51

L

Labour bureau, 45, 61, 108-111, 112, 114, 116, 149
Lamb, David, 97, 168, 179, 180, 181
    Mrs Minnie, 168
Lancet, The, 92
Langdon, George, 185
Laurie, John, 97, 185
Lawford, Mr, 175
Leeds, 41, 73
Leigh-on-Sea, 157, 158
Lewis, John, 185
Life and Labour of the People in London, 83
Light Brigade, 147
Limehouse, viii, 7, 8, 9, 12, 58, 84, 87, 108, 123
Liverpool, 79, 90
Loch, Lord Henry, 168
Lockwood, Mr, 164
London Orphan Asylum, 55

Lord's Supper, the, 124
Lovatt, Roy, 186

M

Maiden Tribute of Modern Babylon, The, 20, 42
Manitoba, 177
Manpower Services Commission, 169
Mansion House Committee, 111, 168
Margate, 3
Marylebone, 8
Match Industry, 117-120, 144
Maternity homes, 26, chapter 3, 149
   Chelsea, 30
   Hackney
      (27 Devonshire Road) 31, 32, 33
      (Ivy House, 271 Mare Street) 31, 32, 35, 36, 37
   Pimlico, 30
Maternity receiving house, Brent House, 32
Matrimonial bureau, 45-47, 149
Mayfair, 23
Mayflower training centre, 82
McAllister, William, 186
McLaren, Walter, 142
Melbourne, 9, 43, 75, 78
Men's Social Services, 184
Men's Social Work, 71, 97, 168
Metropoles, 90-91, 149
   Men's: Southwark, 90, 91, 106, 147
   Women's:
      Cardiff, 90, 102
      Hanbury Street, 90
      Liverpool, 90
Mexborough, 49
Middlesbrough, 14
Midnight patrol, 12, 22-23, 29, 149
Midnight soup kitchens, 98, 149
Mile End Waste, vii, 1, 10
Milner, Captain, 41
Mingay, Albert, 186
Missing persons, 21, chapter 4, 149
Moore, Harold E, 160-161
Morley, John, 155
Mother and baby homes, 26, chapter 3
   Chelsea, 29, 30, 126
   Notting Hill, 30, 31
   Pimlico, 29, 30, 31

Mothers' and childrens' homes, The Nest, 62
Mothers' meetings, 3
Muirhead, Dorothy, 186

N

Nash, Mrs Frazer, 34
Nash, Tom, 181, 183
Newberry, Mrs, 129
Newcastle, 12
New York, 39, 43, 51
Nicol, Alex, 69
Ninfield, 41
Northampton, 18
Norway, 156
Nottingham, vii
Notting Hill, 30, 31, 102
Nuneaton, 137
Nunn, George, 119
Nurses' home, 35, 37
Nursing,
    district, 38, 149
    midwifery, 35, 36, 38
    training, 35, 36, 38

O

Old-age pensions, 154-155
Old Ford, 117, 119
'Old Telegraph', 88-89, 94
Onslow, the Earl of, 146
Orders and Regulations for
    first farm colony (1891) 158
    first food and shelter depot (1888) 7
    rescue homes (1892) 24, 143
Orsborn, Albert, 72, 186
    Mrs Phillis (see also Taylor, Mrs Phillis) 72
Out-of-Love Fund, 25, 26
Oversea Colony, 141, 149, 163, 164, 172-176
Ozanne, Clara, 107

P

Paisley, 82
Paris, 43

208

Penny banks, viii
Pepper, Mrs Ellen, 62, 100, 111
Piccadilly, 20, 22, 23
Pimlico, 29, 30, 31
Pindred, Leslie, 182-183
    Mr, 182
Plymouth, 12, 28, 81, 82, 173
Police court work, 26, 70, 79, 81, 82, 149
    Cardiff, 81
    Plymouth, 81
Pollard, George, 166
Pollett, Agnes, 122-123
Poor Law, 99, 155
    Guardians, 173
        Camberwell, 164, 166
        Whitechapel, 94
    Conference, 154
    Relief, 5, 153, 180
Poor man's bank, 149
Poor man's lawyer, 26, 149, 153
Poplar, 2, 5, 8, 32, 71, 99
Povlsen, Mrs Agnes, 185
Prison gate homes, 67, chapter 7, 149, 169
    Devonshire House, 75, 77, 78, 79, 88, 105, 177
    The Bridge, 67, 68, 69, 78, 103, 115, 116, 143
    Glasgow (women's), 82
Prison gate work, chapter 7, 149
    Wandsworth, 74
Prison visitation, chapter 7
    Aberdeen, 82
    Ayr, 82
    Dundee, 82
    Edinburgh, 82
    Glasgow, 82
    Greenock, 82
    Paisley, 82
    Plymouth, 82
Prison work, chapter 7
    Hastings, 73
    Leeds, 73
Probation officers, 70
Probation of First Offenders Act (1887) 67, 68
Probation of Offenders Act (1907) 70

Q

Quarterman, Ensign, 62

R

Rabbits, Edward, 147-148
Ragged schools, viii, 10, 17
Railton, George Scott, 1, 2, 3, 75, 182
   Mrs Marianne, 74, 75
Reading rooms, viii
Reconciliation bureau, 47-48
Reed, Henry, 143
Rees, Captain, 54
Reid, Mrs Flora, 10, 12
Relief, viii, chapter 1, 10, 75
Rescue work, chapter 2, 34, 42, 43, 44, 51, 53, 63, 71, 75, 101, 105-107,
     111, 126, 127, 129, 143, 148, 149, 176
  Bayswater, 23
  Cardiff, 12, 90
  Charing Cross, 22, 30
  Chatham, 12
  Chelsea, 29, 30
  Glasgow, 12, 13, 87
  Guernsey, 28, 29
  Hackney, 22, 32, 36
  Hastings, 11, 73
  King's Cross, 23
  Limehouse, 12
  Mayfair, 23
  Middlesbrough, 14
  Newcastle, 12
  Northampton, 18-19
  Notting Hill, 30, 31
  Piccadilly, 22, 23
  Pimlico, 29, 30, 31
  Plymouth, 12, 28, 81
  St Leonards, 12
  Shoreditch, 10
  Soho, 12, 23
  Whitechapel, viii, 11, 12, 13, 14, 16, 17, 27, 87, 176
Reynolds, Mrs Caroline, 26, 32, 43, 129
Rhodes, Cecil, 168
Royal commission (1871), 20

S

St James's Hall, Piccadilly, 20, 142
St Leonards, 12
St Peter Port, 124
Salisbury, 62, 100

Salvation Army, change of name to, 6, 131
Salvation ship, 149, 173, 180, 181
Sapsworth, Elizabeth, 15, 19, 24, 26, 36-38, 88, 142
Scotland, 12, 13, 70, 71, 82, 87, 90, 106, 115, 182
Scott, Molly, 23, 26
Servants home, Notting Hill, 103, 149
Servants registry, 26, 100, 101-102, 103, 105
   Cardiff, 102,
   Hackney, 101
   Notting Hill, 102, 103
Seven Dials, 56
Sewing classes, 99
Sheffield, 71
Sheltered housing, 156
Shelters: men's, 60, 61, 70, 78, 80, chapter 8, 112, 114, 116, 128, 130
   131, 133, 147, 149, 159
   Birmingham, 97
   Blackfriars, 92, 94, 95, 96
   Bristol, 92
   Burne Street, 96
   Cardiff, 96
   Clare Market, 92
   Clerkenwell, 82, 92, 93, 108
   Limehouse, viii, 7, 58, 84, 87, 108, 114
   Lisson Grove, 92
   Middlesex Street, 96
   Poplar, 71
   Quaker Street, 91, 92, 96
   Royal Mint Street, 92
   Southwark, 90, 91, 106
   Spa Road, 96
   Westminster, 92, 96, 97
   Whitechapel,
      272 Whitechapel Road, 92, 94
      Victoria Homes, 97
   Whitecross, 96
Shelters: women's, 61, chapter 8, 149
   Cardiff, 90, 102
   Hanbury Street, 86, 87, 88, 89, 90, 92, 107
   Liverpool, 90
Shop Assistants Act (1900) 152
Shoreditch, 10, 67
Short, Jane, 3, 10
Simmonds, Mrs Rose, 24
Simpson, Staff-Captain, 83
Singapore, 111
Situations Department, 101
Sloss, 'Old Dad', 76, 77

Slum work, 38, 56, 59, 117, 127, 131, 133, 149, 155
Small holding settlement, Boxted, 169-172
Smith Falls, 182-183
Smith, Frank, 109, 111, 118, 119, 132, 133, 135-137, 138, 154, 185
'Social Boom', 144-145, 147
Social League, 145, 147
Social Reform Wing, 46, 52, 59, 69, 80, 103, 109, 111, 115, 116, chapter
        11, 177
Social Trust Deed, 184
Soho, 12, 23
Somerset, Lady Henry, 142
Soper, Lilian, 81
Soup kitchens, viii, 6, 14
    Poplar, 2
    Whitechapel, 2, 11
South Africa, 106, 173
Southend, 157-158
Southport, 51
Southwark, 90, 91, 95, 106, 108
Sowden, Mrs Annie, 36-38
Sowton, Charles, 185
Spitalfields, 10
Stamford Hill, 129
Stanley, H. M., viii, 138
Stead, W. T., 20, 42, 132-133, 135, 136, 165
Stepney, 8
Stitt, Samuel, 164-166, 167, 172, 175
    Mrs, 157
Stittsville, 182
Stockton, 3
Stoke Newington, 107
Stratford, 110
Sturgess, Randolph, 185
'Submerged tenth', vii, 45, 92, 139, 141, 157
Sweating Commission (1888) 117, 118, 119
Swift, Susie, vi, 56, 61, 62, 69, 78, 84, 85, 87, 103, 105, 106, 107, 108, 116,
        127, 128, 154, 155, 156, 160-162, 166, 178
Sydney, 43

                                T

Tasmania, 143
Tassie, Captain, 87, 90
Taylor, Mrs Phillis (see also Orsborn, Mrs Phillis) 72, 185
Temperance, 56, chapter 10, 138, 160, 170
Thrift clubs, 3

Thundersley, 6
Thurman, Colonel, 116
Tickner, Julia, 186
Tilbury, 158
Topley, Ronald, 181
Toronto, 43, 182
Townsend, 99
Toynbee Hall, 136
Trade Department, 46-47, 63, 90, 102, 108, 134
Training homes, 6, 24, 34, 50, 55, 73, 75, 125, 126
Training home nursery, 54-55, 59, 62, 63
Training of Children, The, 55-56, 65
Training of
  nurses, 33, 35, 36, 38
  officers,
    evangelical (1880) 6, 24
    rescue (1889) 24, 149
    men's social (1891) 151
Tyler, William, 13

U

USA, 39, 43, 51, 58, 109, 116, 133, 173
Unsworth, Isaac, 45
  Madge, 36

V

Victoria, Australia, 92
  Queen, 74, 77, 80, 88, 96, 136, 168

W

Wakefield, 74
Walker, Mrs, 29
Wales, 12, 71, 81, 90, 96, 102
Walthamstow, 155
Wandsworth, 74
War,
  Boer, 106
  Crimean, 167
  Egyptian, 116
  First World, 44, 96, 169
  Second World, 23, 44, 169

Ward, Corps Sergeant-Major, 74, 75, 79, 88
Welfare State, viii, 184
Wesley,
   Charles, 61
   John, 61
Westcott, Herbert, 186
West Ham, 110
Westminster, 92, 94, 96, 97, 142
Weston-super-Mare, 151
Whitby, 131
Whitechapel, viii, 2, 3, 8, 11-19, 27, 59, 60, 62, 86, 87, 88, 89, 92, 94, 97,
      105, 106, 113, 121, 123, 125
Williams, Richard, 44
Wills, Mr Justice, 59
Wilson, Dr, 34
Women's rights, 111, 125, 151
Women's Social Services, 184
Women's Social Work, 20, 39, 72, 82, 111, 146, 148, 155
Wood Green, 60

X

Xenia Field Foundation, 82